The Institutior
of the Foreign E

European University Studies
Europäische Hochschulschriften
Publications Universitaires Européennes

Series V
Economics and Management

Reihe V Série V
Volks- und Betriebswirtschaft
Sciences économiques, gestion d'entreprise

Vol./Bd. 2691

PETER LANG
Frankfurt am Main · Berlin · Bern · Bruxelles · New York · Oxford · Wien

Jörg Zeuner

The Institutional Economics of the Foreign Exchange Market

A Comparison of the Present Market Structure with Alternative Arrangements

PETER LANG
Europäischer Verlag der Wissenschaften

Die Deutsche Bibliothek - CIP-Einheitsaufnahme

Zeuner, Jörg:

The institutional economics of the foreign exchange market : a comparison of the present market structure with alternative arrangements / Jörg Zeuner. - Frankfurt am Main ; Berlin ; Bern ; Bruxelles ; New York ; Oxford ; Wien : Lang, 2000
(European university studies : Ser. 5, Economics and Management ; Vol. 2691)
Zugl: Würzburg, Univ., Diss., 1999
ISBN 3-631-36648-5

D 20
ISSN 0531-7339
ISBN 3-631-36648-5
US-ISBN 0-8204-4803-6

To my mother

Acknowledgements

Many people have contributed to my knowledge and thinking over the years about the institutional economics of the foreign exchange market, whether consciously or not. Among them, there are a number of people to whom I owe a particular debt of gratitude.

My supervisor Peter Bofinger as well as Norbert Schulz both from the Bayerische Julius-Maximilians-Universität Würzburg. Furthermore, Andrea Schächter from the International Monetary Fund, Washington, DC, and Adalbert Winkler from IPC, Frankfurt. I would also like to express many thanks to the Commerzbank AG, Frankfurt, and Michael Rühl, for facilitating this research.

Financial support is gratefully acknowledged. This has come from the Konrad-Adenauer Foundation in the form of a research grant throughout my studies.

From all these people as well as Michael Diehm, Thomas Greinwald, Bettina Maucher, Gerald Oertel, Britta Schmitt, Rainer Tölle, and many others, I have benefited from advice, comments and criticism over the time that I have been studying economics, and especially over the gestation period of this thesis. I am sure that the end product is better for this advice. I would also like to thank Brendan Goff and Stephan Grollius for their editorial support. However, the responsibility for the final text is, of course, mine alone.

In conclusion, I must tribute to my family Heinz and Sonja Zeuner for their support and encouragement over the past years.

Jörg Zeuner

Zusammenfassung in deutscher Sprache

Internationale Wirtschaftsbeziehungen kennzeichnen sich unter anderem dadurch aus, daß Ansprüche aus grenzüberschreitenden Vertragsvereinbarungen nicht ohne weiteres durchgesetzt werden können. So endet etwa die Zuständigkeit jeder Gerichtsbarkeit an den Grenzen des entsprechenden Rechtsraumes. In der Regel sind dies nationale Grenzen. Internationalen Güter- und Finanztransaktionen fehlt daher der verbindliche Rechtsrahmen.

Gleichzeitig vollzog sich die Entstehung und Entwicklung des Devisenmarktes ohne staatlichen Einfluß gleichsam evolutorisch. Der Handel mit Devisen unterliegt auch heute noch keiner staatlichen Regulierung, da er nicht ortsgebunden ist. Staatlicher Aufsicht konnte und kann damit stets ausgewichen werden. Mit anderen Worten, Regierungen können den Handel mit Devisen innerhalb ihrer Landesgrenzen zwar einschränken bzw. ganz unterbinden, dessen weltweite Organisation können sie jedoch nicht nachhaltig beeinflussen.

Die Besonderheit der *Devisentransaktion* als internationale Transaktion erlaubt eine originäre Anwendung der Institutionenökonomik auf den Devisenmarkt. Die Institutionenökonomik geht davon aus, daß der Durchführung von Resourcentransfers ein verbindliches System zur Durchsetzung von Verträgen fehlt. Die Rahmenbedingungen des Handels mit Devisen sind damit zutreffend beschrieben und transaktionsspezifische negative Externalitäten (insbesondere die asymmetrische Verteilung von Information) können als Erklärung für die institutionelle Ausgestaltung des Devisenmarktes herangezogen werden. Alle Institutionen, die im folgenden erfaßt sind (wie etwa Market Making oder Kursspannen), werden daher auf eine oder mehrere Unvollkommenheiten im Handel mit Devisen (wie etwa das Kreditrisiko) zurückgeführt.

Die Besonderheit der Entstehung und Entwicklung des *Devisenmarktes* gestattet darüber hinaus den Versuch, eine Theorie der Effizienz des Devisenhandels zu entwerfen. Nach Hume, Menger, Hayek und Sugden müßte die heutige Organisationsform des Devisenmarktes das Resultat einer außerordentlich erfolgreichen Arbeit der 'unsichtbaren Hand' sein. Nach ihrer These dürften auf dem 'Markt für institutionelle Rahmenbedingungen' nur diejenigen Institutionen ausgewählt worden sein, die in ihrem Zusammenspiel und für den Handel mit Devisen effizient sind. Sie sind wiederum effizient, wenn sie nutzenmaximierend und sich selbst durchsetzende Vereinbarungen sind, da private Wirtschaftssubjekte den institutionellen Rahmen für ihr Handeln selbst gestaltet haben.

Die folgende Analyse definiert daher nicht nur den institutionelle Rahmen des Devisenmarktes, um ihn dann einer mikroökonomischen Erklärung zuzuführen. Vielmehr werden darüber hinaus alternative Organisationsformen vorgestellt, die dann mit den existierenden im Hinblick auf ihre jeweilige Effizienz verglichen werden. Unterscheidungsmerkmal sind dabei die spezifischen Transaktionskosten, die jedes institutionelle Arrangement verursacht, wenn es zur Überwindung einer bestimmten Unvollkommenheit herangezogen wird. Für Marktformen (wie etwa Aktienmärkte im Vergleich zu Warenbörsen oder dem Kunsthandel) sind dies im einzelnen (i) Such- und Informationskosten, (ii) Verhandlungs- und Entscheidungskosten sowie (iii) Kosten der Vertragsabwicklung und -durchsetzung.

Als Ergebnis der Arbeit ergibt sich folgende Effizienzhypothese:

Das Such- und Informationssystem des Devisenmarktes ist effizient in seiner derzeitigen Ausgestaltung. Gleiches gilt für die Organisation der Preisverhandlungen. Es gilt jedoch nicht für das Abwicklungssystem des Devisenmarktes. Der institutionelle Rahmen des Handels mit Devisen ist somit nicht effizient zum jetzigen Zeitpunkt. Die bereits von den Marktteilnehmern angekündigten Änderungen in der Abwicklung von Devisentransaktionen lassen jedoch eine effiziente Organisation des Devisenmarktes in naher Zukunft erwarten. Voraussetzung dafür ist die Anpassung des Such- und Informationssystems an die neuen Verhältnisse, da es transaktionsspezifische Unvollkommenheiten antizipiert, die durch die Umgestaltung des Abwicklungssystems verschwinden werden.

CONTENTS

Tables

Figures

CHAPTER I

Introduction

The division of labour results in transactions. Transactions, in turn, result in coordination and cooperation problems as soon as their characteristics give rise to opportunistic behaviour or other negative externalities. Prominent examples for the failure to coordinate or cooperate have been drawn from the markets for used cars (Akerlof 1970), insurance contracts (Spence and Zeckhauser 1971, a/o), labour (Arrow 1972, Spence 1973, Lundberg and Startz 1983, Akerlof 1985, Milgrom and Oster 1987, a/o) and loans (Stiglitz and Weiss 1981, a/o). They all have in common that either a profitable agreement is not reached at all (coordination failure) or that it is not reached because a violation of a possible agreement is rationally expected (cooperation failure).

With reference to Coase (1937), Alchian and Demsetz (1972), Arrow (1974), Williamson (1975, 1985), and Chandler (1977), a/o, the competitive solution to market failures of the above kind is the implementation of coordination and cooperation mechanisms that lie beyond the neoclassical market structure for the certainty case and the idealized Arrow-Debreu economy for the uncertainty case. According to their view, certification, efficiency wages, or collateral, more generally, any market-specific rules and regulations have their origin in some kind of imperfection in the interpersonal and intertemporal resource transfer. Linking organizational characteristics to imperfections, finally, is well-established as the agenda of New Institutional Economics.

New Institutional Economics has been subject to considerable debate[1]. Consequently, it has come to the point where it is sufficiently mature to be applied to specific organizations. Nevertheless, a rigorous analysis of certain types of firms or a complete analysis of such well-defined organizations as markets can rarely be found in the literature. On the one hand, most analyses are purely academic. The practical relevance of their findings for policymakers and regulators is, therefore, severely restricted. On the

---

1 See, e.g., Terberger (1994).

other hand, they generally fall short of being comprehensive in the sense of covering the characteristics of a specific organization in their entirety. In other words, applied institutional economics is still in its infancy.

A category of organizations for which this is particularly true is the one of international financial and commodity markets. This is even more surprising given that international trade and finance meets the basic requirement for applying institutional economic reasoning appropriately. By their very nature, international trade and financial relations lack a contract enforcement system in the form of governments, law, or courts, a/o. For being agreements on the international transfer of resources, international contracts cannot be enforced because contracts cannot be enforced across national borders. Consequently, the development of market-specific rules and regulations has been and will be competitive by nature. Any deviation of existing coordination and cooperation mechanisms from the idealized alternative of the Arrow-Debreu economy, therefore, must have its origin in some kind of imperfection, if the economic theory of institutions is correct.

Whatever is true for international financial markets with respect to missing regulation, it is particularly true for the foreign exchange market. On the one hand, trading foreign exchange in New York is a perfect substitute to trading foreign exchange in London, which is a perfect substitute to trading foreign exchange in Frankfurt, etc. Any attempt to regulate today's foreign exchange market centres would therefore result in the market participants moving from one market place to the other (depending on which national authority would try to restrict foreign exchange trading). On the other hand, Einzig (1970) demonstrates that the development of the foreign exchange market structure has lacked public intervention, at least since the foreign exchange market centres were connected with each other by modern communication technologies. Hence, the foreign exchange market is the ideal object for extending the frontier of applied institutional economic analysis given that a comprehensive theory of the market-specific rules and regulations of the foreign exchange market is also missing as yet.

But the following analysis can even go one step further. Given that the wealth maximizing behaviour of private economic agents is at the heart of economic reasoning and that the development of the foreign exchange market structure has lacked public intervention such that the development of market-specific rules and regulations has been competitive in nature, it should be possible to derive a theory of the efficiency of the foreign exchange market structure from first principles. According to Hume (1739/40), Menger (1883), Hayek (1978), and Sugden (1986, 1989), the current foreign exchange market structure is the result of the invisible hand for both conditions. The current foreign exchange market structure should, therefore, be efficient if the invisible hand theory is taken for granted.

Summarizing, the following analysis is the attempt to explain why

'the structure of the foreign exchange market is inherently different from that of equity or commodity markets' (Frankel, et al. 1996, p. x).

More precisely, it is the attempt to explain why

'it lacks their centralization and transparency' (Frankel, et al. 1996, p. x).

Furthermore, the following analysis is the attempt to establish a theory of the efficiency of the foreign exchange market structure based on wealth maximization. Arguments are brought forward that shall explain why the market for foreign exchange differs from the one for arts, antiques, stocks, futures, or, most elementary, potatoes (interestingly, however, arguments are also brought forward that explain why the market for foreign exchange would resemble the market for *hot* potatoes if such a market existed).

The analysis proceeds as follows. Chapter II briefly reviews the economic theory of institutions, with special emphasis on market organizations and the differences of the presented view to the one that underlies New Institutional Economics. Chapter III then starts the institutional economic analysis of the foreign exchange market. Choosing the comparative approach to institutions, more precisely, it maps out the scope of the analytical chapters, chapters IV-VI below. Most importantly, the set of alternative market structures is defined. Based on a review of the foreign exchange market practice, each alternative arrangement is furthermore described by emphasizing the essential differences to the foreign exchange market practice.

Dividing the foreign exchange market into three subsystems, Chapter IV analyzes the search and information system. The imperfections, that have already been addressed in Chapter III once, are translated into transaction costs. Moreover, the alternative search and information systems are compared with respect to the specific costs that they entail. This comparative method is subsequently applied in Chapter V on the pricing system and Chapter VI on the settlement system. Chapter VII, finally, summarizes the key findings of each of the analytical chapters and concludes the presentation at the same time. Most importantly, it argues that the foreign exchange market structure is (almost) efficient.

CHAPTER II

The Institutional Economic Theory of Markets

'In the modern textbook, the analysis deals with the determination of market prices, but discussion of the market itself has entirely disappeared' (Coase 1988, p. 7).

Imagine a foreign exchange (FX) deal between two commercial banks. More precisely, let a Bank B sell some amount of US dollars (USD) to a Bank A. Bank A, furthermore, pays for the US dollars in terms of Euros (EUR). Similar transactions (definition II.1) are constantly repeated, all over the world and for 24 hours a day. Not surprisingly, therefore, there exists a foreign exchange market (definition II.2) for this purpose. In other words, there exists an organization (definition II.3) for the sole purpose of trading foreign exchange. Consequently, other markets provide the platform for trading other objects instead (the members or market participants may or may not be identical). Firms, therefore, provide the institutional environment (definition II.4) for production purposes and international policy coordination, finally, facilitates international trade, a/o.

DEFINITION II.1 (TRANSACTION): 'the alienation and acquisition, between individuals, of the rights of future ownership of physical things' (Commons 1934, p. 58).

DEFINITION II.2 (FOREIGN EXCHANGE MARKET): the economic location where private economic agents exchange deposits denominated in different currencies among each other. Each of the foreign exchange transactions is price-mediated such the foreign exchange market is always engaged in price discovery (Kreps 1990, p. 187). Furthermore, all potential parties to a foreign exchange market transaction are, a priori, equally entitled. In other words, all market participants always have the same rights unless they choose to give them up (Williamson 1985, pp. 70, 73).

DEFINITION II.3 (ORGANIZATION): a limited and well-defined group of people who repeatedly interact with each other subject to a well-defined institutional environment. The interactions, which are all of the same kind, always take place between two members of the group (Schmoller 1900, p. 61; North 1990, p. 239).

DEFINITION II.4 (INSTITUTION AND INSTITUTIONAL ENVIRONMENT): an institution can be defined as a working rule (Ostrom 1990, p. 51). An institutional environment is thus 'the sets of working rules that are used to determine who is eligible to make decisions in some arena, what actions are allowed or constrained, what aggregation rules will be used, what procedures must be followed, what information must or must not be provided, and what payoffs will be assigned to individuals dependent on their actions ... All rules contain prescriptions that forbid, permit, or require some action or outcome. Working rules are those actually used, monitored, and enforced when individuals make choices about the actions they will take' (Ostrom 1990, p. 51).

OPPORTUNISM OR THE ORIGIN OF ORGANIZATIONS: Imagine private economic agents and ignore transaction-specific characteristics until further notice. It is far from obvious, in this case,

- why existing organizations differ with respect to the corresponding institutional environments, and
- why each member, therefore, commits himself to the different rules and regulations that characterize each organization.

In other words, it is far from obvious,

- why the market for arts differs from the one for stocks, the market for stocks from the one for used cars, why markets differ from firms, and why firms differ from international organizations, a/o.

Furthermore, it is far from obvious

- why traders follow the rule of trading stocks on the floor and during operation times only, why they follow the rule of trading foreign exchange with market makers only, or why they report private information to a counterparty truthfully, a/o.

For constant returns to scale, standard microeconomic theory does not provide any answer to either of these questions. In fact, it cannot even explain the existence of organizations in the first place.

'Suppose that perfect competition exists, that information is freely available, and that individuals can credibly commit to honoring all agreements. The financial system performs flawlessly in this environment. The absence of informational frictions and the ability of contracting parties to make credible promises implies that everyone is able to lend and borrow freely at risk-corrected rates of interest. Market forces consequently allocate income efficiently between consumption and saving, and then in turn allocate saving efficiently across investment projects. Each individual adjusts his saving to equalize the marginal utility of a unit of foregone consumption with the expected marginal benefit - the expected product of the gross return on saving and the discounted marginal utility of future consumption. The total funds furnished from saving flow to equalize risk-corrected marginal returns across investment projects. Competitive forces ensure that lending and borrowing rates adjust to clear markets and that no one earns extra-normal profits. And the entire process is costless; the flow of funds from savers to borrowers does not absorb any resources. ... Finally, the perfect markets paradigm is silent about the role of financial contracts and institutions. The theory only makes predictions about real allocations. Financial structure is both irrelevant and indeterminate, in keeping with the Modigliani-Miller theorem. ... Because it is costless to obtain information and enforce contracts, individuals can enter financial relationships without the aid of institutions. That is, financial intermediaries are not essential. The theory accordingly offers no particular predictions about the evolution of financial relationships and institutions' (Gertler and Rose 1996, pp. 15-17).

In other words, for the standard assumptions of perfect competition, perfect information, and non-strategic behaviour, any transfer of property rights is frictionless. Consequently, the institutional environment that governs this transfer is irrelevant for private economic agents[2].

However, the various financial and currency crises have repeatedly demonstrated that the institutional environment *does* matter[3]. And even Marshall (1920) admits that, by ignoring institutions, standard microeconomic theory falls significantly short of the demands that reality and policy making poses on it (Marshall 1920, p. 200). Based on this critique of the neoclassical paradigm, therefore, the economic theory of institutions suggests to account for a number of frictions in order to overcome the obvious shortcomings. Most importantly, it allows for

- strategic behaviour and
- imperfect information

in order to explain the existence, the variety, and the stability (the legal force) of institutions. The basic idea is the following.

Transaction-specific characteristics often give rise to imperfections. Among others, they give rise to information imperfections. At the same time, it is well-established that, based on strategic behaviour, information imperfections provide an incentive for free-riding on a counterparty's innocence. More precisely, asymmetric information gives rise to moral hazard and adverse selection problems. Since it is also known from the economics of information that signalling, screening, and self-selection are the basic alternatives to rationing (Milgrom and Roberts 1992, pp. 149-69, 185-91), therefore, organizations may have their origin in cutting down opportunism (definition II.5). In other words, the

---

2 See Williamson (1979) for more details.

3 See, e.g., World Bank (1998) on the Asian crisis.

selection of members and any other rule and regulation that characterizes an arbitrary organization may well be interpreted as a signalling, screening, or self-selection device[4].

DEFINITION II.5 (OPPORTUNISM): 'by opportunism I mean self-interest seeking with guile. This includes but is scarcely limited to more blatant forms, such as lying, stealing, and cheating. Opportunism more often involves subtle forms of deceit. ... opportunism refers to the incomplete or distorted disclosure of information, especially to calculated efforts to mislead, distort, disguise, obfuscate, or otherwise confuse' (Williamson 1985, p. 47).

Since information imperfections differ with respect to the underlying transaction, furthermore, it is not only the existence of institutions that can be explained on the above grounds. On the contrary, allowing for transaction-specific characteristics, organizations, most likely, differ from each other. Consequently, imperfections also explain the variety of different organizations.

Opportunism can explain the origin of organizations and their variety as it has just been demonstrated. But, finally, it cannot (yet) explain the stability of organizations.

- The economic theory of institutions must abandon the assumption of 'legal centralism' (Williamson 1983, p. 520) that underlies standard microeconomic theory. This step is important because there would still be no answer to the issues that were raised above should contract enforcement be perfect. Rules and regulations would again be irrelevant because there would be no incentive for opportunistic behaviour. For private economic agents, a theft is worth the risk if and only if there is a high enough chance *not* to be caught in the end. For a well-functioning legal system, this is, however, not the case (Williamson 1983, pp. 520-21).
- For abandoning legal centralism, on the other hand, opportunism is at least as much likely to explain why the members of an organization do *not* commit themselves to specific rules and regulations as it is likely to explain why they do so (Terberger 1994, pp. 187-90).

Hence, an explicit theory of collective decision making is required that can seriously replace the assumption of legal centralism which, again, must be abandoned for being able to explain the stability of organizations in the first place.

THE ABSENCE OF LAW AND SELF-ENFORCEMENT OR THE REQUIRED THEORY OF COLLECTIVE DECISION MAKING: Incorporating a theory of collective decision making into the economic theory of institutions is the point of departure of the present view on the economics of institutions from the standard

---

4 For details, see Furubotn and Richter (1997, chapter 1), a/o.

approach to it, namely, the one of New Institutional Economics. The most straightforward theory of collective decision making is, furthermore,

- to assume the absence of law (definition II.6) and
- to require each rule and regulation to be a self-enforcing agreement among all members of a specific organization (definition II.7).

DEFINITION II.6 (ABSENCE OF LAW): law is absent if there is no possibility at all for making recourse to regulators for designing and/or enforcing rules and regulations. In other words, law is absent if any kind of ordering is private (Williamson 1983, pp. 520-21).

DEFINITION II.7 (SELF-ENFORCING AGREEMENT): 'a self-enforcing agreement between two parties remains in force as long as each party believes himself to be better off by continuing the agreement than he would be by ending it' (Telser 1980, p. 27).

More precisely, the existence of a benevolent dictator in the form of a contract enforcement system and/or a regulatory authority is rejected in what follows. It is, however, assumed instead that any conflict of interest must be resolved by mutual agreement for an organization to be stable. Reflecting individual rationality, this is implicit in the self-enforcement condition. In other words, it is assumed below that any rule or regulation survives if and only if each member of an organization is better off by following it than he would be otherwise.

EFFICIENCY AND THE ECONOMIC THEORY OF THE DESIGN OF ORGANIZATIONS: Individual rationality, the absence of law, and self-enforcement provide the ground for explaining the stability of organizations without running into the methodological problems that have just been addressed. But these underlying assumptions also allow for the most straightforward application of Hayek's (1978) invisible hand theorem below, if the focus is on the institutional environment of organizations.

'There is, therefore, no reason why a polycentric order in which each element is guided only by rules and receives no orders from a centre should not be capable of bringing about as complex and apparently as 'purposive' an adaptation to circumstances as could be produced in a system where a part is set aside to perform such an order on an analogue or model before it is put into execution by the larger structure. In so far as the self-organizing forces of a structure as a whole lead at once to the right kind of action (or to tentative actions which can be retraced before too much harm is done), such a single-stage order need not be inferior to a hierarchic one in which the whole merely carries out what has first been tried out in a part. Such a non-hierarchic order dispenses with the necessity of first communicating all the information on which its several elements act to a common centre and conceivably may make the use of more information possible than could be transmitted to, and digested by, a centre' (Hayek 1978, p. 74).

In other words, the absence of law guarantees competition on the level of organizing economic activity. Individual rationality and self-enforcement, furthermore, ensure that the outcome of the competitive selection of rules and regulations is efficient (definition II.8), which is the 'miracle' that market forces can do. Most importantly, therefore, the invisible hand metaphor provides the basis for deriving theories of the efficiency of different institutional environments that are based on economic reasoning.

DEFINITION II.8 (EFFICIENCY): any individually rational institution or institutional environment is efficient if it maximizes each group member's wealth subject to the constraint that it is self-enforcing[5].

It is the 'discovery' of transaction costs (definition II.9) by Coase (1937) that removes the final obstacle to deriving a rigorous theory of the economics of institutions. This is the case because the concept of cost minimization is a widely used and well-established one in microeconomic analysis. Translating the imperfections that were discussed above into costs, therefore, Coase (1937) provided the final key for economists to address the problem of why and how to organize economic activity.

DEFINITION II.9 (TRANSACTION COSTS): 'the costs of drafting, negotiating, and safeguarding an agreement' (Williamson 1985, p. 20).

THE COMPARATIVE AND THE EVOLUTIONARY APPROACH TO THE ECONOMICS OF INSTITUTIONS: Economists can focus on the design of institutional environments in two, respectively, three different ways.

- In a dynamic framework, North (1981, 1990, a/o) and his associates investigate the evolution of particular organizations *over time*. In other words, they investigate if,

---

5 Note that this definition does not correspond to the familiar definition of Pareto efficiency. It does, however, come close to the concept of interim incentive efficiency as it is suggested by Holmström and Myerson (1983). The difference between both concepts has its origin in the different view on collective decision making that is presented here compared to the one that underlies New Institutional Economics. New Institutional Economics does not require institutions to be self-enforcing. The theory simply assumes that the invisible hand always selects the Pareto optimal institutions and that these institutions are stable for precisely this reason. But this rather naive belief in market forces creates the methodological problems that have already been referred to. Many Pareto efficient institutions are not self-enforcing. If they are assumed to stable, therefore, theory must refer to some kind of legal centralism assumption on the level of organizing economic activity in order to explain why this is the case. But this is a contradiction in terms The recourse to legal centralism, strictly speaking, destroys the grounds on which economic institutionalism is based altogether (Terberger 1994, pp. 187-190).

how, and why organizations respond to changes in the transaction-specific characteristics (that may reflect changes in the environment such as technical progress).

- In a comparative-static framework, Williamson (1979, 1985, 1991, 1993, a/o), most prominently, started to provide reasons for why there are differences in organizations *at the same point in time*. In other words, he started to provide reasons for the variety of different organizations, each one based on a given set of transaction-specific characteristics.
- As it is the case for the present analysis, finally, the comparative-static approach can be extended such that *different* institutional environments are investigated with special emphasis on their respective efficiency when it comes to governing *the same transaction*, namely, the foreign exchange transaction.

COMPARATIVE ANALYSIS OF MARKETS: The institutional economic analysis of the foreign exchange market below is restricted to a comparison of alternative institutional environments with respect to trading foreign exchange. Referring to these institutional environments as market structures, chapters III-VI below are therefore restricted as follows.

- The basic unit of analysis is constantly given as an exchange transaction.
- The traded object is constantly given as foreign exchange.
- The group members are constantly given as the set of foreign exchange traders.
- The alternative institutions and market structures are constantly given as the set of institutions and institutional environments that can govern trade in principle.

Methodologically, the following analysis is furthermore restricted such that any hypothesis concerning the (in)efficiency of a particular market structure is a hypothesis concerning the *relative* (in)efficiency of this market structure. For the comparative approach, any institution and/or market structure is only (in)efficient compared to the alternatives that are investigated. It may not be so otherwise.

Following Dahlman (1979), finally, the comparative analysis of the foreign exchange market can be simplified as follows. Adopting a functional approach to organizations, a market must accomplish four main tasks, namely,

- organizing the search for potential trading partners,
- organizing the acquisition of information on the potential trading partners, the traded object and/or the market conditions in the most general sense,
- specifying the price/quantity negotiations that select the counterparty from the set of potential trading partners, and
- organizing payment and delivery between two parties to an agreement (Dahlman 1979, pp. 141-148).

Since, furthermore, these objectives find their expression in

- a search and information system,
- a pricing system, and
- a settlement system (Dahlman 1979, pp. 141-148),

the foreign exchange market is analyzed below such that each of these systems is addressed separately. In terms of transaction costs, this approach is equivalent to analyzing separately

- the search and information costs,
- the bargaining costs, and
- the settlement costs

as it is done in chapters IV-VI below.

SOME CHARACTERISTICS OF FOREIGN EXCHANGE AND THE FOREIGN EXCHANGE MARKET: Restricting the economic analysis of the foreign exchange market to the comparative analysis of different market structures, the following paragraphs can finally rely on three additional specifications.

In the descriptive literature, the foreign exchange market is generally viewed as a set of four closely interrelated markets. The spot is distinguished from the forward market and the respective interbank segment is separated from the customer or commercial one (Riehl and Rodriguez 1983, Anthony 1989, Burnham 1991, Weisweiller 1991, Fischer-Erlach 1995, and Souren 1995, a/o). Undoubtedly, this approach contributes to a better understanding of foreign exchange trading in the operational sense. It does, however, not serve the purpose of the present analysis. On the contrary, adopting the standard view is seriously misleading.

- The interbank forward market is not engaged in the discovery of the exchange rate. It is, thus, not a market in the sense of definition II.2 above. The forward rate is the sum of the spot rate plus the swap rate. But the spot rate is the result of spot trading and the swap rate is determined on the international credit markets (Fischer-Erlach 1995, pp. 64-71).
- The customer markets are not markets for foreign exchange for the same reason. The quoted spot and forward rates are the sum of the interbank rates plus a premium. The premium, however, depends on the customer's identity. Hence, it is constant for normal market conditions (Fischer-Erlach 1995, pp. 32-35).

For both reasons, the interbank spot market is the only market in the sense of definition II.2 above. The following analysis of the foreign exchange market is thus restricted to commercial banks and the interbank spot market.

According to definition II.2 above, a major characteristic of market transactions is, secondly, that the parties to an agreement have the same rights. In the absence of law, therefore, screening devices must be ignored below for any two-sided problem of asymmetric information. By assumption, there is no reason to provide any one bank with a right to monitor that the counterparty does not have.

Finally,

'the foreign exchange market is seen no longer as a market where the flow supply and demand over time determine the equilibrium price - as in the case of perishable agricultural goods - but as a market where the price is determined by expectations of income that can be generated by holding assets denominated in a certain currency' (Frankel, et al. 1996, p. 1).

Exchange rate movements, in other words, relate to expected future changes in the value of one currency relative to another one rather than changes in the current net flows of goods and capital between the corresponding two countries (Frankel, et al. 1996, p. 1). Adopting the asset approach to foreign exchange, therefore, a currency is viewed below as a common-value object (definition II.10).

DEFINITION II.10 (COMMON-VALUE OBJECT): if a trader updates his own belief about the future value of the traded object as soon as he comes to know another trader's belief about the future value of the same object, the object is a common-value object (McAfee and McMillan 1987, pp. 720-21).

Conveniently, the first specification reflects the assumption of individual rationality. The agents that the following analysis is concerned with are profit maximizing banks. More importantly, however, restricting the analysis to interbank foreign exchange trading underlines how appropriate the foreign exchange market is as an object for applied institutional economic research. The assumption of the absence of law, which is critical for national organizations, reflects the reality on the interbank foreign exchange market. Foreign exchange trading banks are based in different countries. Hence, they are not all subject to the same legal system which creates transaction-specific problems because contracts cannot be enforced across national borders.

The absence of law when trading foreign exchange is also reconfirmed when reviewing the Code of Conduct of the foreign exchange market because it suggests a mechanism for the resolution of controversies that is typical for a world that lacks a contract enforcement system. On the foreign exchange market, a typical dispute is resolved in mutual agreement. If no other agreement is reached, losses are covered in equal shares (Association Cambiste Internationale 1996, p. 25).

CHAPTER III

The Comparative Analysis of the Foreign Exchange Market

> 'The analysis thus directs attention to the point that institutions fulfil an economic function by reducing transaction costs and therefore ought to be treated as variables determined inside the economic scheme of things (Dahlman 1979, pp. 161-62).

Chapter III puts the comparative approach of the institutional economic theory of markets in concrete terms with respect to foreign exchange trading. In other words, it identifies the relevant imperfections as well as presents the set of possible institutional and organizational responses to each of the FX transaction-specific problems. The analytical chapters IV - VI below, therefore, all rely on Chapter III.

The analysis starts with identifying the three main characteristics of foreign exchange trading. Details are given on the implications of customer trading (sections 1.1 and 1.2) and on the detached settlement of the two legs of a foreign exchange transaction (section 1.3). Chapter III then translates these findings into imperfections that give rise to the deviation of the optimal market structure from the idealized alternative above (Chapter II). Not surprisingly, information imperfections are identified as the one force that perforates the foundation of the Arrow-Debreu economy (sections 2.1, 3.1, and 4.1). Outlining the alternative market structures that may overcome these imperfections follows. In doing so, sections 2.2, 3.2, and 4.2 include the current FX market practice. They also demonstrate that

'market organizations develop into types as:
auction or customer markets
markets in experience or search goods
'organized' or 'nonorganized' markets' (Furubotn and Richter 1997, p. 288),

or anything in between. Chapter III concludes with the presentation of a simple asset demand and supply model that underlies most of the formal analysis below (section 5).

1. Characteristics of Foreign Exchange Trading

1.1 Exogeneity of Foreign Exchange Positions

Although customer trading was suggested above to be analytically different to interbank trading, the dual role of commercial banks as traders of foreign exchange and, at the same time, as intermediaries for their customers' FX business cannot be ignored. On the contrary, given that customer trading is

- continuous trading[6],
- trading for their own account[7], and
- final[8] (Fischer-Erlach 1995, pp. 32-35),

each FX trading bank faces the problem that it cannot perfectly control its foreign exchange positions. If it were not for interbank trading, in fact, each bank's foreign exchange positions would be entirely exogenous, assuming that customer deals are not rejected.

1.2 Monopolistic Information on the Trade Price of Foreign Exchange

'In the foreign exchange market, one potential source of private signals at the dealer level is order flow from nondealer customers' (Lyons 1996, p. 186).

The view that customer trading provides private information on future exchange rates is also taken in Goodhart (1988, p. 456), Lyons (1995), and Perraudin and Vitale (1996), a/o. It is supported by the fact that, unanimously, FX trading banks do not regard customer business as a burden. On the contrary, they view it as a prerequisite for successfully participating in interbank foreign exchange trading. According to market participants, the banks extract relevant information on future exchange rate movements from the execution prices of customer deals as well as the size and direction of customer order flows (Gallant 1991, p. 5/15). The monopolistic information clearly results from the fact that all three variables affect the trade price of each bank's current FX holdings on the interbank market. Customer orders are ultimately processed there.

---

6 Customer orders are processed as they arrive (Cohen, et al. 1986, p. 12).

7 Customer orders are satisfied from the banks' own account (Cohen, et al. 1986, pp. 18-19).

8 The settlement is irrevocable and unconditional (Bank for International Settlements 1996, p. 63).

Frankel and Froot (1990a, 1990b), furthermore, demonstrate that there is no consensus view among banks on the relevant information for exchange rate forecasting. Hence, a second source of monopolistic information on future exchange rates is as simple as there being a 'different opinion' (Varian 1989, p. 6) on future developments among traders. Thinking of chartists, these differences in opinion may not be due to 'information as such' (Varian 1989, p. 6). For common-value objects, however, they are themselves valuable information since they would influence the forecasts of all other market participants if they were known. This is for the same reason as above. The traders' opinions influence the trade price of current foreign exchange holdings[9].

1.3 Asynchronous Settlement of Payment and Delivery Leg

DEFINITION III.1 (PAYMENT-VERSUS-PAYMENT): 'a mechanism in a foreign exchange settlement system that ensures that a final transfer of one currency occurs if and only if a final transfer of the other currency or currencies takes place' (Bank for International Settlements 1996, p. 64).

Imagine the US dollar/Euro currency pair. Furthermore, let the US dollar be the base currency such that the Euro is the traded currency. Ignoring cash settlement, an interbank USD/EUR transaction is therefore settled such that

- funds denominated in USD are transferred from one nostro account to another for which a US-based payments system is used (payment leg) and
- funds denominated in EUR are transferred in the opposite direction for which, however, an EU-based payments system must be used (delivery leg).

Payments systems are restricted to a single currency (Van den Bergh 1994, pp. 31-36)[10]. Hence, the intermediated settlement of the payment leg of a foreign exchange transaction is necessarily detached from the intermediated settlement of the corresponding delivery leg (figure III.1).

For payment being detached from delivery, however, the two legs of a foreign exchange transaction are not necessarily settled payment-versus-payment (definition III.1)[11]. In

---

9 For details on the price determination of common-value objects, see the rational expectations literature, e.g., Fama (1976, chapter 5) or Blanchard and Fischer (1989, pp. 213-74). See also Chapter IV, section 2 below.

10 For further details on payments systems, see also Blommestein and Summers (1994), a/o.

11 For foreign exchange transactions, the terms payment and delivery can obviously be used synonymously without loss of generality. Conventionally, therefore, the synchronous settlement of a foreign exchange transaction is referred to as payment-versus-payment rather than delivery-versus-payment.

fact, it has not yet been possible to synchronize the settlement of the two legs of a foreign exchange transaction.

- Payments systems are based in different time zones,
- none of them operates on a 24-hour basis, and
- some systems settle net debit positions periodically (netting systems) whereas others do so in terms of gross amounts and continuously (real-time gross settlement systems) (Bank for International Settlements 1998, pp. 23-25).

FIGURE III.1: Settlement of a Foreign Exchange Transaction

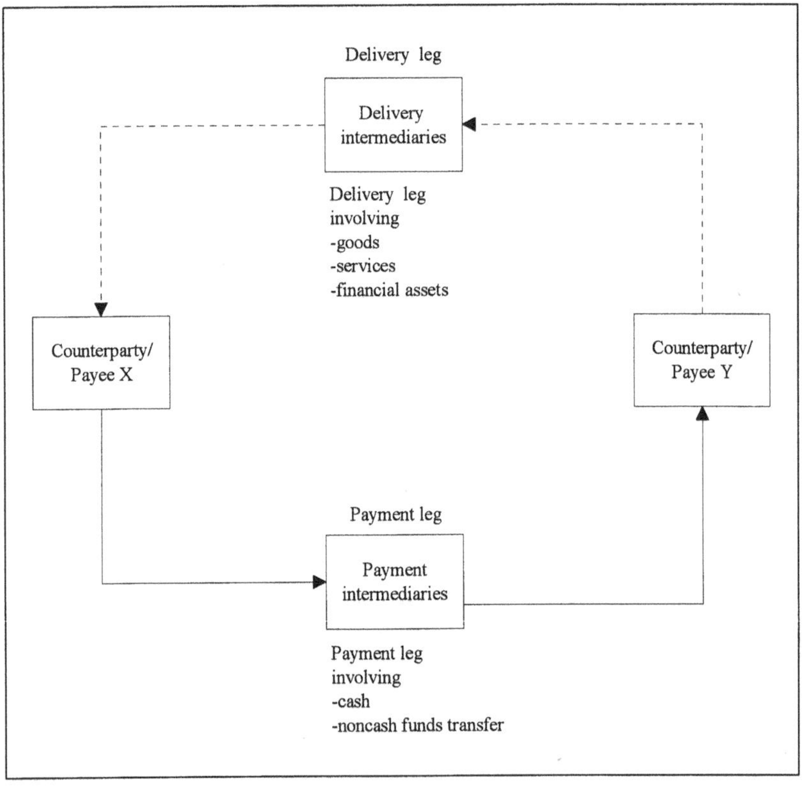

Source: Van den Bergh and Veale (1994, p. 90, chart 1)

All three characteristics combined clearly violate the conditions for perfect synchronization, namely, overlapping operation times and identical settlement times (Shen 1997, p. 54; figure III.2)[12]. The transaction costs of synchronizing payments systems of minor importance within one time zone have also prevented the wide implementation of payment-versus-payment mechanisms given that the three major traded currencies, the US dollar, the Japanese Yen, and the Euro, represent three different time zones (Shen 1997, pp. 54-55).

2. Comparative Analysis of the Search and Information System

2.1 Imperfections

2.1.1 Position Risk Exposure

Ceteris paribus, a bank's foreign exchange position is exogenously determined by the unknown customer order flow. Hence, the bank faces the risk of running out of payment reserves provided that the buy orders do not exactly set off the sell orders, not even in the long run. At some point in time, the bank may thus no longer be able to settle incoming customer orders due to a lack of funds. In other words, the bank faces position risk (definition III.2)[13].

DEFINITION III.2 (POSITION RISK): the risk that a bank runs out of foreign exchange holdings.

Position risk translates into one out of altogether three trading motives. Following Tirole (1982), trade generally relies on

- opinion or differences in prior beliefs,
- attitudes towards risk,
- diversification, and/or
- 'irrational' behaviour (Tirole 1982, pp. 1163-64).

---

[12] For an in-depth analysis of the major payments systems in the Group of Ten countries, see Bank for International Settlements (1993). Restricting the analysis to the G-10 countries follows the approach of the Bank for International Settlements to interbank foreign exchange trading as it is expressed in Bank for International Settlements (1996, 1998).

[13] With a few exceptions, the discussed imperfections are identical to what the Bank for International Settlements introduced as the types of settlement risk of foreign exchange transactions (Bank for International Settlements 1996, p. 4). Settlement risk is furthermore understood as the 'general term used to designate the risk that settlement in a transfer system will not take place as expected' (Bank for International Settlements 1993, p. 544). Hence, settlement risk is finally at the heart of deviating from the idealized market structure when organizing a spot market. See also Van den Bergh and Veale (1994) for a discussion of settlement risk.

FIGURE III.2: Operation and Settlement Times of Selected Group of Ten (G-10) Payments Systems in 1998

Current or planned opening hours of selected G-10 payment systems

The differences in time zones shown are those applying during winter time

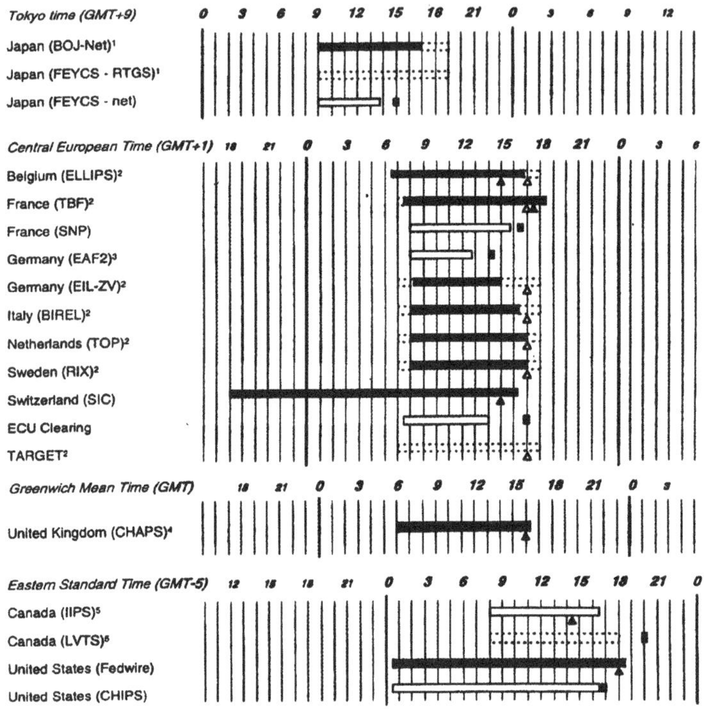

Key

RTGS system (current hours) ....

Net system (current hours plus settlement time).....................

Planned hours (for new or existing systems) ....

Cut-off time for third-party payment orders (where applicable)... ▲ Current △ Planned

[1] Dates of planned times: FEYCS-RTGS introduction (in December 1998 with closing time of 17:00, to be extended to 19:00 in 2000), BOJ-Net extension (2000). [2] The operating hours (i.e. opening, closing and third party cut-off times) for ELLIPS, TBF, EIL-ZV, BIREL, TOP and RIX will be standardised on those shown for the TARGET RTGS system when the latter is introduced (January 1999). [3] EAF2 is a net settlement system that combines features of liquidity saving and early finality. [4] CHAPS hours shown are for the existing GBP service. As part of the introduction of TARGET, an additional CHAPS service (handling Euro and with the standard TARGET hours shown) will be introduced (January 1999). [5] IIPS settles next day at 12:00; this system will be withdrawn when LVTS is introduced (Autumn 1998).

Source: Bank for International Settlements (1998, p. 24, chart C)

Since, however, banks may differ with respect to many features, each bank is nevertheless strongly expected to behave rationally. Irrational behaviour is thus ignored. Turning to risk aversion and private information below, therefore, the exposure to position risk clearly motivates trade for the purpose of diversifying a bank's portfolio. In other words, commercial banks engage in FX trading because they wish to reallocate their inventory positions which are imbalanced due to customer trading. In this sense, they engage in liquidity trading.

Liquidity trading, finally, initiates a process of search for potential trading partners. More precisely, an arbitrary Bank A with a 'surplus' in the base currency US dollar looks for a counterparty Bank B that has a 'shortage' in the same currency and vice versa. Concluding section 2.1.1 with a brief outlook on the formal analysis below, Chapter IV, section 4, therefore, classifies different search and information systems with respect to their efficiency of reallocating inventory. The relevant criteria is search costs. As it turns out, they differ with respect to the design of the search and information system of a market.

2.1.2 Market Risk Exposure

Due to uncertainty, future exchange rates are random variables. Consequently, any non-zero balance of foreign exchange is subject to the risk of adverse price movements compared to the purchase price. In other words, each FX position is subject to exchange rate risk or market risk (definition III.3).

DEFINITION III.3 (MARKET RISK): 'the risk that an institution or other trader will experience a loss on a trade owing to an unfavourable exchange rate movement' (Bank for International Settlements 1996, p. 64).

Given the possibility of default, market risk gives rise to replacement risk (definition III.4). On the FX market, furthermore, replacement risk is restricted to exactly two business days. With respect to the problem of market design, however, replacement risk can be treated as if it were market risk. It differs from market risk only with respect to the origin of the open position. But the origin of open positions is irrelevant in the present context[14].

[14] The settlement delay of two business days on the FX market results from various factors. Among others, the asynchronous settlement of each leg of a foreign exchange transaction prevents real-time settlement. So does the involvement of correspondent banks, or multilateral netting *prior* to settlement, a/o. Each of these reasons has already been addressed or will still be addressed below (Chapter VI). It is not pointed out on each occasion, however, that the settlement of FX transactions requires a certain delay.

DEFINITION III.4 (REPLACEMENT RISK): 'the risk that a counterparty to an outstanding transaction for completion at a future date will fail to perform on the settlement date. This failure may leave the solvent party with an unhedged or open market position or deny the solvent party unrealised gains on the position. The resulting exposure is the cost of replacing, at current market prices, the original transaction' (Bank for International Settlements 1996, p. 64).

Finally, market risk gives rise to foreign exchange trading due to different attitudes towards risk. If a bank is risk averse as opposed to risk neutral, e.g., the desire for reallocating 'excessive' market risk exposure follows each disturbance of the optimal portfolio. The bank then wants to hedge its involuntary open position on the interbank foreign exchange market. The transaction-specific problem is thus again the efficient search for potential trading partners. This time, however, it arises from the exposure to market risk such that the search and information system must ensure the optimal reallocation of market risk rather than the optimal reallocation of inventory. The problem is addressed in Chapter IV, section 3 below.

2.1.3 Dispersed Information

For monopolistic information that has its origin in each bank's customer business, the information on future exchange rates is extremely dispersed on the FX market. On the one hand, therefore, monopolistic information gives rise to information trading. In other words, it motivates trading because of differences in opinion or differences in prior beliefs among market participants.

'Because each dealer has sole knowledge of his own-customer order flow, ... it is private information, which can be exploited in interdealer trading' (Lyons 1996, p. 186).

On the other hand, search and information systems differ with respect to the degree of preserving information imperfections during the process of searching for potential trading partners. In other words,

- they differ with respect to the *degree of centralization* or the degree of 'information aggregation' (Grossman and Stiglitz 1976, p. 249). Furthermore,
- they also differ with respect to the *degree of transparency* or the degree of making the aggregated information available to the public.

For *given* search costs, therefore, different search and information systems can be investigated as to whether they entail high or low costs of information acquisition. This question is followed up in Chapter IV, section 2.

2.1.4 Credit Risk Exposure

If the settlement of a foreign exchange transaction involves different time zones, payment precedes delivery or vice versa. Only the first move can be observed. If it takes place within the same time zone, the payments systems are still not synchronized and the problem remains the same in principle. The only difference is that *neither* the first *nor* the second move can now be observed, for equally entitled banks and as long as the market is in a normal state. In other words, one payment is always analytically equivalent to a loan to the counterparty assuming settlement to be final. For settlement in the same time zone, both banks rationally treat their respective payment obligations as loans. Given that banks can fail, therefore, one bank always is and the other sometimes thinks that it is exposed to credit risk (definition III.5).

DEFINITION III.5 (CREDIT RISK): 'the risk that a counterparty will not settle an obligation for full value, either when due or at any time thereafter' (Bank for International Settlements 1996, p. 63).

As in any credit relationship, the likelihood of default varies with respect to the debtor. Furthermore, the information on the own reliability is private information. Consequently, for two types of banks,

- reliable banks that do not fail and
- unreliable banks that may or may not fail,

an arbitrary Bank B must attach a positive probability to its counterparty, Bank A, being of one type or the other.

But Bank B's belief about Bank A's type affects Bank B's decision with respect to delivering. For a non-zero proportion of unreliable banks in the population, settlement is less likely, ceteris paribus. This, in turn, provides incentives for other banks not to pay. Ultimately, the market may fail and Bank B's belief about Bank A's type can therefore be referred to as the adverse selection component of credit risk in the sense of Stiglitz and Weiss (1981, pp. 395-401). By the very nature of credit risk, furthermore, it is the search and information system of the foreign exchange market that can prevent the crisis scenario, if anything.

It is Chapter IV, section 1 that addresses the adverse selection problem. The following example of the attempted Soviet coup d'état in 1991, furthermore, illustrates the point of adverse selection once again. A change in the expected reliability of trading partners affected the payment decisions of both, creditors and debtors, such that they almost triggered a crisis. Finally, figure III.3 below summarizes the present section.

FIGURE III.3: Demands on the Optimal Search and Information System

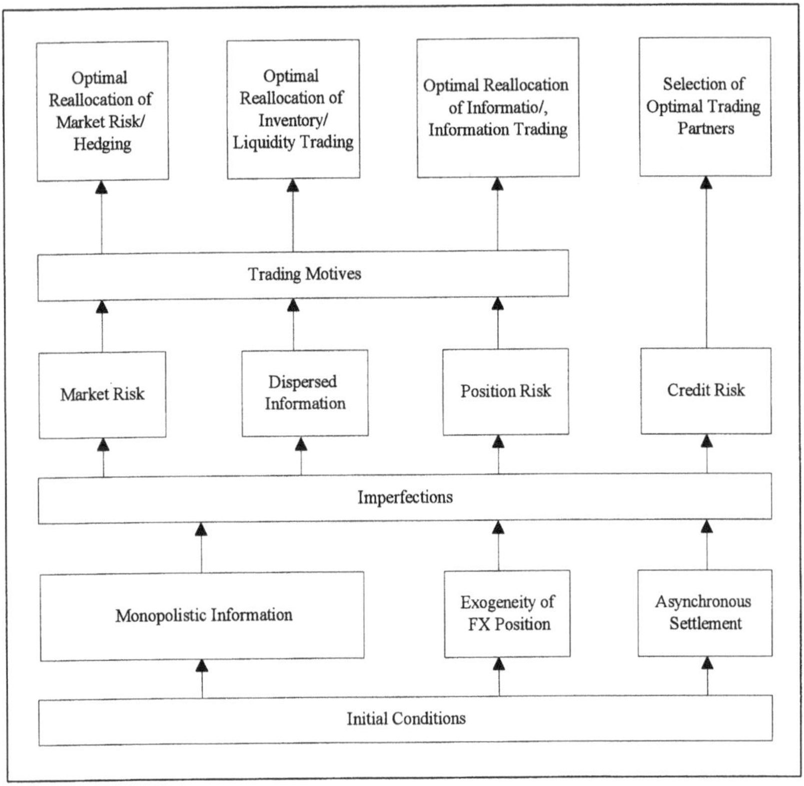

EXAMPLE: 'The short-lived coup d'état in Moscow in August 1991 led to uncertainty about the status ... of certain financial institutions based in, or owned by institutions in, the then Soviet Union. For a few days the uncertainty had a disruptive effect on settlement in the foreign exchange market, in which these institutions were active traders. Some of their market counterparties were unwilling, given the political climate, to expose themselves to what they saw as potentially very acute principal risk in settling their maturing FX contracts. They instead pressed for the receipt of countervalue (or a guarantee from an acceptable third party) in advance of releasing funds. As a result, some deals were not settled when due. There were also some instances of unwillingness on the part of the Soviet-based institutions' correspondent banks to release funds even when countervalue had been received' (Bank for International Settlements 1996, p. 7)[15]. END OF EXAMPLE

2.2 Alternative Search and Information Systems

2.2.1 Decentralized Market

2.2.1.1 Foreign Exchange Market

Imagine the following communication on an electronic trading system. Most institutional arrangements, not only concerning search and information, can be illustrated referring to this fictitious deal (table III.1)[16].

TABLE III.1: A Standard Foreign Exchange Deal

Bank A:	HELLO FRIENDS THIS IS NATIONAL BANK OF AMERICA NY
Bank B:	HIHI FRDS WHAT CAN I DO FOR U?
Bank A:	SPOT DOLLAR EURO IN 10 DLRS PSE
Bank B:	MOM PSE
	20/27
Bank A:	AT 27 I BUY 5 DOLLARS
Bank B:	OK ALL DONE MY EUROS TO DRESDNER FFT
	WHERE YOUR DOLLARS?
Bank A:	MY DOLLARS DIRECT
Bank B:	OK TKS BIBI

Source: Cartledge (1991, p. 11/39)

15 Correspondent banks are treated as if they were branch offices. Agency problems in the relationship bank-corespondent bank are thus ignored.

16 Detailed information on the operation of the foreign exchange market is most importantly provided in Weisweiller (1991) and Fischer-Erlach (1995). But excellent surveys on the foreign exchange market practice can also be found in Riehl and Rodriguez (1983), Anthony (1989), Burnham (1991), and Souren (1995).

INSTITUTION 1 (PARTNER-SPECIFIC TRADING): With reference to Williamson (1983) who characterizes investments in durable assets as transaction-specific (Williamson 1983, p. 522), foreign exchange trading can be referred to as partner-specific trading.

- The FX market practice is to convey the desire to trade to a preselected set of potential trading partners only. Bank A contacts Bank B and a limited number of other Banks C, D, etc. The knowledge of a trading opportunity is thus exclusive to the market participants who have been called upon. It is not the same to all traders at all times and FX trading is pairwise in this sense (Wolinsky 1990, p.1).
- It is also common practice on the FX market that each asking bank reveals its identity at the very beginning of each contact. Hence, FX trading is furthermore non-anonymous.

INSTITUTION 2 (SEALED TRADING): Foreign exchange trading can be referred to as sealed trading, a term which is borrowed from auction theory (McAfee and McMillan 1987, p. 702, a/o). On the FX market, prices are quoted privately in the sense of Wolinsky (1990, p. 1).

- The access to the determination of the terms of trade is restricted to the bargaining partners Bank A and Bank B. No other market participant or third party can observe or participate in ongoing price/quantity negotiations.
- The outcome of the bargaining process is private information to both banks.
- Foreign exchange is traded for multiple execution prices.

INSTITUTION 3 (CONTINUOUS TRADING): On the FX market, orders are obviously processed as they arrive. They are not registered for later execution. Bank A and Bank B above agree or they separate. In other words, FX trading is continuous (Cohen, et al. 1986, p. 12).

INSTITUTION 4 (DEALING, MARKET MAKING, AND STANDARD DEALING AMOUNTS): A market participant is a dealer if and only if he is engaged in price discovery *and* trades for his own account at the same time (Cohen, et al. 1986, pp. 18-19). Bank A and Bank B above are dealers in this sense. So are all other foreign exchange trading banks due to partner-specific trading (institution 1) combined with membership (institution 5). But each FX market participant is also a special kind of dealer. With reference to Bank B's behaviour above, each FX *dealing* bank is making a market (definition III.6) for the USD/EUR currency pair.

DEFINITION III.6 (MARKET MAKING):

- standing ready for a deal (purchase or sale) upon request and
- being prepared to make a firm price offer

- for standard dealing amounts (the equivalent to USD 1-10 million)
- at any time during the business day provided that
- the market is in normal condition (Fischer-Erlach 1995, pp. 29-31).

'A market maker [therefore] ... does not initiate a deal but responds to a request for a price' (Cartledge 1991, p. 11/23).

INSTITUTION 5 (MEMBERSHIP): By quoting a price to Bank A, Bank B acquires the right to ask for a quote specifically at Bank A. It is in fact strongly expected to do so following a (small) number of deals initiated by Bank A. In other words, FX dealing is reciprocal (Fischer-Erlach 1995, pp. 29-31; definition III.7). Consequently, entry to the foreign exchange market is restricted. Market makers only trade with other market makers.

DEFINITION III.7 (RECIPROCITY): 'reciprocity transforms a unilateral supply relation - whereby A sells X to B - into a bilateral one, whereby A agrees to buy Y from B as a condition for making the sale of X and both parties understand that the transaction will be continued only if reciprocity is observed' (Williamson 1983, pp. 530-31).

Restricting entry to the FX market to market makers, however, implies that trading is simultaneously restricted to banks that have invested in transaction-specific trading facilities (definition III.8) in the past. Market making requires the installation and operation of a highly sophisticated dealing room.

DEFINITION III.8 (TRANSACTION-SPECIFIC INVESTMENTS): investments that are realized 'in advance of the contemplated exchange ... Their value in alternative uses, or by alternative users, is greatly reduced' (Williamson 1983, p. 522).

Concluding the characterization of the FX market practice, the comparative analysis of the following chapters can obviously be described as an attempt to develop a theory that explains if and how the combination of

- partner-specific trading,
- sealed trading,
- continuous trading,
- dealing, market making, and standard dealing amounts, and
- membership

responds efficiently to the problems of

- credit risk exposure,
- dispersed information,
- market risk exposure, and
- position risk exposure.

The remainder of this section, thus, gives details on the possible organizational alternatives to the current market practice. Their existence is necessary in order to derive meaningful propositions on the efficiency of market structures given that the approach to the economics of institutions is comparative-static. The selection of the organizational alternatives is finally presented in the appendix to the present chapter below.

2.2.1.2 Free Entry Foreign Exchange Market

Due to the absence of any better real-world example, the first alternative to the current FX market practice is the free entry foreign exchange market. It differs from the existing market structure only in that

- trading would be non-reciprocal and
- transaction-specific investments would not be a prerequisite to participating in FX dealing.

Market makers would therefore face other banks, non-banks as well as other market making banks when being asked for a price. They would not consider the additional information that the asking party is also a market maker as valuable information. They would also not acquire the right to ask for a price at any other bank in the future.

2.2.2 Organized Exchange

2.2.2.1 Frankfurter Wertpapierbörse

Similar to the FX market, organized exchanges in general and the Frankfurter Wertpapierbörse (FWB) in particular are membership markets. The access to FWB requires that

- market participants are banks or brokers who have the necessary organizational capacities and human resources that ensure a smooth operation of trading and settlement,
- market participants deposit a collateral, and
- market participants pay an annual membership fee (Deutsche Börse 1994, §§ 14-23; Deutsche Börse 1996, pp. 8-9).

In contrast to the FX market, however, the membership in exchanges is formal instead of informal. In other words, the legal force of the rules and regulations concerning membership does *not* result from them being self-enforcing agreements. On the contrary, it results from screening. FWB implements, monitors, and enforces the set of criteria that each market participant must comply with in order to be permitted to trading. Hence, FWB is not equally entitled in relation to the stock traders. By design, it is a regulatory authority instead. By the very nature of membership, it cannot be a member of the organization 'stock market'.

FWB also differs from the FX market in its degree of centralization.

- All buy and sell orders for a particular stock are collected in a single order-book,
- they are subsequently matched according to a specific algorithm, hence,
- the buy and sell orders are processed in regular intervals rather than as they arrive (with the frequency depending on how actively the stock is traded) (Frankfurter Wertpapierbörse 1991, pp. 5-19; Deutsche Börse 1994, §§ 26-39; Deutsche Börse 1996, p. 16).

Consequently, trading is not continuous, nor can it be referred to as dealing. Price discovery is beyond the control of any trader.

Finally, FWB is also the reverse to the FX market with respect to the degree of transparency.

- Submitting orders to a monopolistic broker implies equal access to all trading opportunities for all traders at all times.
- The use of a matching algorithm based on price, quantity, and order type implies random matching.
- Monopolistic brokerage guarantees a single execution price.
- The brokers at FWB provide price information prior to closing their books with finality. All traders, therefore, have access to the determination of the terms of trade (Frankfurter Wertpapierbörse 1991, p.12; Deutsche Börse 1994, § 32)[17].

2.2.2.2 London Stock Exchange

The London Stock Exchange (LSE) is equivalent to the Frankfurter Wertpapierbörse with respect to membership and the degree of transparency. It is, however, similar to the FX market with respect to the degree of centralization. At LSE, a market maker system is in operation.

---

[17] Major institutional changes that have recently taken place on the international stock markets and of which more have to be expected in the close future are ignored. It is the organizational alternative of the *current* market structure of FWB that matters in the present context. Whether or not FWB is going to survive the next decade or whether all trading activities move to the electronic XETRA trading system (which actually comes close to the FX market practice) is an interesting but irrelevant question with respect to the present focus. So is the expected merger of major European stock markets (which could for example be driven by the fact that identical assets are meanwhile traded on each market, something that has always been the case for different foreign exchange market places but not for the different stock market centres, until recently).

'In London, the dealers (called jobbers) stand at a post on the trading floor (or sometimes operate by telephone) and write on a chalkboard the names of the stocks handled and the midspread prices (i.e., prices halfway between their bids and asks). Floor brokers holding customer orders walk around to competing jobbers and get bid-ask quotations (but without quantity offers) from each jobber without disclosing whether they wish to buy or sell or are 'just looking'. The broker selects the best counterpart jobber quotation for his customer. The chosen jobber will normally take the full amount of the broker's order at the quoted price so long as the order is not a large block (about $500,000 for major issues)' (Cohen, et al. 1986, p. 19).

The distinguishing feature of the LSE market maker system compared to the one of the FX market is, however, the fact that the number of jobbers is strictly limited to a number *less* than the number of all market participants. Market making is therefore a privilege which LSE grants to a few traders only (Cohen, et al. 1986, p. 24)[18].

2.2.3 Centralized Market

2.2.3.1 Sotheby's

The market for arts in the form of Sotheby's, e.g., is the most familiar centralized market structure. Yet, at the same time, it is the complete opposite to the FX market.

- Participation in trading is not restricted.
- The English auction (definition III.10) with a single auctioneer guarantees the highest degree of centralization that can possibly be achieved. There is no discretion left to any dealer, nor can continuous trading be exploited for strategic reasons or create a broken environment.
- The English auction mechanism guarantees the highest degree of transparency that a market can provide. Except for the identity of the potential trading partners, everything is at all times known to all market participants. Trade is extremely easy to survey[19].

2.2.3.2 Free Entry London Stock Exchange

For the sake of completeness only, a free entry version of the London Stock Exchange provides the final alternative to the current market practice with respect to search and information acquisition. Compared to the free entry FX market, however, it would not

[18] For the rules and regulations of the London Stock Exchange, see also London Stock Exchange (1999).

[19] For details on the rules and regulations of Sotheby's, refer to the terms and conditions which are published together with each catalogue.

only be the preselection of market participants that would be impossible if there was no membership. More importantly, the number of market makers could not be predetermined if the access to the market was open.

3. Comparative Analysis of the Pricing System

3.1 Imperfections

3.1.1 Position Risk Exposure Revisited

Ceteris paribus, position risk is the risk of running out of foreign exchange due to customer trading. FX dealing banks, therefore, engage in interbank trading in order to overcome the exogeneity of their inventories. Based on this idea, the pricing system determines the efficiency of the reallocation of inventory on the interbank market as follows.

Given that the search for potential trading partners was successful, the pricing system directs

- the selection of the counterparty to a transaction as well as
- the selection of the execution price.

Not surprisingly, therefore, different pricing systems (may) lead to different outcomes in this respect. Consequently, different bargaining games (may) entail different bargaining costs when it comes to liquidity trading. Chapter V, section 1 is concerned with this issue.

Given that FX dealing banks are market makers on the interbank market, position risk would still be non-zero even if there was no customer business. Hence, position risk has a second dimension which, in analogy to the adverse selection component of credit risk, could be referred to as the interbank component of position risk. Since, furthermore, the exchange rate is not exogenous to market makers, FX dealing banks can control the inflow and outflow of foreign exchange from interbank trading by setting the exchange rate accordingly. A price increase reduces the excess demand for a particular currency and vice versa. Apart from the search and information system, therefore, it is again the pricing system that can (also) respond to position risk exposure. The design of the bargaining game determines each market makers' ability to set prices efficiently in the sense of minimizing the risk of running out of foreign exchange. The interbank component of position risk is subject of Chapter V, section 3 below[20].

---

[20] Any result of Chapter V, section 3 can of course be applied to the customer market in analogy. Given that the banks set the prices on the customer market, any institution that minimizes the interbank

3.1.2 Dispersed Information Revisited

Monopolistic information on future exchange rate movements gives rise to information trading. *Given* institution 4 (dealing), however, pricing systems differ with respect to if and how they allow for the truthful communication of private information among banks. But the truthful communication of private information is the necessary condition for information trading.

- Spontaneously, no bank reports private information truthfully.
- If, therefore, the pricing system ignores the existence of private information altogether, any Bank B rationally prefers to step back from any proposed deal that Bank A would accept and vice versa. In other words, adverse selection of the Akerlof-type emerges. Agreements always point to a loss which is why the market collapses (Akerlof 1970).
- If, however, the pricing system is designed such that the expected outcome of the bargaining game is always incentive compatible, both banks agree upon each and every profitable deal.

Consequently, different pricing systems entail different bargaining costs since they differ with respect to the incentive compatibility of the expected outcome of the bargaining game. Chapter V, section 2 addresses the incentive compatibility of different bargaining games, figure III.4 below, finally, summarizes the demands on the optimal pricing system.

3.2 Alternative Pricing Systems

3.2.1 Auctions

3.2.1.1 Foreign Exchange Market

INSTITUTION 6 (BID-ASK SPREAD): Returning to table III.1 above, market makers obviously quote a shortened version of the USD/EUR exchange rate, namely, 20/27. The so called big figure is always assumed to be known by all market participants. Let it be USD/EUR 1.10 for simplicity. But, more importantly, quoting 20/27 implies that, on the FX market, two prices are actually quoted instead of one. USD/EUR 1.1020 and USD/EUR 1.1027. The two prices are known as bid and ask rate, respectively. The bid rate, 1.1020, is Bank B's buying price (Bank B pays EUR 1.1020 for USD 1). The ask rate, 1.1027, is its selling price (Bank B charges EUR 1.1027 for USD 1). The difference of seven basic points is the bid-ask spread (Fischer-Erlach 1995, pp. 29-31).

---

market-specific position risk can also reduce the customer market-specific position risk. Both risk categories are analytically equivalent.

FIGURE III.4: Demands on the Optimal Pricing System

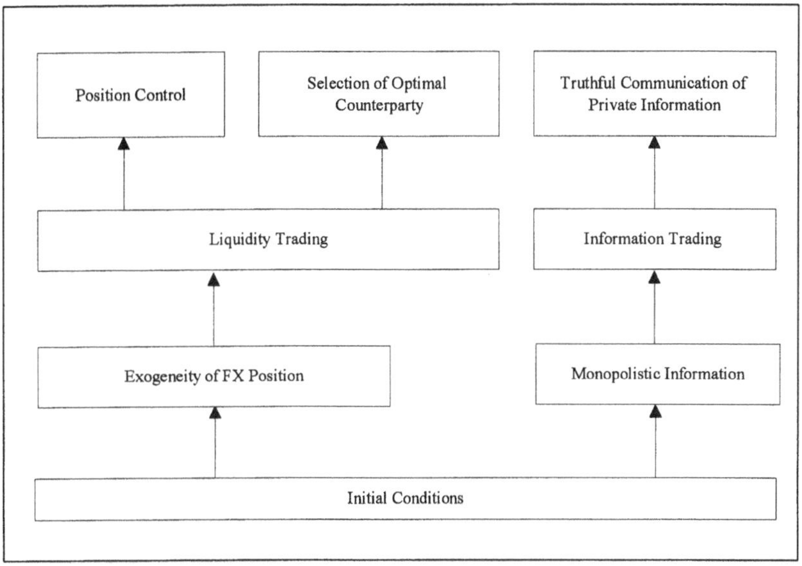

INSTITUTION 7 (FIRST-PRICE SEALED-BID AUCTION AND COMPETITION): Turning from the outcome of the price negotiations to the procedures, the determination of the exchange rate or execution price seems to take place in the form of a simple 'take-it-or-leave-it' price offer.

- Bank A announces its desire to trade by asking for a quote (first move).
- Bank B quotes a bid-ask spread (second move).
- Bank A accepts or rejects (third move).
- The game is not repeated[21].

But the negotiations only seem to be bilateral. If the deal had been recorded in Bank A's dealing room rather than in Bank B's, it would have turned out that Bank A contacted other market makers as well. The determination of the terms of trade is not bilateral but multilateral (Fischer-Erlach 1995, pp. 40-42). Furthermore, the negotiations take place as an auction. Bank B and its competitors are the bidders and Bank A the auctioneer (Flood 1991, p. 59). Even more precisely, the negotiations take place as a first-price

[21] Bank A can individually determine the dealing amount in table III.1 above only because it is below the maximum standard dealing amount of USD 10 million.

sealed-bid auction (definition III.9). In other words, they completely lack transparency with respect to the bidding process. The only information Bank B has is that Bank A 'most likely' contacted other banks as well. In other words, Bank B only knows with certainty that bidding is competitive[22].

DEFINITION III.9 (FIRST-PRICE SEALED-BID AUCTION): 'with a first-price sealed-bid auction, potential buyers submit sealed bids and the highest bidder is awarded the item for the price he bid' (McAfee and McMillan 1987, p. 702).

For illustrative reasons, finally, the first-price sealed-bid auction is frequently used for tendering government procurement contracts. Sometimes, it is also used for selling mineral rights or real estate, a/o. But it is rarely used for selling commodities (McAfee and McMillan 1987, p. 702).

3.2.1.2 Sotheby's and Other Auction Markets

Analytically, there are three basic types of auctions apart from the first-price sealed-bid auction,

- the English auction (definition III.10),
- the Dutch auction (definition III.11), and
- the second-price sealed-bid auction (definition III.12) (McAfee and McMillan 1987, pp. 701-703, a/o)[23].

DEFINITION III.10 (ENGLISH AUCTION): 'in the English auction, the price is successively raised until only one bidder remains. This can be done by having an auctioneer announce prices, or by having bidders call the bids themselves, or by having bids submitted electronically with the current best bid posted. ... The essential feature of the English auction is that, at any point in time, each bidder knows the level of the current best bid (McAfee and McMillan 1987, p. 702).

---

[22] Viewing the price determination as a first-price sealed-bid auction is in contrast to Flood (1991, p. 59) who characterizes the exchange rate determination as open-bid. But execution prices are quoted privately such that not all market participants have simultaneous access to them. In other words, institution 2 (sealed trading) and open bidding are not compatible. The fact that market makers publish quotations on the Reuters FXFX page, e.g., does not make the auction open-bid. The quotes are not binding and, usually, they are not the execution prices (Goodhart, et al. 1996, p. 108).

[23] With respect to the selection of the alternative market structures to the FX market practice, there is no other institutional alternative to the bid-ask spread, a two-tier price, other than a unique price. Furthermore, institution 6, the bid-ask spread, and institution 7, the first-price sealed-bid auction, are not interrelated. Any self-enforcing agreements concerning the bargaining game can be discussed irrespective of whether the price quotation itself is two-tier or unique. For the sake of brevity, therefore, a discussion of the bid-ask spread is first of all postponed to Chapter V, section 3. Secondly, the alternative auction mechanisms are discussed below such that, finally, the emphasis can be on the alternatives to auctions. Section 3.2.2 below on bargaining arrangements thus concludes the presentation of the set of organizational alternatives to the FX market practice.

DEFINITION III.11 (DUTCH AUCTION): 'the Dutch auction is the converse of the English auction. The auctioneer calls an initial high price and then lowers the price until one bidder accepts the current price' (McAfee and McMillan 1987, p. 702).

DEFINITION III.12 (SECOND-PRICE SEALED-BID AUCTION): 'under the second-price sealed-bid auction, bidders submit sealed bids having been told that the highest bidder wins the item but pays a price equal not to his own bid but to the second-highest bid' (McAfee and McMillan 1987, p. 702).

The most prominent example for the English auction is the market for arts and antiques as it is provided by Sotheby's. Price offers can constantly be observed and revised by all bidders and the bidder with the highest bid wins the object and pays the equivalent amount.

'The basic difference between the first-price sealed-bid auction and the English auction is [therefore] that, with the English auction, bidders are able to observe their rival's bids and accordingly, if they choose, revise their own bids; with the sealed bid auction, each bidder can submit only one bid' (McAfee and McMillan 1987, p. 702).

Many goods markets can furthermore be characterized as Dutch auctions. The Dutch auction is for example used for selling cut flowers in the Netherlands, fish in Israel, and tobacco in Canada. Finally, there is, however, no empirical equivalent to the second-price sealed-bid auction. It only has useful theoretical properties (McAfee and McMillan 1987, p. 702) which is why it was originally developed by Vickrey (1961).

3.2.2 Bargaining Arrangements

DEFINITION III.13 (AUCTION): 'an auction is a market institution with an explicit set of rules determining resource allocation and prices on the basis of bids from the market participants' (McAfee and McMillan 1987, p. 701).

Pricing systems cannot unilaterally be classified as auctions in the sense of definition III.13 above. On the contrary, on a more general level, auction markets have to be distinguished from the larger set of decentralized markets that all use some kind of bargaining arrangement (definition III.14) for determining the execution price.

DEFINITION III.14 (BARGAINING): 'following Nash we use the term 'bargaining' to refer to a situation in which (i) individuals ('players') have the possibility of concluding a mutually beneficial agreement, (ii) there is a conflict of interest about which agreement to conclude, and

(iii) no agreement may be imposed on any individual without his approval' (Osborne and Rubinstein 1990, p. 1).

Bargaining arrangements can be thought of in countless numbers. Take-it-or-leave-it offers can turn into repeated offers, repeated offers can be alternating offers, the time horizon can be finite or infinite, etc. But bargaining theory also developed a modelling technique that allows for treating all these arrangements simultaneously which is why more details on possible bargaining arrangements are not required[24].

Finally, the analysis ignores customer markets since the efficiency arguments related to fixed prices (Barro 1972; Mussa 1981; Okun 1981) are based on an inequality assumption concerning the supply and demand for a traded object. The behaviour of firms, the supply side, is systematically distinguished from the behaviour of households, the demand side. But this assumption is not at all justified for FX dealing banks. Matching algorithms are also ignored since they are unique to centralized markets. But the discussion of the pricing system in Chapter V starts with the assumption that the search and information system is a dealing system.

4. Comparative Analysis of the Settlement System

4.1 Imperfections

4.1.1 Credit Risk Exposure Revisited

EXAMPLE 1: On June 26, 1974, 3.30 p.m., Frankfurt time, Bankhaus Herstatt, a Cologne-based bank that was very active on the FX market was closed by the German authorities. By this time, the German interbank payments system had already closed. Hence, the DEM-denominated legs of all USD/DEM transactions that were due that day had already been settled with finality. In other words, Herstatt's trading partners had settled their payment obligations. But when the closure of Herstatt was announced, it was only 10.30 a.m. in New York and Herstatt's correspondent bank had not yet even ordered any settlement of the corresponding USD-denominated legs. It never did. All outgoing US dollar payments from the Herstatt account were suspended. Herstatt's

[24] Refer to Chapter V below. See also Osborne and Rubinstein (1990), Rasmusen (1994), or any intermediate textbook on bargaining theory for a more extensive discussion on bargaining arrangements.

trading partners were left with the loss of the principal amount (Bank for International Settlements 1996, p. 6; Shen 1997, p. 50)[25]. END OF EXAMPLE

EXAMPLE 2: On July 5, 1991, BCCI SA, Luxembourg, was shut down. The day before, on July 4, the London branch of BCCI had sent a payment instruction to its American correspondent bank to settle the USD-denominated leg of a USD/Sterling transaction with a London-based trading partner for value on July 5. On July 5, however, this payment was delayed beyond the normal settlement time (7 a.m., New York time) because the correspondent bank had already exceeded its credit limit with the interbank payments system. The payment, therefore, remained in the queue. Meanwhile, the message from the liquidator of BCCI reached the correspondent bank which immediately cancelled the order. This was the case at about 4 p.m., New York time, when the London interbank payments system had already closed and the Sterling payment had been made with finality. The London-based trading partner, therefore, lost the principal amount of the contract (Bank for International Settlements 1996, p. 7).

END OF EXAMPLE

Both examples clearly demonstrate that

'it is generally not possible to close a bank which is active in the foreign exchange market at a time when all the relevant payments systems have settled all its transactions due on a given day. ... [In the case of BCCI, e.g.], the closure required the Luxembourg Court to appoint a liquidator, an action which under Luxembourg law can take place only within the normal business day of the Court' (Bank for International Settlements 1996, p. 7).

Both examples, therefore, demonstrate that there is an inherent risk in foreign exchange transactions that the counterparty fails *after* receiving a payment but *prior* to delivering. Due to its very nature, the risk must be referred to as credit risk. But, at the same time, it is analytically different to the adverse selection component that was introduced in section 2 above. More precisely, losing the principal amount half-way through the settlement process can be interpreted as arising from moral hazard due to the counterparty's hidden knowledge of its own insolvency.

A solvent Bank B must generally choose between the two actions 'deliver' and 'fail to deliver' not yet knowing the counterparty's action. Bank A's action, however, depends on whether or not it has turned insolvent (assuming until further notice that it is optimal for Bank A to deliver if it is solvent). Hence, Bank B would need to know Bank A's

[25] The Herstatt failure was the first serious international settlement failure ever to occur. The overall settlement risk is therefore often referred to as the Herstatt risk which is; strictly speaking, inappropriate.

status in order to correctly anticipate the counterparty's action. Unfortunately, however, the settlement procedures only allow for the reverse. Consequently, Bank B can only learn Bank A's status from observing Bank A's action, in other words, when it is 'too late'. Bank B loses the principal amount if unfortunate (figure III.5).

FIGURE III.5: Bank B's Exposure to the Moral Hazard Component of Credit Risk

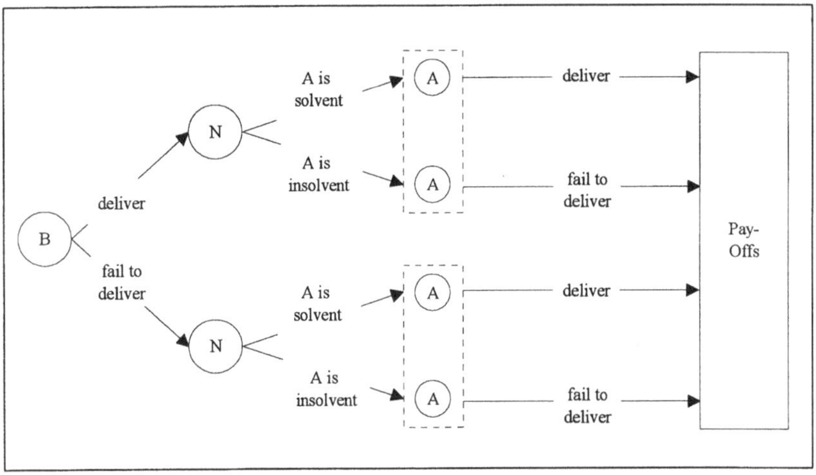

Nevertheless, rational behaviour requires that Bank B takes the possibility of Bank A's failure into account. It does so by attaching a certain probability to the event 'insolvency'. As long as bank failures occur, this probability is non-zero. Moreover, the likelihood of the event 'insolvency' can be interpreted as the moral hazard component of credit risk as opposed to the adverse selection component of credit risk for the following reasons.

- The likelihood of insolvency cannot be equivalent to the adverse selection component of credit risk. On the contrary, it must be *conditional* on the event that the trading partner is unreliable because reliable banks do not fail (the likelihood of which is the adverse selection component of credit risk).
- The information asymmetry is due to Bank A's hidden knowledge (solvent or insolvent) instead of its hidden type (reliable or unreliable). In this sense, the probability is not partner-specific but transaction-specific.
- Bank A's failure to deliver does not result from opportunistic behaviour ex ante[26].

[26] See Milgrom and Roberts (1992, pp. 149-69, 185-91), a/o for details on the characteristics of adverse selection compared to moral hazard.

FIGURE III.6: Bank B's Exposure to the Adverse Selection and Moral Hazard Component of Credit Risk

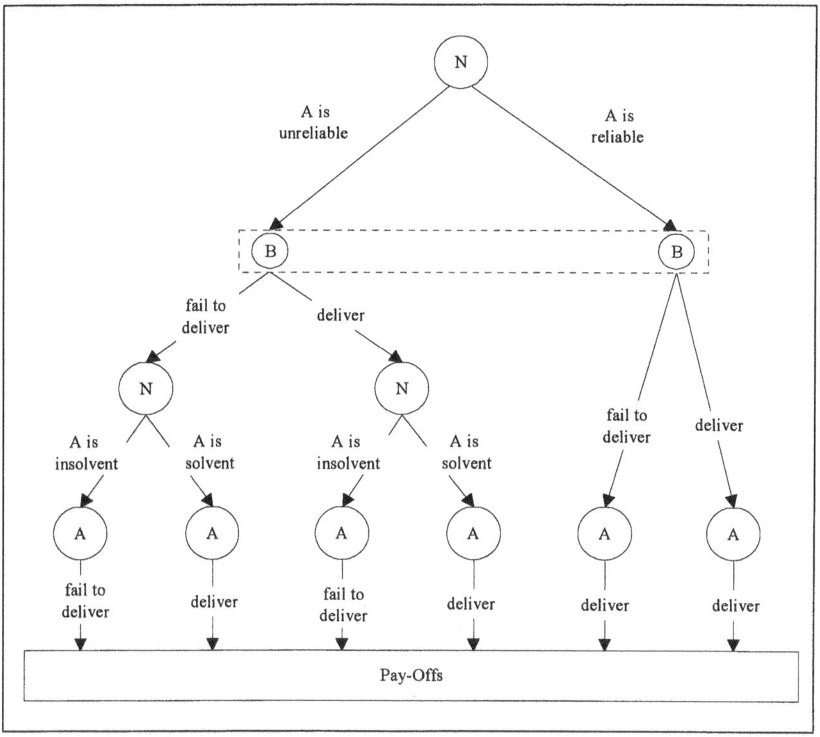

Interpreting credit risk as a problem of moral hazard, finally, implies that it must be accounted for when designing the settlement system. Returning to example 2 above, it is the settlement procedures that can adjust to the business day of Luxembourg Courts, if anything. In other words, settlement systems and settlement systems only differ with respect to if and how they expose their member banks to credit risk which is subject of Chapter VI, section 1 below. The moral hazard and adverse selection component of credit risk combined find their expression in the game tree above (figure III.6).

4.1.2 Liquidity Risk Exposure

Exogenous shocks such as a counterparty's default, large customer orders, or a breakdown in communications affect a bank's willingness or ability to pay. Since, however, the settlement failure in this case is temporary (communications will be re-established sooner or later and an unexpected outflow of funds can be neutralized on the interbank foreign exchange market and/or on national money markets), the relevant risk category must be referred to as liquidity risk (definition III.15) as opposed to credit risk.

DEFINITION III.15 (LIQUIDITY RISK): 'the risk that a counterparty (or participant in a settlement system) will not settle an obligation for full value when due. Liquidity risk does not imply that a counterparty or participant is insolvent since it may be able to settle the required debit obligations at some time thereafter' (Bank for International Settlements 1996, p. 63). In this sense, liquidity risk shall include operational risk, 'the risk of incurring interest charges or other penalties for misdirecting or otherwise failing to make the settlement payments on time owing to an error or technical failure' (Bank for International Settlements 1996, p. 64).

With respect to institutional responses, liquidity risk only matters *because* there is credit risk. Otherwise, communications still break down, etc. Since, however, it would be common knowledge that banks do not turn insolvent, the settlement agent of a payments system would guarantee all obligations and/or Bank A would have unlimited credit with Bank B. But a temporary situation may actually be a permanent one for non-zero credit risk and imperfect information. Settlement failures may thus signal

- a temporary shortage of funds,
- unreliability combined with a temporary shortage of funds, or
- unreliability combined with insolvency (figure III.7).

Consequently, there is generally no settlement guarantee. Furthermore, however, settlement systems differ with respect to if and how they expose their member banks to liquidity risk as Chapter VI, section 2 outlines.

EXAMPLE: In 1990, the Drexel Burnham and Lambert (DBL) group collapsed. The London subsidiary Drexel Burnham Lambert Trading (DBLT) which was an active trader on the FX market, however, was still solvent. The situation nevertheless resulted in DBLT concerns about its trading partners' behaviour. The bank suspected that its counterparties would not settle their obligations even if DBLT itself did but use the funds for offsetting amounts that were due to them from other companies in the group. In other words, liquidity risk emerged for both DBLT and its counterparties because neither of the parties was temporarily willing to settle its obligations due to an exogenous shock, the failure of DBL. This was the case although DBLT was known to be solvent (Bank for International Settlements 1996, pp. 6-7)[27]. END OF EXAMPLE

FIGURE III.7: Bank B's Exposure to Credit Risk and Liquidity Risk

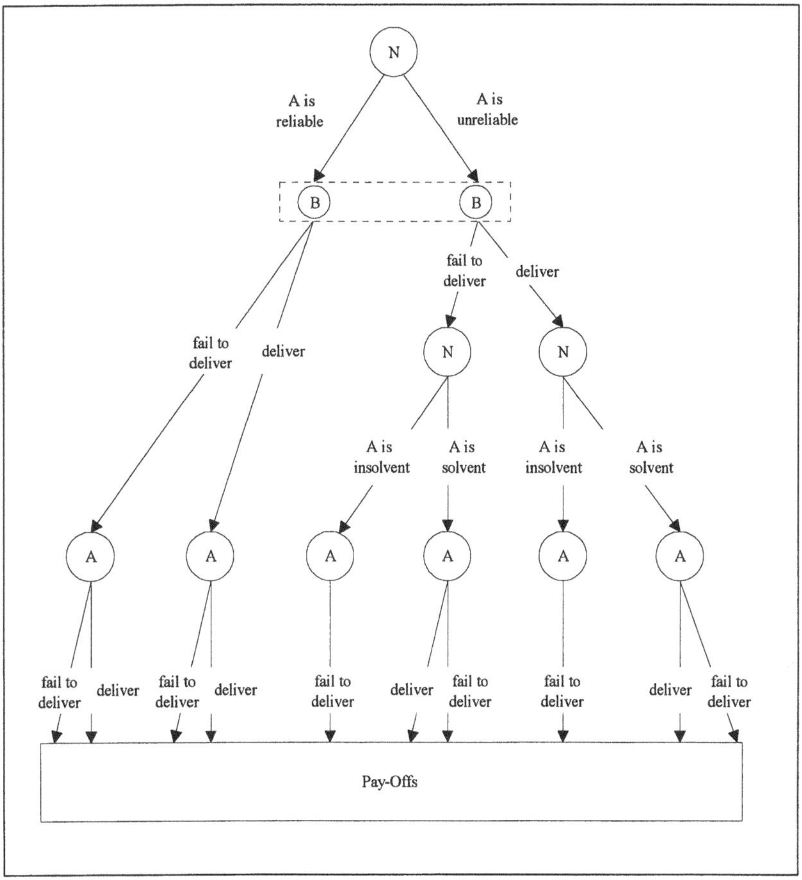

27 The gridlock was finally overcome by the Bank of England establishing a settlement facility that operated according to the following principle. The transfer of funds to the settlement facility is not final until the counterparty has also paid in the equivalent amount (Bank for International Settlements 1996, pp. 6-7).

4.1.3 Systemic Risk Exposure

DEFINITION III.16 (SYSTEMIC RISK): 'the risk that the failure of one participant in a transfer system, or in financial markets generally, to meet its required obligations when due will cause other participants or financial institutions to be unable to meet their obligations (including settlement obligations in a transfer system) when due. Such a failure may cause significant liquidity or credit problems and, as a result, might threaten the stability of financial markets' (Bank for International Settlements 1996, p. 65).

Systemic risk (definition III.16) results from implementing multilateral arrangements, in the present case, payments systems. Furthermore, it clearly depends on the likelihood of individual settlement failures. Given, therefore, that

- credit risk and liquidity risk are both non-zero and
- the Bank for International Settlements estimated that FX settlement accounted for something between 50 and 90 per cent of the daily turnover value of major national payments systems in 1996 (Bank for International Settlements 1996, p. 4),

systemic risk exposure is likely to be significant. This is even more important since it equally affects all market participants.

For gross settlement, which is one of the two alternatives for operating a payments system, systemic risk arises because one payer's failure to settle an obligation may cause a liquidity problem for the corresponding payee. The funds may have been anticipated such that they were destined for settling one of the payee's obligations with a third party. Any delay of this payment may in turn threaten the third party with a liquidity shortage, etc. The more banks fail to settle, therefore, the more likely is a situation where each bank lacks funds in the end. The result is obviously a chain reaction of unrealized payment obligations (Shen 1997, pp. 48-50).

With respect to netting, the second alternative for operating a payments system, systemic risk arises because the settlement necessarily requires that each bank is capable of covering negative balances on its account with the settlement agent. If, however, the funds are missing, the netting of all transactions that the bank was involved in must be unwound. This, however, leads to other banks not having the necessary funds available since they have calculated a different balance with respect to their own account, etc. Finally, none of the transactions is likely to be settled leading to a potential breakdown of all payments services. The actual liquidity situation of each bank may differ significantly from the one that was expected. The outcome is again a chain reaction of unfulfilled payment obligations (Shen 1997, pp. 51-52; table III.2). Concluding section 4.1 with the following example on systemic risk and figure III.8 below, Chapter VI, section 3 returns to the spill-over effects of individual settlement failures.

EXAMPLE: In February 1995, Barings Brothers collapsed. The administrator was appointed on Sunday, February 26. On Friday, one of Barings' trading partners had already sent a payment instruction addressed to Barings' correspondent. The settlement was to occur through the ECU clearing system, a netting system, on Monday. On Monday, of course, the trading partner tried to reverse the transaction but, at the end of the day, it turned out that this was legally impossible as well as not allowed according to the rules of the ECU clearing system. Hence, Barings' trading partner, who did not anticipate this outcome, ended up with an unexpected net debit position which it was unable to cover. Hence, the settlement of the daily turnover of ECU 50 billion among altogether 45 banks were suddenly at risk creating major liquidity problems for most participating banks (Bank for International Settlements 1996, p. 8). Speaking with the Bank for International Settlements (1996),

'this demonstrates the potential problems which can be caused when banks do not have a thorough understanding of the rules of the clearing systems through which they will pay or receive the currencies of their market transactions. If the sending bank had not eventually agreed to borrow in order to cover its payment, the end-of-day settlement would have been frustrated. The clearing would have had to be unwound, so that no payments between any of the 45 ECU clearing banks would have been settled on the due day, even though less than 1% of those payments had anything to do with Barings. The failure to settle could have had very serious consequences for the banks, and for their customers, in the ECU market and more widely' (Bank for International Settlements 1996, p. 8). END OF EXAMPLE

4.2 Alternative Settlement Systems

4.2.1 Single-Currency Settlement

4.2.1.1 Foreign Exchange Market

INSTITUTION 8 (SINGLE-CURRENCY SETTLEMENT): The settlement of FX transactions is equivalent to the settlement of any purchase of goods, services, or assets that is paid for using money in the form of bank deposits. Each leg is always and ultimately settled using national payments systems which process payment instructions that are denominated in the same currency. In this sense, the settlement of foreign exchange transactions is single-currency.

FIGURE III.8: Demands on the Optimal Settlement System

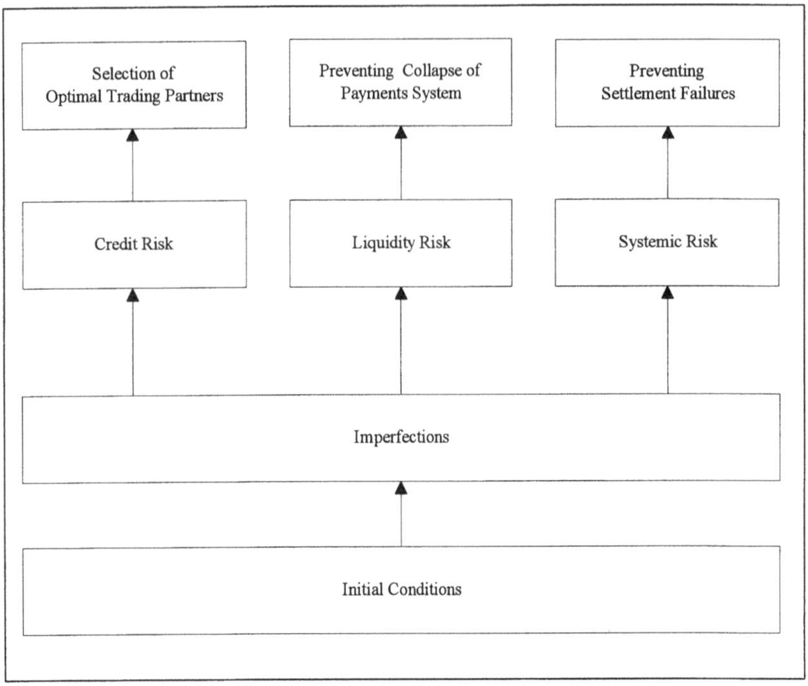

INSTITUTION 9 (BILATERAL SETTLEMENT): The settlement of FX transactions is also bilateral as opposed to multilateral since (until recently) there have not existed any transaction-specific settlement arrangements that required the participation of more than two banks (Fischer-Erlach 1995, p. 140).

INSTITUTION 10 (GROSS SETTLEMENT): With reference to definition III.17 below, the settlement of foreign exchange transactions can finally be interpreted as a settlement in gross amounts as opposed to net amounts since (until recently) neither leg has somehow been processed *prior* to entering the national payments system. In other words, a payment instruction has been issued for the principal amount of each spot contract. This has been the case even for a number of more than one payments to the credit of the same counterparty (Fischer-Erlach 1995, p. 140).

DEFINITION III.17 (GROSS SETTLEMENT SYSTEM): 'a transfer system in which the settlement of funds or securities transfers occurs individually on an order-by-order basis according to the rules and procedures of the system, i.e. without netting debits against credits' (Bank for International Settlements 1993, p. 538).

Summarizing institutions 8-10, a settlement system for foreign exchange transactions has in effect not existed. It has been the national payments systems that have been used 'as if' foreign exchange transactions were domestic transactions.

INSTITUTION 11 (CREDIT LIMITS): FX dealing banks impose credit limits on each of their counterparties. In other words, they restrict the partner-specific trading volume to a maximum. Most generally, these limits apply to the total exchange turnover that is allowed to mature on the same day. Sometimes, however, these limits are furthermore supplemented by a partner-specific limit for all outstanding transfers or for all outstanding transfers over a certain period (Fischer-Erlach 1995, pp. 131-33).

4.2.1.2 Bilateral Netting

Although gross settlement has just been introduced as the FX market practice, the information technologies used in international banking (FXNET, Valunet, S.W.I.F.T. Accord, a/o) provide netting services (definition III.18) on a bilateral basis. More precisely, in 1997, 77 per cent of surveyed Group of Ten banks engaged in processing payment obligations prior to forwarding them to national payments systems.

- (Expected) incoming and outgoing payments
- with the same counterparty
- denominated in the same currency

were aggregated such that only the eventually resulting negative balance was actually settled. Overall settlement flows were at the same time reduced by 15 per cent (Bank for International Settlements 1998, pp. 2, 5, 15-16)[28].

DEFINITION III.18 (NET SETTLEMENT, POSITION NETTING): 'the settlement of a number of obligations or transfers between or among counterparties on a net basis' (Bank for International Settlements 1996, p. 540) for netting being understood as position netting in the sense that 'the netting of instructions in respect of obligations between two or more parties ...

[28] Given that the overall settlement flow reduced by only 15 per cent although 77 per cent of the surveyed banks participated in bilateral netting (Bank for International Settlements 1998, pp. 15-16), it is still justifiable to interpret gross settlement as common practice. This is also convenient for methodological reasons since the settlement of foreign exchange transactions is currently undergoing major changes and gross settlement can be referred to as the benchmark model for demonstrating the efficiency gains related to the envisaged system.

neither satisfies nor discharges those original individual obligations' (Bank for International Settlements 1996, p.542)[29].

EXAMPLE: Let the following payment obligations enter a netting system.

Transaction 1: Bank C pays Bank A USD 20 million.
Transaction 2: Bank A pays Bank B USD 15 million.
Transaction 3: Bank B pays Bank A USD 10 million.
Transaction 4: Bank A pays Bank C USD 10 million.

In this case, the total debit of each bank is subtracted from its total credit and the bank only settles any negative difference or its net debit position. The net debit position of the payments system is thus always equal to zero (table III.2).

TABLE III.2: Net Settlement
(amounts in USD million)

Payer\Payee	Bank A	Bank B	Bank C	Total Debit
Bank A		15	10	25
Bank B	10			10
Bank C	20			20
Total Credit	30	15	10	55
Total Debit	25	10	20	
Net Receipt (Net Payment)	5	5	(10)	

Source: Shen (1997, p. 53)

END OF EXAMPLE

[29] Any other form of netting is not permitted in most G-10 countries since the original contracts must in one way or another be replaced by a new, offsetting contract otherwise which however does not entail the same information on quantities and prices as the original ones. In particular, the exchange rate that equalizes the net obligations is not the execution price. It is the result of simple algebra. Speaking with most national supervisory authorities, therefore, netting could be used to 'hide' unfavourable deals or collusive behaviour (Bundesaufsichtsamt 1982; Fischer-Erlach 1995, pp. 140-42).

4.2.1.3 Exchange Clearing House

'ECHO (Exchange Clearing House Limited) is a London-based clearing house for the multilateral netting and settlement of spot and forward foreign exchange obligations between its users' (Bank for International Settlements 1998, p 18).

Effectively, therefore, ECHO extends position netting per currency with respect to the counterparties beyond the number of two.

ECHO is, however, not a settlement system in the sense that it circumvents the use of national payments systems. On the contrary, ECHO operates nostro accounts for each currency such that it has access to the national payments systems in the same way as FX dealing banks have. The major difference to gross settlement and bilateral netting is therefore that, in regular intervals,

- ECHO notifies any net payer *with the entire clearing house* about their debit positions
- which the net payers settle by transferring the necessary funds *to the ECHO accounts*
- for *sending on* to the net creditors with the system.

Though ECHO is multilateral, therefore, it remains a single-currency netting arrangement.

But for operating nostro accounts, furthermore, ECHO is not merely a services provider for calculating net debit positions. This is due to the 'zero sum' property of netting arrangements (all imbalances always sum up to zero at settlement time). Ceteris paribus, the 'zero sum' property enables ECHO to always settle each obligation although it is not at all capitalized. Hence, ECHO indeed guarantees the settlement of all the payers' obligations to the credit of any payee (as long as both parties are members of the system, of course). In other words, ECHO replaces the payer in any transaction that is reported to it. Similar to commercial banks, therefore, ECHO intermediates rather than brokers financial transactions. The clearing house is in the dual role of being a creditor (with respect to the payer) *and* a debtor (with respect to the payee) at the same time.

Finally, however, ECHO guarantees each member bank's obligations up to a pre-specified level only. Most importantly, this level is determined by the collateral that the bank deposits with ECHO in terms of US treasury bills. In other words, the settlement guarantee is subject to bank-specific credit limits[30].

---

[30] A detailed description of the operations of ECHO was not readily available at the time of writing. The above paragraphs are therefore based on extensive discussions with FX market participants and the Exchange Clearing House Limited. So is the following section 4.2.4 on the CLS Bank.

With respect to the relevance of multilateral netting compared to gross settlement and bilateral netting, the Bank of International Settlement outlines that 23 per cent of the G-10 banks that were included in the already familiar survey engaged in this activity in 1997. Overall settlement flows were at the same time reduced by 0.8 per cent only (Bank for International Settlements 1998, p. 16). In fact, according to market participants, the use of ECHO is expected to increase dramatically in the close future. Furthermore, ECHO is from now on referred to as the clearing house that resulted from the merger of the original ECHO with Multinet (US-based) and CLSS (Continuously Linked Settlement Services, Belgium). All of them were providers of the same services with respect to the settlement of FX transactions (Bank for International Settlements 1998, p. 19).

4.2.2 Multi-Currency Settlement

4.2.2.1 Continuously Linked Settlement Bank

The Continuously Linked Settlement (CLS) Bank is not yet operational. But

'although the details of the CLS Bank design continue to evolve, the underlying principle is clear. ... The CLS Bank will act as a settlement intermediary between the two counterparties to an FX trade or between their correspondents. Participants will hold multicurrency accounts at the CLS Bank, which will settle trades by debiting the account of the seller of the currency and crediting that of the buyer. Both sides of each trade will settle simultaneously on the CLS Bank's books ... While settlement of the trades will be on a gross basis across the accounts at the CLS Bank, the funding and defunding of the accounts by the participants will be on the basis of the net amounts in each currency of the trades they are settling that day' (Bank for International Settlements 1998, p. 19).

In other words, the CLS Bank will provide the one and only payments system for the settlement of foreign exchange transactions. Each member bank of the CLS Bank, thus, circumvents the use of national payments systems. The objective of settling foreign exchange transactions separately is achieved by the banks holding their nostro accounts for *each* currency with *one and the same* settlement agent, the CLS Bank. Consequently, the CLS Bank will be the one and only multi-currency arrangement. By definition, settlement is multilateral. It has finally been chosen to be gross settlement.

Having all accounts concentrated at the CLS Bank, the settlement will occur payment-versus-payment. More precisely, monitoring all nostro accounts, the CLS Bank can and will verify prior to processing two corresponding payment instructions that the seller *and* the buyer have the necessary working balances on their respective accounts. It will then transfer the funds in gross amounts. It will however not do so otherwise.

Gross settlement, finally, requires that each participant holds sufficiently high balances with the CLS Bank (per currency and/or overall including overdraft facilities). The Bank will thus issue clear rules in this respect. Ceteris paribus, therefore, the accounts only need to be (re-)funded for neutralizing a net debit position at the end of a settlement day and vice versa. Settlement could thus take place 'all day long'. Nevertheless, the CLS Bank will only process each currency pair during times where there is a window-of-opportunity (definition III.19).

DEFINITION III.19 (WINDOW-OF-OPPORTUNITY): the time period during which the national payments systems that correspond to a currency pair are both operational.

4.2.2.2 Multi-Currency Netting

For the sake of completeness, the organizational alternatives to the FX market practice shall include multi-currency netting. The settlement system can be thought of as the CLS Bank, the only difference being that the total credit and debit positions are set off against each other prior to settlement. The payments system is furthermore assumed not to guarantee settlement, as was the case for ECHO, the second multilateral netting arrangement that enters Chapter VI below[31].

5. Supply and Demand for Foreign Exchange

Chapters IV-VI adopt the general approach of the microstructure literature to asset markets. But starting with Garman (1976), who first formalized an inventory control problem, and Copeland and Galai (1983), who introduced information trading, most authors have taken the market structure as given, mainly focusing instead on price behaviour, the bid-ask spread, and the trading volume[32]. The following asset demand model, which can be found in Kreps (1990, pp. 93-98), therefore, differs from the

---

[31] There are three organizational alternatives to the FX market practice that are ignored. (i) Multi-currency, bilateral, and net settlement are ignored because any advantage of bilateral netting over gross settlement is independent of whether the settlement is single-currency or multi-currency. (ii) Multi-currency, bilateral, and gross settlement are ignored because it describes the situation of a single payments system for the settlement of all transactions worldwide. It is therefore reasonable to ignore this alternative. (iii) Single-currency, multilateral, and gross settlement are ignored because there are no efficiency gains to be expected by any multilateral arrangement that does not process the payment flow in one way or the other.

[32] For a recent overview, see O'Hara (1995).

standard framework in as much as it necessarily remains in an early stage, at least for the beginning.

Imagine bank $n \in N = (A, B, \ldots)$ to be initially endowed with EUR_0 units of Euros and USD_0 units of US dollars. The positions may result from customer business or any other of the bank's activities. For each time $t = 1, 2, \ldots, T-1$, let bank *n* furthermore be allowed to trade ΔUSD_t units of US dollars against Euros on the FX spot market at the 'market' exchange rate e_t. It values the US dollars in terms of Euros, which shall be the unit of account, by the reservation price or 'private' exchange rate v_t. Due to the nature of foreign exchange, bank *n*'s final period portfolio P_T is thus given as

$$\text{(III.1)} \qquad \mathrm{P}_T = \left(EUR_0 - \sum_{t=1}^{T-1} \Delta USD_t e_t \right) + \left(USD_0 + \sum_{t=1}^{T-1} \Delta USD_t \right) v_T .$$

For each trading session *t*, the initial Euro position decreases by $\Delta USD_t e_t$ units for a purchase of US dollars and vice versa. At the same time, the USD position increases by the equivalent amount of ΔUSD_t and vice versa.

Bank *n*'s objective is to maximize $u(\mathrm{P}_T)$. For a risk averse bank *n*, therefore, its preferences can be expressed as a von Neumann-Morgenstern utility function $U(\cdot)$ which is strictly increasing, concave, and differentiable. This case is referred to below (Chapter IV, section 3). Now turning to a risk neutral bank *n*, the preferences over P_T are given such that

$$\text{(III.2)} \qquad u(\mathrm{P}_T) = a\mathrm{P}_T - b, \qquad \text{for } a > 0.$$

Maximizing equation (III.2) with respect to either or both of the bank's decision variables, more precisely, the exchange rate and/or the dealing amount, the first-order conditions would not depend on the initial endowments. Reflecting a standard result, risk neutral agents maximize trading profits only. They do not consider their inventories in absolute terms. Hence, let the model be simplified such that $a = 1$ and $EUR_0 = USD_0 = b = 0$. bank *n*'s decision problem is then equivalent to

$$\text{(III.3)} \qquad \text{Max} \quad v_T \sum_{t=1}^{T-1} \Delta USD_t - \sum_{t=1}^{T-1} \Delta USD_t e_t .$$

For each trading opportunity, bank n needs to compare the exchange rate with its own reservation price and submit the following market orders[33] in order to maximize utility.

(III.4) $$\Delta USD_t \begin{matrix} >0 & if & v_T - e_t > 0 \\ <0 & if & v_T - e_t < 0 \\ =0 & if & v_T - e_t = 0 \end{matrix}.$$

Finally, note that

- the model is for discrete variables,
- it is (still) one of certainty,
- selling short is not restricted,
- credit limits can be introduced by restricting USD_t such that $USD_{limit,low} \leq USD_t \leq USD_{limit,up}$ (in which case, a credit limit for EUR_t is automatically implemented as well), and
- the dealing amounts can be standardized such that $\Delta USD_t = \Delta USD$ if bank n is a buyer and $\Delta USD_t = -\Delta USD$ if it is a seller[34].

---

[33] The analysis is restricted to market orders. For a discussion of limit orders, see Harris (1991) and Madhavan (1992).

[34] Introducing standard dealing amounts is not only useful since it reflects the reality on the foreign exchange market. Due to the linear nature of the model with risk neutral agents, any solution is necessarily a corner solution and the decision variables must therefore be restricted. In fact, if a linear model adequately describes a bank's decision problem, standardized dealing amounts may be explained on these grounds. The price fluctuations that would result from changes in a bank's valuation of a currency such that it wants to switch from buying to selling could be enormous otherwise. The bank would not only square out an undesired position, but also try to immediately reverse it during the same trading session. Further explanation is provided in Chapter IV, section 4 below.

Appendix: Alternative Search and Information Systems

The comparative method of the present analysis requires contrasting the existing arrangements of the current market practice with a set of alternatives. The selection of the possible alternatives to the search and information system is the focus of this appendix. Section 1 introduces the alternatives on the institutional level and section 2 identifies the possible institutional environments or organizational arrangements.

1. Institutional Alternatives

Table III.3 below compares each of the implemented institutions 1-5 above with the corresponding alternative arrangement. A similar inventory with respect to search and information systems can be found in Cohen, et al. (1986, pp. 9-14, 16-25) and Wolinsky (1990, p. 1) who have already served to identify the various institutional arrangements that determine the search and information system of the FX market. Pagano and Roell (1992, pp. 3-6) also adopt this view whereas Madhavan (1992, pp. 607-10) uses slightly different categories in his analysis of different search and information systems. He refers to a less detailed classification of order versus quote-driven systems.

TABLE III.3: Set of Institutional Alternatives to Institutions 1-5

	FX Market Practice	Alternative
Institution 1	Partner-Specific Trading	Centralized Trading
Institution 2	Sealed Trading	Open Trading
Institution 3	Continuous Trading	Periodic Trading
Institution 4	Dealing and Market Making	Order Matching
Institution 5	Membership	Free Entry

ALTERNATIVE 1 (CENTRALIZED TRADING): Trading is centralized as opposed to partner-specific trading whenever each market participant has access to identical trading opportunities at all times (Wolinsky 1990, p. 1). Trading shall also be referred to as centralized when it is anonymous.

ALTERNATIVE 2 (OPEN TRADING): Trading is open when prices are quoted publicly (Wolinsky 1990, p. 1). In other words, trading is open as soon as there is unlimited access for all market participants to price negotiations and all other trade information.

Open trading, therefore, implies that the object of trade is always exchanged at a singe execution price.

ALTERNATIVE 3 (PERIODIC TRADING): Trading is periodic rather than continuous if orders are not processed as they arrive but collected for execution all at once at a specific, predetermined time.

ALTERNATIVE 4 (ORDER MATCHING): A matching system is different from a dealing system in as much as the market participants who are engaged in price discovery do not deal for their own account (Cohen, et al. 1986, pp. 18-19). Whereas the only dealing system in operation is the market maker system, various matching systems can be identified. The present analysis shall however be restricted to intermediated trading (definition III.20), which is also known as order-book trading (Cohen, et al. 1986, p.20)[35].

DEFINITION III.20 (INTERMEDIATED TRADING): trading is intermediated if orders are collected by a single, independent agent (broker, automated trading system, etc.) who tries to match them according to a certain algorithm which must determine a unique execution price (Cohen, et al. 1986, pp. 20-21).

For free entry to be self-explanatory compared to membership, table III.3 suggests that, strictly speaking, there are 32 (2^5) alternative market structures for organizing search and information acquisition. In other words, 32 alternative systems would have to be investigated with respect to their specific costs if it was not for the following.

- Order matching cannot be continuous by definition. In a matching system, a sell order can be processed if and only if a corresponding buy order has already been submitted and vice versa. Orders, therefore, cannot be processed as they arrive.
- Dealing is always continuous. Ceteris paribus, immediacy is preferred to delay by both the dealer and the trader. Both parties would be exposed to avoidable market risk otherwise.
- Matching systems are always centralized trading systems. Given that intermediation is monopolistic, order matching is equivalent to centralized trading by definition.
- Partner-specific trading is not compatible with open trading. For partner-specific trading, public price quotations cannot be firm price offers by definition.
- Centralized trading is always open trading. Whereas the other propositions result from straightforward contradictions in terms, this final suggestion results from the

[35] For details on other matching systems, see Cohen , et al. (1986, pp. 20-23). Since order matching allows for splitting up large orders, furthermore, standard dealing amounts do not require separate attention.

analysis of the Walrasian auction compared to the open-outcry auction in Chapter IV, section 2.2.1 below.

The set of 32 possible search and information systems is thus reduced to altogether 6 market structures including the FX market practice itself (table III.4).

2. Organizational Alternatives

HORIZONTAL INTEGRATION: Consolidating each row in table III.4 above allows for a clear description of the institutional choice problem that FX dealing banks face.

- Transparency versus privacy.
- Centralization versus decentralization.
- Free entry versus membership.

The market participants went for the second alternative in each case (table III.5).

TABLE III.4: Set of Alternative Search and Information Systems

FX Market	System 2	System 3	System 4	System 5	System 6
Partner-Specific Trading	Partner-Specific Trading	Centralized Trading	Centralized Trading	Centralized Trading	Centralized Trading
Sealed Trading	Sealed Trading	Open Trading	Open Trading	Open Trading	Open Trading
Continuous Trading	Continuous Trading	Periodic Trading	Continuous Trading	Periodic Trading	Continuous Trading
Dealing	Dealing	Order Matching	Dealing	Order Matching	Dealing
Membership	Free Entry	Membership	Membership	Free Entry	Free Entry

VERTICAL CONSOLIDATION: A similarly useful contribution to a better understanding of the banks' decision problem is to consolidate each column of table II.4 above because it is the same as determining the 'real world equivalents' to the systems 1-6. In so doing, the choice among all possible search and information systems turns out to be the choice among

- the current FX market practice,
- a free entry foreign exchange market,

- a market equivalent to the German stock exchange 'Frankfurter Wertpapierbörse (FWB)',
- the London Stock Exchange (LSE),
- the market for arts and antiques as it is provided by Sotheby's, and
- a free entry LSE.

Each of these market structures (table III.6) is described in section 2.2 above.

TABLE III.5: Set of Alternative Search and Information Systems Revisited I

FX Market	System 2	System 3	System 4	System 5	System 6

Transparency	
Partner-Specific Trading	Centralized Trading
Sealed Trading	Open Trading

Centralization	
Continuous Trading	Periodic Trading
Dealing	Order Matching

Openness	
Membership	Free Entry

TABLE III.6: Set of Alternative Search and Information Systems Revisited II

<table>
<tr><td>System 1</td><td>FX Market</td><td rowspan="2">Decentralized Market</td></tr>
<tr><td>System 2</td><td>Free Entry FX Market</td></tr>
<tr><td>System 3</td><td>FWB</td><td rowspan="2">Organized Exchange</td></tr>
<tr><td>System 4</td><td>LSE</td></tr>
<tr><td>System 5</td><td>Sotheby's</td><td rowspan="2">Centralized Market</td></tr>
<tr><td>System 6</td><td>Free Entry LSE</td></tr>
</table>

The classification of the alternative search and information systems into

- decentralized market,
- organized exchange, and
- centralized market

is finally based on the following two definitions.

DEFINITION III.21 (ORGANIZED EXCHANGE): 'to be classified as an [organized] exchange, a trading system must
provide [public] price information in the form of buy and sell quotations on a regular or continuous basis; ...
have either a formal market-maker structure or a consolidated limit order book, or be a single price auction;
centralize trading for the purpose of trade execution; [and]
have members' (Domowitz 1996, pp. 104-105)[36].

DEFINITION III.22 (CENTRALIZED MARKET):'in such [centralized] markets the trades are carried out at publicly announced prices and all traders have access to the same trading opportunities' (Wolinsky 1990, p. 1).

[36] The quoted definition of organized exchanges is based on The American Securities Exchange Act and decisions by the US-based Securities and Exchange Commission, thus, adopting a functional approach.

CHAPTER IV

The Optimal Search and Information System

> 'The structure of the foreign exchange market is inherently different from that of equity or commodity markets. It lacks their centralization and transparency' (Frankel, Galli and Giovannini 1996, p. x).

The previous paragraphs provided the basis for the comparative analysis of the FX market structure. Chapter III, section 2, in particular, opened the following matrix with respect to the search and information system (table IV.1). The objective of sections 1-4 below is consequently to fill in each of the 36 cells in terms of transaction costs which finally results in the identification of one (or more) efficient arrangements with respect to search and information acquisition.

For *given* search costs,

- section 1 focuses on credit risk exposure and the related information costs in terms of agency costs and
- section 2 analyzes dispersed information and the related information costs in terms of foregone returns on information.

Leaving behind the ceteris paribus assumption of constant search costs and assuming perfect information instead,

- section 3 then turns to market risk exposure and the trade-off between minimizing the costs of delay and minimizing liquidity costs. Liquidity costs are defined as the discount that a trader must pay for stand-by trading opportunities. The costs of delay are therefore given as the costs of waiting for these opportunities. Both the costs of delay and the liquidity costs are search costs by nature. The trade-off situation arises from being exposed to market risk.
- Section 4 finally addresses position risk exposure and the second trade-off between minimizing the costs of delay and minimizing liquidity costs. For the exposure to position risk, however, liquidity costs are referred to as order processing costs as opposed to discounts. Stand-by trading opportunities are not costly for foreign

- exchange being a risky asset. They are costly because market makers give up the control over their inventory positions for standing ready for a deal upon request (figure IV.1)

1. Credit Risk Exposure and the Efficiency of Partner-Specific Trading, Sealed Trading, and/or Membership

1.1 Agency Costs

1.1.1 Foregone Trading Profits

Starting with the most simple case, imagine the risk neutral Bank A above to purchase the standard dealing amount of one US dollar $(\Delta USD = 1)$ from the risk neutral Bank B above for EUR 1.10 at time $t = 1$. The transaction is not repeated such that $T = 2$. Neither payment nor delivery can be monitored because the settlement of the US dollar payment occurs early in the morning, local time, whereas the funds transfer denominated in EUR is instructed late in the afternoon, again, local time. Hence their is no second-mover advantage.

Performing according to this agreement, Bank A as well as Bank B have to deliver EUR 1.10, respectively, USD 1.00 on the settlement day. Both banks do however have the option to violate the agreement (Telser 1980, p. 27). Speaking in game-theoretic terms, they have the choice between the two actions 'deliver (D)' and 'fail to deliver (F)'. Their decision depends on the payoffs to either of the two actions, taking into account the other party's (re-)action. The game is one of simultaneous moves because both payments are analytically equivalent to an advance payment due to the monitoring inability. The relevant payoff matrix is presented in table IV.2 below[37].

Clearly, {F,F} is the only Nash equilibrium in pure strategies in this game. But it is also the only equilibrium in mixed strategies. For any subjective probability associated with the trading partner playing D including a probability of one and, thus, zero credit risk, it is always optimal for both banks to play F. In other words, F is the dominant strategy for each player. Returning to real world terms, therefore, Bank A and Bank B violate the agreement. They do so irrespective of the credit risk that they associate with each other

[37] According to equation III.4 above, the described deal requires $v^B < e < v^A$. For simplicity, the following numerical values are assumed. $v^A = 1.30$ and $v^B = 0.80$. Since the transaction is not repeated, furthermore, the time subscripts can be ignored until interest rates are considered.

which, again, is given as the probability of the trading partner playing F. This gridlock situation of non-cooperation in a one-shot game is a familiar result and, thus, well known as the prisoners' dilemma.

'Therefore, a prudent ruler cannot keep his word, nor should he, when such fidelity would damage him, and when the reasons that made him promise are no longer relevant. This advice would not be sound if all men were upright; but because they are treacherous and would not keep their promises to you, you should not consider yourself bound to keep your promises to them' (Machiavelli 1532, pp. 61-62)[38].

TABLE IV.1: Comparative Analysis of the Search and Information System

Market Structures\ Imperfections	**Credit Risk Exposure**	**Information Trading**	**Market Risk Exposure**	**Position Risk Exposure**
Decentralized Market				
FX Market (Membership)				
FX Market (Open Entry)				
Organized Exchange				
FWB (Order Matching)				
LSE (Market Making)				
Centralized Market				
Sotheby's (Order Matching)				
LSE (Market Making)				
Efficient Arrangement				

[38] Note that, for perfect monitoring, the outcome would have been the same. In a one-shot game, the second mover never pays. But since this is anticipated by the first mover, he does not settle either, irrespective of the credit risk that is associated with his counterparty. For further details on the prisoner's dilemma, see any intermediate textbook on game theory, e.g., Rasmusen (1994).

FIGURE IV.1: Imperfections and Corresponding Costs

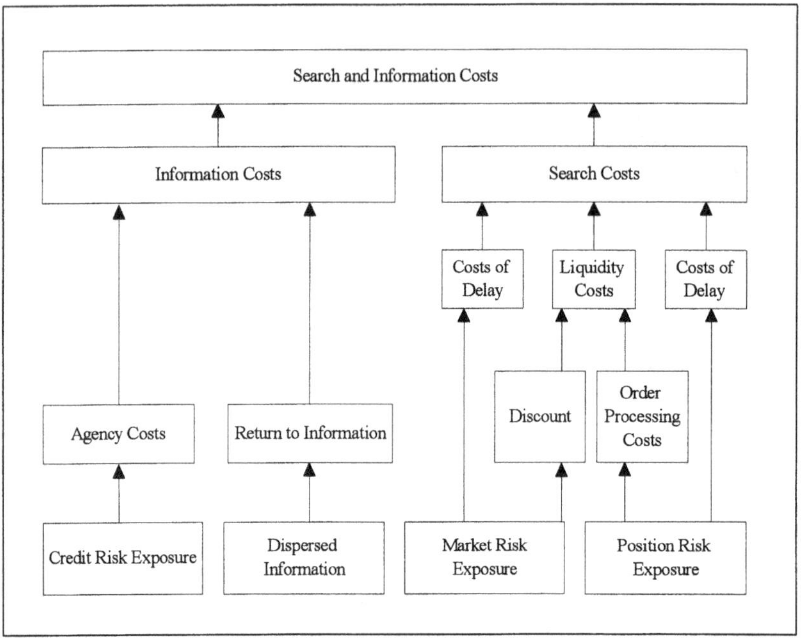

The violation of a non-repeated agreement is rationally anticipated by both banks. The solution is always 'no trade'. The agency costs C_A that result from cooperation failure are therefore given as the foregone trading profits $v^A - e$ or EUR 0.20 for Bank A, respectively, $v^B - e$ or EUR 0.30 for Bank B. Furthermore, they include the foregone, second period interest earnings on the trading profits or $\left(v^{A,B} - e\right)\left(i_2 - i_1\right)$ in absolute terms.

TABLE IV.2: A Non-Repeated Foreign Exchange Deal in Game-Theoretic Terms

Bank A\Bank B	Deliver (D)	Fail to Deliver (F)
Deliver (D)	$v^A - e \; ; \; e - v^B$ (0.20 ; 0.30)	$-e \; ; \; e$ (-1.10 ; 1.10)
Fail to Deliver (F)	$v^A \; ; \; -v^B$ (1.30 ; -0.80)	**0 ; 0**

1.1.2 Opportunity Costs of Collateral

Fortunately, economic agents are inventive and cooperation failure is generally prevented, even in the absence of law. The focus of the present analysis is on mechanisms that are self-enforcing in the sense of definition II.7 above which is repeated as definition IV.1 below.

DEFINITION IV.1 (SELF-ENFORCEMENT): 'a self-enforcing agreement between two parties remains in force as long as each party believes himself to be better off by continuing the agreement than he would be by ending it' (Telser 1980, p. 27).

Williamson (1983), furthermore, suggests only one mechanism that self-enforces delivery in a one-shot game, namely, credible commitments. The idea behind credible commitments is to ensure contract performance by leaving a hostage with the counterparty who is known to be suspicious about the own delivery. Contract violation is unattractive since the counterparty would not release the hostage. He would keep it as a compensation for the loss of the principal amount. For advance payments or credit relationships, the hostage must obviously be thought of as collateral c. Cooperation is ensured because the payoff matrix in table IV.2 above changes such that delivery becomes the best policy (Williamson 1983, pp. 519-20). The point is illustrated for Bank A in table IV.3 below[39].

TABLE IV.3: Bank A's Commitment to Cooperation in a Non-Repeated Transaction

Bank A\Bank B	Deliver (D)	Fail to Deliver (F)
Deliver (D)	$v^A - e \; ; \; e - v^B$ (0.20 ; 0.30)	$-e \; ; \; e + c$ **(-1.10 ; 2.30)**
Fail to Deliver (F)	$v^A - c \; ; \; c - v^B$ (0.10 ; 0.40)	$-c \; ; c$ -1.20 ; 1.20

Bank A's failure to cooperate can thus be prevented for the opportunity costs of foregone interest earnings on c during the first period or $C_C = c \cdot i_1$, the opportunity costs of collateral.

39 c must be greater than the extra profit to violation, more precisely, the exchange rate e. c is thus assumed to be equal to EUR 1.20.

But table IV.3 describes a situation which is unreasonable. Bank A can by no means be expected to enter such an agreement because it rationally anticipates Bank B's non-cooperative behaviour. Although Bank A's failure to cooperate would be prevented, therefore, a foreign exchange market is still unlikely to exist. This prediction, however, turns into its opposite as soon as the deposit of collateral is reciprocal. In this case, the Nash equilibrium is 'both players play D' (Williamson 1983, pp. 528, 530-31). For the reciprocal solution, furthermore, the opportunity costs of collateral are equal to zero for each bank. They are offset by the interest earnings related to the trading partner's collateral that is held in its own portfolio.

1.1.3 Transaction-Specific Investments

Apart from collateral, the hostage can also be thought of as transaction-specific investments. If a certain transaction to be carried out requires special equipment that cannot be redeployed for other purposes, any party that is prepared to pay a significant amount for its installation can be expected to perform according to the agreement. It is in the party's interest that the transaction should be carried out successfully since the return to investment, the trading profit, is zero otherwise (Williamson 1983, p. 522). Transaction-specific investments reduce collateral requirements on a one-to-one basis if both mechanisms are combined.

In contrast to collateral, however, the costs related to the acquisition of transaction-specific assets are not just the costs of foregone interest earnings, since the funds could have been used otherwise. On the contrary, the costs related to the realization of transaction-specific investments include the investments themselves because, due to their very nature, they cannot be redeployed for other productive purposes. In other words, they include the costs of acquisition or sunk costs s. For non-repeated transactions, s is a fixed cost. Finally, the above discussion on reciprocity applies analogously. But neither the opportunity costs are offset nor are the costs of acquisition.

Summarizing sections 1.1.1-1.1.3, the agency costs related to a non-repeated foreign exchange transaction come about as a certain combination of the components that have just been listed above - depending on how search and information acquisition is actually organized (table IV.4).

TABLE IV.4: Agency Costs Related to a Non-Repeated Transaction

Foregone Trading Profits Foregone Interest Earnings	$\lvert v^{A,B} - e \rvert$ $\lvert (v^{A,B} - e)(i_2 - i_1) \rvert$
Opportunity Costs of Collateral (Non-Reciprocal Solution)	$c^{A,B} \cdot i_1$
Opportunity Costs of Collateral (Reciprocal Solution)	Zero
Transaction-Specific Investments Foregone Interest Earnings	$s^{A,B}$ $s^{A,B} \cdot i_2$

1.1.4 Investments in Reputation

Whenever a trader knows that his counterparty wishes to renew a deal, he can eventually rely on threatening with the termination of business relations in order to enforce contract performance (Telser 1980, pp. 27-28). Hence, for the absence of any commitments, the dynamics of repeated play require the following, separate analysis compared to the static model of the previous sections[40].

The settlement of a repeated transaction between Bank A and Bank B is self-enforcing if and only if

(IV.1) $\quad \mathrm{P}_{j-1} + v_T^A \leq \mathrm{P}_T, \quad$ for Bank A,

and

(IV.2) $\quad \mathrm{P}_{j-1} + e_j \leq \mathrm{P}_T, \quad$ for Bank B.

In other words, the trading profits for $j-1$ rounds of trading plus the one-time extra profit at the time of the violation j must be less than or equal to the trading profits for all

40 Since the choice of sanctions determines whether or not an agreement is self-enforcing, the most severe punishment, namely, the termination of the business relationship, is assumed. On the one hand, no forgiveness is a reasonable assumption as long as there are more than one trading opportunities for the non-violating party. It can simply turn to other trading partners. On the other hand, the assumption reflects the reality on the FX market (Fischer-Erlach 1995, p. 29).

$T-1$ rounds of trading for a repeated agreement to be self-enforcing. Otherwise, a violation occurs at time j (Telser 1980, pp. 37-38).

Reflecting the exposure to credit risk, however, neither Bank A nor Bank B can reasonably be assumed to know with certainty at any time t

- when the counterparty intends to exit the market, in other words, whether $T^{A,B} < T$ and the counterparty is unreliable (thus, reflecting the adverse selection component of credit risk as it is discussed below) and
- whether condition (IV.1), respectively, (IV.2) holds for the current round of trading, in other words, whether $t = j$ and the counterparty plays F instead of D (thus, reflecting the moral hazard component of credit risk as it is discussed below).

But, at the same time, both information together determine each bank's action at time t. For $t = T^{A,B} - 1$, e.g., the counterparty would not deliver if it was known. The relevance of asymmetric information, which was of no significance in the one-shot game, is therefore the second major deviation of the following analysis compared to the previous one (the first one was repeated play).

Unfortunately,

'giving a complete specification of the equilibrium that is obtained [in a repeated prisoners' dilemma with asymmetric information] is extraordinarily tedious, because it is based on some very involved recursions' (Kreps, et al. 1982, 267).

Hence, imagine the following for simplicity.

(a) There are two types of banks in the population.
(b) Reliable, type-R banks have a horizon T and a return of zero to playing F[41].
(c) Unreliable, type-U banks have a horizon $\mathrm{T} < T$ and a positive return to playing F as it was the case in the original prisoners' dilemma game.
(d) The share of type-R and type-U banks in the entire population is common knowledge. It is given as $1-\rho_0$ and ρ_0, respectively.
(e) Bank A is type-R, which is private information.
(f) Bank B is also type-R. But, in this case, it is common knowledge.
(g) Bank B is the seller in all transactions and Bank A is therefore always the buyer.
(h) Interest rates are zero until further notice.

41 A zero return to playing F is the finite horizon equivalent to assuming a bank to be reliable since reliable banks, strictly speaking, have an infinite horizon. Infinite horizon models are however more complicated without contributing to the general outcome. See Kreps, et al. (1982) for a detailed discussion on this issue as well as related matters.

Describing the so called one-sided prisoners' dilemma of assumptions (a)-(h)[42], Bank B does not know Bank A's horizon according to assumption (e). The player can only assign a subjective probability $1-\rho_t^A$ to Bank A being a type-R bank. In other words, at each time t, Bank B expects to play the game given in table IV.5 below with probability $1-\rho_t^A$ [43]. With probability ρ_t^A, however, it expects to play the game presented in table IV.6 instead[44].

TABLE IV.5: A Cooperative Game

Bank A\Bank B	**Deliver (D)**	**Fail to Deliver (F)**
Deliver (D)	$v_T^A - e_t \,;\, e_t - v_T^B$ **(0.20 ; 0.30)**	$-e_t \,;\, 0$ (-1.10 ; 0)
Fail to Deliver (F)	$0 \,;\, -v_T^B$ (0 ; -0.80)	0 ; 0

ρ_t^A is equivalent to the adverse selection component of credit risk because it stands for Bank B's uncertainty with respect to repeating the foreign exchange transaction, which is the driving force behind Bank A's delivery strategy. Delivery, therefore, depends on Bank A's hidden type. No matter what happens, if Bank A has horizon T, it will fail to deliver sooner or later. More importantly, ρ_t^A is equivalent to the adverse selection component of credit risk because asymmetric information with respect to each bank's horizon is analytically equivalent to asymmetric information with respect to each bank's reliability. This is the case because an unsound business strategy adversely affects the time period that a bank can stay in business. Having a short horizon is therefore equivalent to being unreliable.

Apart from the uncertainty on Bank A's type, however, the asymmetry of information also implies that Bank B faces a second uncertainty which immediately results from the former. Assuming that it plays the prisoners' dilemma, Bank B does not know with certainty whether or not the incentive compatibility constraint for Bank A holds at time t, or more precisely, whether $t = j$. Hence, Bank B also assigns a positive probability

---

42 Assumptions (a)-(h) are largely drawn from Frank (1996, pp. 47-49). Rasmusen (1994), furthermore, points out that turning a two-sided prisoners' dilemma into a one-sided version is not associated with a loss of generality (Rasmusen 1994, pp. 129-31). On the contrary, focusing on agency costs, the simplifications will even turn out to be useful since they restrict the analysis to one bank only, namely, Bank A.

43 {D;D} is the Nash equilibrium in a one-shot game.

44 {F;F} is the Nash equilibrium in a one-shot game. Furthermore, see the game tree in figure III.7 above for illustration of the non-cooperative game.

$1-\pi_t^A$ to the event that Bank A delivers, respectively, π_t^A to the event that it does not deliver at time t. $0<\pi_t^A<1$ is conditional upon the event that Bank A is type-U because if it was type-R, π_t^A would of course be equal to zero. If it was equal to one, on the contrary, there would no longer be any uncertainty on Bank A's type. Finally, π_t^A is the moral hazard component of credit risk because $t=j$ is analytically equivalent to the event that Bank A turns insolvent[45].

TABLE IV.6: A One-Sided Prisoners' Dilemma

Bank A\Bank B	**Deliver (D)**	**Fail to Deliver (F)**
Deliver (D)	$v_T^A - e_t$; $e_t - v_T^B$ (0.20 ; 0.30)	$-e_t$; 0 (-1.10 ; 0)
Fail to Deliver (F)	v_T^A ; $-v_T^B$ (1.30 ; -0.80)	**0 ; 0**

BANK A: Following these extensive, preliminary remarks, let the actual analysis start with Bank A. The player knows that a long-term business relationship is envisaged. But since this is private information, Bank A must take into account that this asymmetry affects Bank B's actions. Player B certainly plays 'more carefully'. For example, it may start playing F and await Bank A's reaction. In addition to having the desire to trade repeatedly, therefore, Bank A also has to signal this desire in a credible manner to Bank B in order to induce it to cooperate. For exactly this reason, Bank B's behaviour is crucial for Bank A's decision making.

BANK B'S BEHAVIOUR AT TIME t=1: Bank B's expected profit at the end of the first round of trading is given as

$$\text{(IV.3)} \qquad \mathrm{P}_1^B = \rho_1^A \pi_1^A \left(-v_T^B\right) + \rho_1^A \left(1-\pi_1^A\right)\left(e_1 - v_T^B\right) + \left(1-\rho_1^A\right)\left(e_1 - v_T^B\right),$$

for $a_1^B = D$, respectively,

$$\text{(IV.4)} \qquad \mathrm{P}_1^B = 0, \qquad \text{for } a_1^B = F.$$

---

45 The moral hazard component of credit risk is introduced for the sake of completeness. It is also needed for the formal analysis below. With respect to institutional responses to it, however, the moral hazard component of credit risk is subject of Chapter VI, section 1 below. It turns out to be constant throughout the following paragraphs. Hence, it is not affected by the design of the search and information system.

In other words,

- if Bank A is type-R, it delivers with probability $1-\rho_1^A$. Hence, the expected return to cooperation is equal to $\left(1-\rho_1^A\right)\left(e_1-v_T^B\right)$ or the third term of equation (IV.3).
- If Bank A is type-U, which has a likelihood of ρ_1^A, it is expected to play D with probability $1-\pi_1^A$, which determines the second term of equation (IV.3).
- If Bank A is type-U, it is however also expected to play F with probability π_1^A, which determines the first term of equation (IV.3).
- Equation (VI.3) is finally conditional on Bank B playing D because the return to playing F is zero by assumption, which finds its expression in equation (IV.4).

Bank B rationally delivers in the first round if and only if the expected return to playing D is greater than the expected return to playing F. In other words, Bank B delivers if and only if equation (IV.3) is greater than zero. This is the case as long as

(IV.5) $$\rho_1^A < \frac{e_1 - v_T^B}{\pi_1^A e_1}.$$

Thus, the subjective probability to meet a cooperative trading partner or $1-\rho_1^A$ must be sufficiently high to induce Bank B to deliver after the first round of trading. For the time being, it is rationally given as the share of type-R compared to type-U banks in the population, namely, $1-\rho_0$.

BANK B'S BEHAVIOUR FOR $1<t<T$[46]: At least as important for Bank A to determine its strategy as Bank B's behaviour in the first round is Bank B's behaviour in the second as well as all future rounds of trading. If Bank A plays D in the first round, Bank B for example anticipates that Bank A's horizon is greater than one. In other words, Bank B learns about Bank A's type from his past behaviour. More precisely, let Bank B update ρ_t^A according to Bayes' rule such that

(IV.6) $$\rho_{t+1}^A = \frac{\pi_t^A \rho_t^A}{\pi_t^A \rho_t^A + 1 - \rho_t^A}, \qquad \text{for } a_t^A = D.$$

[46] The final-round calculations are ignored for keeping the analysis simple. On the one hand, Kreps, et al. (1982) demonstrate that the final-round problem in a finitely repeated prisoners' dilemma with symmetric information always leads to non-cooperation in each round. Since both players know that, in the final round, they both play non-cooperatively, they rationally do so in each round prior to the last one. The argument is based on backward induction and goes back to Selten (1978) and his equilibrium concept of subgame perfection. On the other hand, they also demonstrate that, for asymmetric information, this is no longer the case which justifies this simplification. For details on the final-round calculations, however, see Frank (1996, p. 72).

Bank B's remaining calculations are then equivalent to the one during the first trading session. The player's action at any time t is therefore determined by whether or not equation (IV.7) below holds.

(IV.7) $$\rho_t^A < \frac{e_t - v_T^B}{\pi_t^A e_t}.$$

BANK A REVISITED: Returning to Bank A, the player knows that playing D brings him the loss of the principal amount as long as equation (IV.7) does not hold. If, therefore, Bank B played F in the first round, Bank A would not deliver in any round of trading, if it was not for what had been learned according to equation (IV.6) above, in other words, if it was not for

(IV.8) $$\rho_{t+1}^A < \rho_t^A, \qquad \text{for } a_t^A = D.$$

But learning implies that, sooner or later, Bank B starts playing D. Hence, Bank A has an incentive to deliver since playing D will be interpreted as a signal in favour of the bank's reliability. In other words, Bank A has an incentive to deliver because it builds up reputation (definition IV.2) and Weber's view holds that, for repeated play, 'honesty is the best policy' (Weber 1990, p. 383).

DEFINITION IV.2 (REPUTATION): 'In common usage, reputation is a characteristic or attribute ascribed to one person (firm, industry, etc.) by another (e.g., 'A has a reputation for courtesy'). Operationally, this is usually represented as a prediction of likely future behavior (e.g., 'A is likely to be courteous'). It is, however, primarily an empirical statement (e.g., 'A has been observed in the past to be courteous'). Its predictive power depends on the supposition that past behavior is indicative of future behavior' (Wilson 1985a, p. 27)[47].

AGENCY COSTS: The model as it has just been presented is based on Frank (1996, pp. 45-74). He also demonstrates that signalling is costly. If condition (IV.7) does not hold at times $t = 1,2,\ldots,k$[48], Bank A's incentive compatibility constraint in equation (IV.1) above turns into equation (IV.9) below.

---

47 Following the seminal contributions of Selten (1978) and Rosenthal (1981), it was Kreps, et al. (1982) who initiated the discussion on reputation and imperfect information in their famous series of papers. The theory was further developed by Fudenberg and Maskin (1986), Fudenberg and Levine (1988), and Hart (1985), a/o.

48 Bank A approximates k since v_T^B and π_t^B are private information to Bank B. For simplicity, however, let the expected value of k be equal to k.

(IV.9) $$P_{j-1}^{A} + v_{T}^{A} \leq P_{T}^{A} - \sum_{t=1}^{k} e_{t}\,.$$

Since Bank B plays F instead of D for k times, the return to cooperation or the right-hand side of equation (IV.9) is reduced by an amount equivalent to

(IV.10) $$\sum_{t=1}^{k} e_{t}$$

which obviously represents the relevant agency costs, namely, the costs of building up reputation as a reliable trading partner. Even for type-R banks, therefore, the return to participating in FX dealing is reduced due to credit risk. It is further reduced for non-zero interest rates (table IV.7).

1.1.5 Adverse Selection and Market Failure

The importance of the result of the previous section must be re-emphasized. Adding agency costs that are identical for reliable and unreliable banks to equation (IV.1), the incentive compatibility constraint no longer holds for many unreliable banks that are on the edge of leaving the market. The shorter their horizon, furthermore, the less likely is equation (IV.9) to hold for them, ceteris paribus. But, more importantly, delivery is also no longer the incentive compatible strategy for many a priori reliable banks that are nevertheless on the edge of non-profit making. Ceteris paribus, honesty is suddenly 'too expensive'.

Since the described scenario is anticipated by Bank B, it rationally raises ρ_1^A above ρ_0. But this, in turn, reduces the number of type-R banks further, ceteris paribus, because the agency costs increase according to equation (IV.7) above, etc. The familiar process of adverse selection sets in and no bank plays D any longer. Consequently, the equilibrium is 'no trade' which is surprising given that reputation is generally referred to as an effective self-selection device and that market failures due to the failure of self-selection are generally not observed. The following section explains what 'went wrong'. The agency costs related to market failure are furthermore presented in table IV.7 below[49].

[49] For a sufficient number of banks with long enough T, adverse selection is not imperative, of course. Assuming market failure does however serve a better understanding of the following discussion.

1.2 Comparative Analysis

Having introduced a complete set of possible solutions to the prisoners' dilemma on the level of a single transaction between two traders, namely,

- collateral (credible commitment),
- transaction-specific investments (credible commitment), and
- reputation (credible threat),

the remaining task is to investigate if and how the different search and information systems apply these tools and to identify the specific costs related to each of the uses. In this respect, it is clearly the institutions that discriminate among traders which are of interest due to the nature of the adverse selection component of credit risk, which is a counterparty risk. Most importantly, it is membership which is immediately followed by partner-specific trading and sealed trading. The market participants' decision problem can thus be described as 'find the optimal degree of transparency and the optimal degree of openness'. With respect to the vertically consolidated set of institutional arrangements (table III.6), therefore, the market participants' choice is among the search and information systems of the FX market, the free entry FX market, the Frankfurter Wertpapierbörse, and Sotheby's. In the present context, the London Stock Exchange is analytically equivalent to FWB and the Free Entry LSE is analytically equivalent to Sotheby's. In other words, the choice is among

- the decentralized market with or without membership,
- the organized exchange, and
- the centralized market.

TABLE IV.7: Agency Costs Related to Repeated Trading

Market Failure	$\sum_{t=1}^{T-1} \lvert v_T^{A,B} - e_t \rvert$ $\sum_{t=1}^{T-1} \lvert (v_T^{A,B} - e_t)(i_T - i_t) \rvert$
Investments in Reputation Foregone Interest Earnings	$\sum_{t=1}^{k} e_t$ $\sum_{t=1}^{k} e_t (i_k - i_t)$

1.2.1 Centralized Market

REPUTATION: Starting with the reference market structure that does not make recourse to either membership or decentralized trading, trading on a centralized market is analytically equivalent to playing a one-shot prisoners' dilemma even for repeated transactions. As it was outlined for Sotheby's, buyers and sellers are matched randomly and, thus, trading is anonymous. Furthermore, market entry is not restricted such that the population of market participants varies over time. For both reasons, centralized trading does not allow for the building up of a reputation. But even if the extreme 'no reputation' condition is relaxed, the outcome is still market failure.

Imagine that the anonymity of trading partners is lifted for settlement. In this case, each bank can record past deals and update private beliefs on the trading partner if both parties happen to be repeatedly matched. For infinite memory and/or a small number of potential traders (such as commercial banks only), therefore, Bank A can gradually build up reputation with Bank B and vice versa. Bank A and Bank B leave the market and establish their 'own' market together with other reliable banks. The risk to meet unreliable market participants due to random matching, anonymous trading, and free entry is zero on this parallel market. This is obviously not a centralized market for exactly this reason. The centralized market is left with the unreliable banks, the lemons (Akerlof 1970). In anticipation of this outcome, reliable banks avoid trading on a centralized market from the outset.

TRANSACTION-SPECIFIC INVESTMENTS: With no formal or informal restrictions to entry, the centralized market does not allow for transaction-specific investments to be an effective screening device. FX dealing would be open to all traders whether or not they were market makers who invest in the installation and operation of dealing facilities. Furthermore, centralized trading does not allow transaction-specific investments to be an effective self-selection and/or signalling device either. Anonymity and random matching imply that Bank A cannot know whether its counterparty is a reliable market maker. More importantly, if there are market makers in the market, they leave a centralized market for exactly the same reason as above. The risk of meeting unreliable market participants can be reduced by establishing a parallel market.

COLLATERAL: The collateral solution to market failure was said to rely on reciprocity. Leaving aside the problem of how to deposit a collateral with an unknown trading partner (if the trading partners' identity is revealed prior to settlement, e.g., this problem can easily be resolved), there is a more fundamental obstacle related to the collateral solution. More precisely, the 'who-monitors-the-monitor' problem arises. Due to the absence of law, there is no incentive to release the hostage following the settlement of a payment obligation. Bank A cannot legally enforce it, nor can Bank B. Thus, the disbursement of the collateral can effectively only be ensured by demanding a collateral for paying back the collateral, etc. This is obviously not reasonable and the collateral solution also fails (Williamson 1983, p. 530).

Summarizing, a centralized market is doomed to failure since neither of the commitment strategies nor the threat strategy works properly. Transaction-specific investments, on the one hand, result in the adverse selection of unreliable market participants. Collateral, on the other hand, does not remove the potential for opportunistic behaviour. It simply transfers the problem to ever higher levels. Reputation, finally, requires non-anonymity or decentralized trading which the market does not provide. The specific costs are given as follows (table IV.8)[50].

TABLE IV.8: Agency Costs of the Centralized Market Structure

	Centralized Market
Collateral	fails
Transaction-Specific Investments	fails
Reputation	fails
Specific Costs	$\sum_{t=1}^{T-1} \left\| v_T^{A,B} - e_t \right\|$ $\sum_{t=1}^{T-1} \left\| \left(v_T^{A,B} - e_t\right)\left(i_T - i_t\right) \right\|$

Concluding with Williamson (1983), therefore, it seems that

'the benefits of cooperation notwithstanding, the achievement of cooperation is ... frustrated by the relentless logic of the prisoner's dilemma. To be sure, it has always been evident that defection can be deterred if payoffs are appropriately altered. But this stratagem is held to be infeasible or is otherwise dismissed' (Williamson 1983, p. 537).

Continuing with the same Williamson (1983), however,

'I [also] submit that the feasibility of crafting superior ex ante incentive structures warrants more attention. A leading reason for its neglect is because the study of the institutions of contract has occupied such a low place on the research agenda. Subtle incentive features that are incorporated

50 Trade is assumed to take place *T-1* times.

in nonstandard contracting practices have gone undetected as a consequence of this nonchalance - on which account the practical significance of the prisoner's dilemma to the study of exchange has been vastly exaggerated' (Williamson 1983, pp. 537-38).

1.2.2 Organized Exchange

Allowing for formal membership, unreliable banks (non-members) can in principle be separated from reliable banks (members). The idea is that having passed a guard, reliable traders only find other reliable traders inside.

'An organized ... market confines trades to those who are its members. This limitation has definite advantages. Each member has a proprietary interest in the survival of the exchange and in the value of his membership. He wants the other members to be reliable. Members who trust each other can trade more quickly at a lower cost' (Telser 1981, p. 12).

For FWB, e.g., these 'economic' entry barriers find their literal expression in the 'physical' entry barriers to the trading floor. Without identity card, access is denied. But once the door is passed, identity no longer matters. Anyone can raise his hands and conclude a deal. Everyone knows that everyone else meets certain criteria since they would not be present otherwise. The question, therefore, is how the 'organizer of a trading platform' (Kolb 1991, p. 4) manages not to adversely select the members of his exchange using the tools reputation, transaction-specific investments, and/or collateral.

REPUTATION: If entry can formally be restricted to reliable banks only, investments in reputation are transaction cost-increasing if anything and, thus, inefficient. Hence, organized exchanges cannot and do not rely on reputation. If they had to, the entry requirements would be misspecified[51].

TRANSACTION-SPECIFIC INVESTMENTS: Investments in transaction-specific assets separate reliable from unreliable banks. For effective formal membership, however, they are also transaction cost-increasing, if anything, because investments in transaction-specific assets are self-selecting. If, therefore, organized exchanges relied on transaction-specific investments, entry requirements would again be misspecified. There would again be no incentive to join such an organized exchange if it was associated with a membership fee - as is generally the case.

---

[51] Methodologically, this outcome implies that membership combined with decentralized trading cannot be a market structure that combines *formal* membership with decentralized trading (as it is not the case).

COLLATERAL: For not being self-enforcing, collateral was demonstrated above as requiring law in order to produce its effects. The most important consequence of formal membership in this respect is that it provides a substitute for law. The monitoring problem above finds an appropriate solution in replacing law by the organizer of the exchange, in other words, by some kind of arbitrator. The infinite regression can be avoided if the organizer is trustworthy. But strategic behaviour on behalf of the organized exchange can easily be prevented by making the traders shareholders of the organized exchange. In order to avoid conflicts of interest, furthermore, many exchanges are non-profit organizations (Telser 1981, pp. 11-14)[52]. Thus, collateral is the mechanism that organized exchanges exclusively rely on. The final advantage of organizing an exchange is that the number of bilateral collateral requirements *N*-1 is reduced to a single collateral requirement with the organized exchange itself, since it acts on behalf of all potential trading partners.

The organized exchange is thus a straightforward application of the collateral solution to the prisoners' dilemma which crucially relies on formal membership and formal membership only. The specific costs of establishing an organized exchange compared to the centralized market are given as follows (table IV.9).

TABLE IV.9: Agency Costs of Centralized Market and Organized Exchange

	Centralized Market	**Organized Exchange**
Collateral	fails	$c^{A,B} \cdot i_{T-1}$
Transaction-Specific Investments	fails	inefficient
Reputation	fails	inefficient
Specific Costs	$\sum_{t=1}^{T-1} \left\| v_T^{A,B} - e_t \right\|$ $\sum_{t=1}^{T-1} \left\| \left(v_T^{A,B} - e_t\right)\left(i_T - i_t\right) \right\|$	$c^{A,B} \cdot i_{T-1}$

[52] For negative consequences of the non-profit status of organized exchanges, however, see Chambers and Carter (1990). They argue that it leads to cross subsidization of the products of an exchange.

1.2.3 Decentralized Market

COLLATERAL: Allowing for partner-specific trading and informal membership in contrast to centralized trading and formal membership, the decentralized market cannot rely on collateral since collateral is not self-enforcing.

TRANSACTION-SPECIFIC INVESTMENTS: Transaction-specific investments separate more reliable banks from less reliable ones. For reciprocity, they effectively restrict market entry to more reliable banks by the means of informal membership. Hence, informal membership reduces credit risk. If, however, the transaction does not require any specific investments, the decentralized market must exclusively rely on reputation if possible.

Since transaction-specific investments are investments in dealing facilities as well as trading personnel, electricity, etc., they consist of a fixed as well as a variable cost component. For repeated play, the variable costs shall be assumed to be constant with respect to time, thus, recurring during each period. More importantly, if the costs were fixed costs only, they would lose their effectiveness as a self-selection mechanism the longer a bank trades. For *T*-1 rounds of trading, therefore, investments in transaction-specific assets can be expressed as

(IV.11) $$s_{fixed}^{A,B} + s_{fixed}^{A,B} \cdot i_T + (T-1)s_{variable}^{A,B} + \sum_{t=1}^{T-1} s_{variable}^{A,B} \cdot i_t \, .$$

REPUTATION: The decentralized market is the only market structure that can (and must) rely on reputation. Partner-specific trading is not anonymous. Furthermore, matching is not random. Hence, the building up of a reputation is an explicit strategy and not only a by-product. Unfortunately, however, the reputational equilibrium is associated with market instability due to the potential for adverse selection. But the likelihood of a market failure is not what the traders are left with because reputational models of the kind presented above ignore that partner-specific trading is sealed trading. In other words, they ignore that the price, the exchange rate e_t, is not publicly quoted and, thus, exogenous. Sealed trading, therefore, allows for multiple execution prices which can be shown to reduce significantly the costs of investing in reputation and, ultimately, the potential for adverse selection. Before turning to the introduction of sealed trading into the above model, however, the point is best illustrated by the following example.

Empirically, it is not observed that a Bank A, let it be a newcomer to the market, faces trading partners who do not deliver for a number of rounds before they are convinced that Bank A is reliable. This observation is very much independent of any market structure. What is observed on decentralized markets, however, is that newcomers pay a premium during the initial periods of a recently established business relation. In other words, newcomers accept worse transaction prices than the 'competitive' one.

THE ONE-SIDED PRISONERS' DILEMMA REVISITED: Bank B's decision with respect to delivery was shown above to be determined by the following inequality.

$$\text{(IV.12)} \qquad \rho_t^A < \frac{e_t - v_T^B}{\pi_t^A e_t}.$$

For price endogeneity, therefore, the realization of the exchange rate e_t determines whether Bank B plays D or F. Hence, as long as it is chosen such that

$$\text{(IV.13)} \qquad e_t > \frac{v_T^B}{1 - \pi_t^A \rho_t^A},$$

Bank B delivers.

Separating e_t into the 'competitive' exchange rate among established banks e_t^c and a risk premium pr_t^A such that

$$\text{(IV.14)} \qquad e_t = e_t^c + pr_t^A,$$

Bank B delivers if and only if

$$\text{(IV.15)} \qquad pr_t^A > \frac{v_T^B}{1 - \pi_t^A \rho_t^A} - e_t^c.$$

Hence, Bank B's action is no longer exogenously determined by the dynamics of Bayes' rule only. On the contrary, Bank A can actively influence Bank B's behaviour if execution prices can vary. Bank A, furthermore, prefers the 'collusive' execution price e_t to the competitive one, e_t^c, as long as

$$\text{(IV.16)} \qquad pr_t^A < v_T^A.$$

In this case, the costs of building up a reputation are smaller for sealed trading than they are for open trading. This is the case because Bank A would lose the amount of $e_t = e_t^c$ to Bank B if trading was open and Bank B played F. Hence, it is willing to pay any premium smaller than or equal to the competitive exchange rate. But it also accepts a slightly higher premium than e_t^c since Bank A is almost prepared to give up its profit from trade, namely, $v_T^A - e_t^c$, in order to guarantee Bank B's delivery.

Summarizing, for

$$\text{(IV.17)} \qquad \frac{v_T^B}{1-\pi_t^A \rho_t^A} - e_t^c < pr_t^A < v_T^A,$$

playing D is strictly preferred to playing F by both players. The fact that, for a dealing amount of USD 1, the premium may actually exceed the market clearing price, supports the view that equation (IV.17) can generally be expected to hold. Thus, decentralized markets can rely on reputation for the reason that sealed trading reduces the agency costs significantly such that adverse selection tendencies and market instability can be avoided. The following calculations may illustrate this further.

For $e_t^c = 1.50$, $v_T^A = 1.70$ and $v_T^B = 1.20$ and for $\pi_t^A = 0.5$ and $e_t = 1.70$, the following holds:

- The right-hand side of equation (IV.12) increases by a factor as high as 1.5. In other words, for a premium pr_t^A equal to EUR 0.20, Bank B's subjective probability that Bank A is unreliable can be 50 percent higher than before and it would still play D.
- Anticipating that Bank A accepts a premium at least as high as 1.50 (Bank B does not know v_T^A, which is why they would probably agree on e_t^c), Bank A and Bank B act cooperatively almost with certainty. According to equation (IV.12) again, ρ_t^A can be close to one for $pr_t^A = 1.50$.
- For any ρ_0 significantly less than one, therefore, the agency costs are strictly lower for sealed trading compared to open trading.

Finally, however, reliability must be established with respect to each trading partner separately[53]. Thus, for N market participants, Bank A has to accept higher execution prices with respect to all other $N-1$ traders when entering the market. The specific costs of building up reputation, therefore, turn out as

---

53 Cheap talk, communication among market participants, etc. is ignored. But this implies that, e.g., reputation does not become common knowledge once it is established with one of the trading partners. For alternative approaches, see Kreps (1990, pp. 403-404, 411-12) and the references therein.

(IV.18) $$\sum_{N-1}\sum_{t=1}^{k}\left(e_t^n - e_t^{c,n}\right) = \sum_{N-1}\sum_{t=1}^{k} pr_t^A .$$

Summarizing, the decentralized market relies on reputation as the self-selection mechanism. In this respect, sealed trading is important because the premium solution is agency cost-reducing. Furthermore, the market is a membership market if the transaction can or must be supported by investments in transaction-specific assets. It reduces credit risk in the form of the subjective probability that the trading partner is not reliable. Finally, the collateral solution is not feasible and the costs induced by decentralized trade are summarized in table IV.10 below.

In conclusion,

PROPOSITION 1: FX dealing banks are exposed to credit risk. Credit risk exposure results in cooperation failure or adverse selection. Preventing either kind of market failure by the appropriate design of the search and information system is possible but costly. The relevant institutional arrangements must discriminate among traders. The costs differ with respect to the choice of institutions. Assuming 'no trade' to be associated with prohibitive costs, this choice is between formal membership, respectively, the organized exchange, and partner-specific trading, eventually supported by informal membership, in other words, the decentralized market. Organized markets rely on the collateral solution to the prisoners' dilemma, decentralized markets make recourse to reputation in order to prevent adverse selection. Sealed trading is a crucial element of the decentralized market with respect to minimizing the specific costs.

A final decision on which market structure is more efficient in discriminating among traders thus cannot be reached on present grounds although the organized exchange looks somehow 'less expensive'. On the other hand, operational costs of running an exchange have been ignored since they do not contribute to credit risk control. But they would of course have to be considered by the traders when designing a market.

Explaining the *coexistence* of decentralized markets and organized exchanges, furthermore, requires a broader theoretical perspective. The exposure to market risk or liquidity risk may, for example, explain differences in institutional design. It may be the reason that, for stocks, the organized exchange seems to minimize overall transaction costs (provided that the market structure is efficient) whereas the same does not hold for foreign exchange. In any case, the above findings are consistent with the empirical evidence in as much as none of the major national and international financial markets is centralized in nature. In all cases,

TABLE IV.10: Agency Costs of Centralized Market, Organized Exchange, and Decentralized Market

	Centralized Market	**Organized Exchange**	**Decentralized Market**
Collateral	fails	$c^{A,B} \cdot i_{T-1}$	fails
Transaction-Specific Investments	fails	inefficient	$s_{fixed}^{A,B} + (T-1) s_{\text{var}\,iable}^{A,B}$ $s_{fixed}^{A,B} \cdot i_T + \sum_{t=1}^{T-1} s_{\text{var}\,iable}^{A,B} \cdot i_t$
Reputation	fails	inefficient	$\sum_{N-1} \sum_{t=1}^{k} pr_t^A$ $\sum_{N-1} \sum_{t=1}^{k} pr_t^A (i_k - i_t)$
Specific Costs	$\sum_{t=1}^{T-1} \left\| v_T^{A,B} - e_t \right\|$ $\sum_{t=1}^{T-1} \left\| (v_T^{A,B} - e_t)(i_T - i_t) \right\|$	$c^{A,B} \cdot i_{T-1}$	$s_{fixed}^{A,B} + (T-1) s_{\text{var}\,iable}^{A,B}$ $s_{fixed}^{A,B} \cdot i_T + \sum_{t=1}^{T-1} s_{\text{var}\,iable}^{A,B} \cdot i_t$ $\sum_{N-1} \sum_{t=1}^{k} pr_t^A$ $\sum_{N-1} \sum_{t=1}^{k} pr_t^A (i_k - i_t)$

'trust is an important lubricant ... It is extremely efficient; it saves a lot of trouble to have a fair degree of reliance on other people's word' (Arrow 1974, p. 23).

2. Dispersed Information and the Efficiency of Sealed Trading and Dealing

Market risk is the risk of adverse price movements. For dispersed information, however, market risk does not only result in hedging activities (section 3) but also information trading if possible. The return on information, finally, depends on the design of the search and information system.

- The more transparent the market structure, the lower is the return on information. Information is made available to the 'uninformed' at close to zero costs. Information is a public good.
- The more centralized the market structure, the lower is the return on information. On the one hand, the 'informed' cannot freely exploit their information. Neither the counterparty nor the execution price is endogenously determined. On the other hand, information is again a public good. Assuming that *prices* communicate information (section 2.1), the trade price of information is zero at time $t+1$ if the execution price is unique for all traders at any time t. In other words, the trade price of information is zero at time $t+1$ because centralized trading equalizes all individual information sets at the end of each trading session t at the latest (section 2.2.1 demonstrates that it may even do so earlier)[54].

2.1 Foregone Return on Information

Currently, there is no general theory of the return on information. In other words, all existing models on information trading need to specify market structures in order to derive the corresponding returns on information[55]. The present section, therefore, starts *and* finishes with the uncertainty case of the basic model of Chapter III, section 5 above.

---

[54] Speculation or the attempt to extract surplus from expected short-term price movements (Aschinger 1995, p. 17) is ignored because market design does not affect speculative trading and vice versa. For any non-zero expected difference in prices or $v_T - e_t \neq 0$, traders engage in speculation on any market. *How* price expectations or v_T are formed, however, very much depends on the design of the search and information system of a market, as the following paragraphs demonstrate. Hence, section 2 focuses on information trading rather than speculation, given the initial condition of information being dispersed among market participants.

[55] See, e.g., O'Hara (1995, chapters 3-6) on trade and information or, more recently, Perraudin and Vitale (1996) on information trading on decentralized markets.

Allowing for private signals on future exchange rates, it provides the maximum of common ground for the comparative analysis below.

Imagine the standardized dealing amount $\Delta USD_t = \pm\Delta USD$ to be an investment in the risky asset foreign exchange. In this case, $\widetilde{v}_T$ is the stochastic gross return to this investment[56]. Focusing on the spot market only, $\widetilde{v}_T$ realizes at time T in the form of the spot rate e_T.

(IV.19) $$v_T = e_T .$$

The expected net return on investment at time $t < T$ is thus the expected trading profit. It results from 'storing' US dollars at time t because they are expected to fetch a higher price at time T.

For simplicity, let each risk neutral bank n have a horizon of $T = 2$. Trade is thus restricted to time 1 only. In addition, let Φ_t^n represent bank n's information set at time t. For each bank, the asset demand problem at time 1 is consequently given as

(IV.20) $$\text{Max} \quad E_1^n\left(\widetilde{\mathrm{P}}_2^n \middle| \Phi_1^n\right) = E_1^n\left[\left(\widetilde{e}_2 - e_1\right)\Delta USD_1 \middle| \Phi_1^n\right].$$

$E_1^n\left[\cdot \middle| \Phi_1^n\right]$ represents bank n's expectations conditional on the information set Φ_1^n.

Turning to Φ_1^n in greater detail, suppose that the market participants independently observe the realization y_1^n of a random variable $\widetilde{y}_1^n$ at time 1. More precisely, $\widetilde{y}_1^n$ shall be given as

(IV.21) $$\widetilde{y}_1^n = e_2 + \widetilde{\varepsilon}_1 .$$

Hence, y_1^n is a private signal on the final-period exchange rate given that $\widetilde{\varepsilon}_1$ is white noise and independently distributed with mean zero and e_2 is the time 2 exchange rate. More importantly, y_1^n determines bank n's *prior* valuation of US dollars such that, ceteris paribus,

(IV.22) $$E_1^n\left(\widetilde{e}_2 \middle| y_1^n\right) = y_1^n .$$

---

[56] Random variables will from now on be denoted by a 'tilde', if necessary.

Following the view that was expressed above on the 'news value' of monopolistic information (Chapter III, section 2.1.3), equation (IV.22) is finally useful information to *all* other FX dealing banks apart from bank n. 'Of course [therefore], the trader's order strategy depends on his or her posterior beliefs' (Madhavan 1992, p. 611) instead of his or her prior ones. Furthermore, the formation of each bank's posterior beliefs is determined by the design of the implemented search and information system. More precisely, the expected value of the time 2 exchange rate is not always given as equation (IV.22) above. It is, for example, determined conditional on the enlarged information set (y_1^n, e_1) instead, provided that the market structure allows for observing the current exchange rate e_1 at time 1 (Madhavan 1992, pp. 610-12).

The uncertainty case of the basic asset demand model with private information is based on two important assumptions.

- Prices are the effective means for communicating private information. The underlying view is of course that

  > 'we must look at the price system as ... a mechanism for communicating information if we want to understand its real function ... The most significant fact about this system is the economy of knowledge with which it operates, or how little the individual participants need to know in order to be able to take the right action ... by a kind of symbol, only the most essential information is passed on' (Hayek 1945, pp. 526-27).

- Time is restricted to $T = 2$.

  > '[This] could be motivated by the Prisoners' Dilemma nature of competition among traders with private information. Since all traders possess private information, a trader who fails to fully exploit his information when he gets a chance to trade runs the risk that his information will already be impounded in prices when he next obtains an opportunity to trade' Madhavan (1992, p. 610).

  Furthermore, restricting the model to one trading session greatly simplifies the required computations[57].

But the above presentation is also based on two simplifications which deviate from the original version of the model in Madhavan (1992).

- Madhavan (1992) originally develops the model for risk averse agents. Since, however, risk aversion 'generates portfolio hedging trade which is not information

[57] Were it not for private information being short-lived, however, a longer time horizon would admittedly provide more room for strategic behaviour. Trades could, for example, be delayed. This kind of strategic behaviour is therefore ignored below.

motivated' (Madhavan 1992, p. 611), the analysis can be kept simple for restricting trade to risk neutral banks only.

- The banks' information sets do not contain public information in the present setting although it is FX dealing that may actually rely on public information more than the exchange of any other financial asset. In any case, the assumption is motivated by orthogonalizing the different information sets up to the point where each trader has only private information (Lyons 1991, p. 10).

2.2 Comparative Analysis

With prices communicating private signals to other market participants, the alternative search and information systems above must be investigated with respect to the observability of e_1 as well as the 'quality' of information that the execution price contains in different settings. In other words, the alternative search and information systems must be investigated by focusing on their degree of transparency (with special emphasis on open versus sealed trading) as well as their degree of centralization (in the form of order matching versus dealing).

- 'We are [thus] interested in ... the process by which information ... is transferred by the ... price system' (Grossman 1977b, p. 433) *and*
- the process by which information is aggregated (definition IV.3),

given that the starting point is dispersed information. According to the above mentioned, any difference in one or both respects should find its expression in changes in the expected return on information. Referring to the appendix to Chapter III above, it is clear that the analysis reduces to comparing

- the current FX market practice with
- the Frankfurter Wertpapierbörse and
- the London Stock Exchange.

This is the case because, concerning transparency and centralization, the FX market is analytically equivalent to the free entry FX market, the Frankfurter Wertpapierbörse is analytically equivalent to Sotheby's, and the London Stock Exchange is analytically equivalent to the free entry LSE (although membership is also readdressed in section 2.2.1 below).

DEFINITION IV.3 (INFORMATION AGGREGATION): 'in some market situations, different individuals have different information, and then the price system may serve to aggregate their information. That is the demand for a risky security of an individual are affected by his information; total demand and accordingly equilibrium market prices thus depend on the information of all the individuals. In this sense the market price aggregates the various pieces of information' (Grossman and Stiglitz 1976, p. 249).

2.2.1 Frankfurter Wertpapierbörse

2.2.1.1 Order Matching and Sealed Trading versus Open Trading

The appendix to Chapter III above relied on the assumption that order matching combined with sealed trading is always second-best compared to order matching combined with open trading. The following paragraphs on the Walrasian auction as opposed to the open-outcry auction illustrate this hypothesis. Demonstrating that order matching perfectly aggregates information, the unique execution price is always fully information-revealing. Hence, a common informational basis is *always* established at the *end* of each trading session. But this implies that any private information, that is obtained *during* a trading session, has a 'news value' of zero. Since, therefore, information trading collapses anyway, all market participants prefer open trading to sealed trading. Ceteris paribus, delaying the publication of the execution price until the end of the trading session is costly compared to publishing all relevant information prior to closing the order book.

ORDER MATCHING AND SEALED TRADING OR THE WALRASIAN AUCTION: In a Walrasian auction, each market participant can only observe his private signal $\Phi_1^n = (y_1^n)$ when he determines his demand schedule. The broker fixes the market clearing price and announces it to the traders *after* the banks have already placed their orders with him (Madhavan 1992, pp. 639-40, a/o). Hence, neither bank can observe the execution price when it is mostly needed in other words, *prior* to deciding on the own asset demand. Furthermore, the exchange rate is exogenous to each trader. With reference to equation (IV.22), therefore, y_1^n is the trader's prior *and* his posterior belief. bank n's objective function is thus given as

$$\text{(IV.23)} \qquad \text{Max} \quad E_1^n\left(\tilde{P}_2^n \middle| \Phi_1^n\right) = \Delta USD_1\left[E_1^n\left(\tilde{e}_2 \middle| y_1^n\right) - e_1\right] = \Delta USD_1\left(y_1^n - e_1\right).$$

The first-order condition requires that bank n places the following limit order with the broker[58].

$$\text{(IV.24)} \qquad \Delta USD_1 = \begin{array}{lll} +\Delta USD & if & y_1^n > e_1 \\ -\Delta USD & if & y_1^n < e_1 \\ 0 & otherwise & \end{array}.$$

58 For exogenously determined, unobservable exchange rates, it is reasonable to assume orders to be limit orders instead of market orders.

e_1 is finally chosen such that

(IV.25) $$\sum_N \Delta USD_1^n(e_1) = 0,$$

in other words, such that the market clears (Madhavan 1992, pp. 639-40).

For a continuous asset demand function, Madhavan (1992) shows that the equilibrium exchange rate would be given as

(IV.26) $$e_1 = \frac{1}{N}\sum_N y_1^n$$

which is a standard result in classical microeconomics. More importantly, however, he also demonstrates that the market clearing price at time 1 already contains all private signals on the time 2 exchange rate such that, optimally,

(IV.27) $$E_1^n\left(\tilde{e}_2 \middle| y_1^n, e_1\right) = e_1 \neq y_1^n,$$

could e_1 be observed. e_1 is the best predictor for the final-period valuation of one US dollar. The market clearing price is fully information revealing and efficient in this sense (Madhavan 1992, pp. 636-40).

More importantly with respect to the present focus, however, equation (IV.27) implies that each market participant would have revised his order strategy had he known e_1, provided that his expectations are rational. In other words, the expected trading profits from the limit order in equation (IV.24) are always and systematically 'wrong' for a Walrasian auction. Due to not being able to observe the market clearing price ex ante, they are, more precisely, 'too high' for this particular matching technology. By the very design of the Walrasian auction,

'traders ignore their effect on price and correspondingly ignore the information contained in price' (Madhavan 1992, p. 639).

This, finally, finds its expression in a higher trading volume for the Walrasian auction compared to the open-outcry auction below. For trading to be costly, however, this is clearly inefficient (Madhavan 1992, pp. 636-40).

Instead of formally deriving identical results for the discrete asset demand function above, the following numerical example shall illustrate the point once again. Furthermore, it is important to emphasize that the present section 2 (as well as Chapter V below) critically depend on the assumption that foreign exchange is a common-value object. If foreign exchange were antiques and the traders were not antiques dealers, in other words, if foreign exchange was an independent private-values object (definition IV.4), $E_1^n\left(\tilde{e}_2 \middle| y_1^n, e_1\right)$ would be equal to $E_1^n\left(\tilde{e}_2 \middle| y_1^n\right) = y_1^n$.

(IV.28) $$E_1^n\left(\tilde{e}_2 \middle| y_1^n, e_1\right) = E_1^n\left(\tilde{e}_2 \middle| y_1^n\right) = y_1^n, \qquad \text{for open } \textit{and} \text{ sealed trading.}$$

DEFINITION IV.4 (INDEPENDENT-PRIVATE-VALUES OBJECT): for independent-private-values objects, any' differences among the bidders' evaluations reflect actual differences in their tastes [only]. ... Any one bidder's valuation is statistically independent from any other bidder's valuation' (McAfee and McMillan 1987, p. 705).

EXAMPLE: Imagine four traders to observe the private signals $y_1^A = 1.20$, $y_1^B = 1.50$, $y_1^C = 1.70$, and $y_1^D = 1.80$, respectively. Furthermore, let the dealing amount be standardized at USD 5 (million). From equation (IV.24), therefore, the banks submit the following orders.

(IV.29a) $$\Delta USD_1^A = \begin{matrix} +5 & if & 1.20 > e_1 \\ -5 & if & 1.20 < e_1 \, , \\ 0 & otherwise & \end{matrix}$$

(IV.29b) $$\Delta USD_1^B = \begin{matrix} +5 & if & 1.50 > e_1 \\ -5 & if & 1.50 < e_1 \, , \\ 0 & otherwise & \end{matrix}$$

(IV.29c) $$\Delta USD_1^C = \begin{matrix} +5 & if & 1.70 > e_1 \\ -5 & if & 1.70 < e_1 \, , \\ 0 & otherwise & \end{matrix}$$

(IV.29d) $$\Delta USD_1^D = \begin{matrix} +5 & if & 1.80 > e_1 \\ -5 & if & 1.80 < e_1 \, . \\ 0 & otherwise & \end{matrix}$$

For the market to clear according to equation (IV.25), therefore, the broker can set the exchange rate equal to $1.50 < e_1 < 1.70$. Yet, announcing $e_1 = 1.60$ to the traders and carrying out altogether two transactions does not result in a trading profit for each Bank A-D. According to equation (IV.27) above, each bank always revises its prior belief such that, ex post, the trading profit is always equal to zero. At the same time, more importantly, none of the market participants would ever have submitted the order that he actually did, had he known e_1. Setting

$$\text{(IV.30)} \qquad E_1^n\left(\tilde{e}_2 \middle| y_1^n, e_1\right) = e_1,$$

they would not have traded at all since each bank would have expected zero profit. The point, however, is that they needed to trade in order to experience this scenario. For trading to be costly, therefore, the outcome is inefficient. END OF EXAMPLE

This illustration may serve as an explanation for the empirical observation that the Walrasian auction is not the prevailing matching technology for frequently traded financial assets[59]. Apart from stochastic non-zero profits, traders cannot win from engaging in trade. On the contrary, the Walrasian auction aggregates all private information perfectly. By design, all market participants are induced to reveal their signals to the broker since they rationally submit their orders contingent on their reservation prices. Since it is assumed that there is no public information and agents are risk neutral, furthermore, they also submit their entire demand schedule. But since it is, finally, only the broker who has access to full information, many transactions are carried out that are inefficient ex post, given that trading is costly.

- If, therefore, a mechanism could be found that reduces the trading volume to an efficient level, at the same time, perfectly aggregating all private information, it should be strictly preferred to the Walrasian auction by each and every market participant. The following paragraphs address such a mechanism.
- Whether or not the perfect aggregation of private signals is the preferred outcome when designing a search and information system is, however, a different matter and remains to be seen (section 2.2.2).

ORDER MATCHING AND OPEN TRADING OR THE OPEN-OUTCRY AUCTION: The open-outcry auction can be interpreted as a Walrasian auction with the broker repeatedly announcing his inside spread *prior* to closing his book. Hence, the open-outcry auction as it is, for example, practiced at FWB anticipates the problem related to the Walrasian auction. In open-outcry auctions as opposed to Walrasian auctions, e_1 is

[59] See any description of major stock or futures markets, which are all organized exchanges, e.g., Cohen, et al. (1986), a/o.

common knowledge to all market participants at all times. Since inefficient trading volumes is the major critique that the microeconomic rational expectations (RE) literature brings forward against classical general equilibrium analysis (Grossman 1976, 1977a, 1977b 1978; Grossman and Stiglitz 1976, 1980, a/o), therefore, the open-outcry auction also comes closest to the RE paradigm that supply and demand decisions are made in full knowledge of the market clearing price. Agents can revise their plans whenever the broker announces a new inside spread.

For an open-outcry auction, the market participants' information sets Φ_1^n are given as

(IV.31) $$\Phi_1^n = \left(y_1^n, e_1\right)$$

and

(IV.32) $$E_1^n\left(\tilde{e}_2 \middle| y_1^n, e_1\right) = e_1, \quad \text{for all } n.$$

In contrast to the Walrasian equilibrium, therefore, a rational expectations equilibrium can obviously be characterized such that

- the differences in prior beliefs disappear,
- the market clearing price e_1 is efficient in the sense that it fully reveals all private information,
- the ex ante profit is zero, implying that, most importantly,
- the trading volume is zero. Each bank's optimal order strategy is given as $\Delta USD_1^n = 0$ (Madhavan 1992, pp. 636-40).

Consequently, the open-outcry auction provides the efficient alternative compared to the Walrasian auction above, if the market applies an order matching technology rather than a dealing technique.

- It efficiently exploits the fully revealing character of the market clearing exchange rate given that trading is costly.
- No market participant would want to revise his strategy. Each bank's strategy is 'regret-free' (Glosten and Milgrom 1985, p. 80).
- It corresponds to the reality on the international financial markets such as FWB.

Finally, therefore, FWB can be referred to as the benchmark model for the following. Having discussed open trading versus sealed trading, the above paragraphs, furthermore, established that order matching perfectly aggregates and reveals private information such that information trading is impossible, whether or not trading is open. The return on information is zero, an outcome which can subsequently be confronted with what the outcome is when order matching is replaced by dealing (section 2.2.2). But first, it is necessary to consider the attainability of order matching in the absence of law.

2.2.1.2 Attainability of Order Matching

Strictly speaking, the open-outcry auction could be an organized exchange *or* a centralized market. But the rational expectations equilibrium is related to a well-known paradox that can be interpreted such that all intermediated markets other than organized exchanges fail due to open entry.

'If, as one would expect, individuals eventually come to realize that the ... price is a perfect predictor of the future spot price, then they will no longer base their demands on their own information, but rather base it solely on the market information. ... But without trade, there is no market; but without a market their beliefs will differ. This paradox can be put another way. If the market aggregated their information perfectly, individuals' demand would not be based on their own information, but then, how would it be possible for markets to aggregate information perfectly?' (Grossman and Stiglitz 1976, p. 250).

From an institutional economic perspective, this familiar paradox is clearly related to the orthodox view that prices are simply 'there'. But they are not because their 'production' is costly.

'Coase's primary lesson is that price discovery entails substantial costs' (Mulherin, et al. 1991, p. 593)[60].

If, therefore, the 'consumption' of prices is not exclusive, as it is implicitly assumed in the RE literature, the paradox is not a problematic or surprising outcome but the most natural result. Negative externalities lead to market failure since there is no economic agent or broker who can profitably engage in price discovery. Every result *other* than the collapse of order matching should thus be much more surprising and the fact that FWB does *not* fail requires explanation.

'What we find interesting about ... [organized exchanges as opposed to centralized markets] is that they are examples of firms that have successfully established markets in financial products. ... the contractual structure of financial exchanges facilitates the production of prices of securities, futures, and other financial instruments. Indeed, we maintain that the establishment of property rights to price quotes is a central function of financial exchanges' (Mulherin, et al.

[60] For details, see Coase (1937, 1960, 1988).

1991, pp. 591-92). 'We define a financial exchange as a firm that creates a market in financial instruments. The product of this particular type of firm is accurate information, as reflected in the prices of the instruments traded on the exchange' (Mulherin, et al. 1991, p. 594).

Mulherin, et al. (1991), therefore, argue that organized exchanges survive because they manage to make the 'consumption of prices' exclusive by establishing a property right on their price quotes. The public good character of public price quotations then dissolves because information can suddenly be traded. Organized exchanges are thus not markets but firms that 'produce' prices.

Most conveniently, Mulherin, et al. (1991) also establish the following conditions that must necessarily hold in order to ensure the survival of organized exchanges as firms. More precisely, conditions (a) and (b) below exclusively allow for the interpretation of organized exchanges as firms. Meeting these requirements explains why FWB does not fail in principle.

(a) Trading *on* the exchange must be restricted to members only and membership must be formal membership.
   (i) The membership must be formal because self-selection is not credible.
   (ii) Non-members must effectively be excluded from receiving price quotes since there is an incentive for traders to become a member of an organized exchange if and only if the organized exchange can effectively restrict the access to information to members only. Otherwise free riding is the optimal strategy (Mulherin, et al. 1991, pp. 593-95, 597, 611).
(b) Members must be restricted in trading *off*-exchange (Mulherin, et al. 1991, pp. 629-34).

   (i) 'The transaction cost argument speaks directly as to why exchanges such as the NYSE do not want to allow members to trade over-the-counter. Through their access to the floor of the NYSE, the members are able to view the currently quoted prices of the exchange specialist. If the members have the option of trading over-the-counter, then the members will only trade with the specialist when the specialist's quotes are inaccurate. This adverse selection problem causes the specialist to widen the spreads. Hence, allowing off-exchange trading, which in effect lessens property rights, leads to higher ... trading costs' (Mulherin 1991, pp. 631-32).
   (ii) 'The transaction cost argument also indicates why exchanges are fearful of the internalization of orders that would be allowed if members could trade off the exchange. If a larger broker such as Merrill Lynch did not have to bring its trades to the floor of the exchange, then Merrill could avoid paying commissions on trades that it matched between its clients. More important, Merrill could withhold the information concerning the size and price of the transaction from the rest of the exchange, while retaining access to the

> information in the prices from all the trades that are conducted on the floor. Of course, if all members engaged in such free riding, prices of exchanges would provide little information' (Mulherin, et al. 1991, pp. 631-32).

As in the previous section, it is again the common-value property that drives the arguments. Markets for independent-private-values objects such as the markets for arts and antiques do not require membership for obvious reasons. But let the analysis, more importantly, turn from the existence of organized exchanges in general to the existence of an organized exchange for FX dealing in particular. In other words, let the following paragraphs turn to the existence of organized exchanges in the absence of law.

The absence of law requires the self-enforcement of conditions (a) and (b) above. Starting with condition (a), there is no conflict of interest between the organized exchange and each *potential* member bank, as long as there is a general interest in the existence of an organized exchange. Hence, there is no enforcement problem as long as brokerage is profitable and the members also profit from reducing the trading volume to an efficient level due to the access to better information. Enforcing formal membership is, furthermore, entirely at the discretion of the organized exchange.

Concerning condition (b), however, the situation is substantially different. A conflict of interest arises between the organized exchange and each *actual* member because members always do better by trading off-exchange, thereby exploiting their informational advantage compared to non-members who still base their decision on the insufficient signal $y_1^{non-member}$. Turning to the already familiar self-enforcing mechanisms for the resolution of conflicts in the absence of law, furthermore,

- Williamson's (1983) commitment solution is obviously not credible. All members always commit themselves not to trade off-exchange irrespective of their actual behaviour.
- Telser's (1981) threat strategy is also not feasible. With modern information technology, a link has been established among all FX markets worldwide. On the one hand, this makes the threat of excluding a party from the trade on one exchange less credible since there are several other options for each member bank. On the other hand, it allows for arbitrage trading among members of different exchanges that cannot readily be sanctioned. Currently, organized exchanges are still *national* private agents by definition. They cannot enforce their rules and regulations across national borders.

For the conflict of interest with respect to condition (b), therefore, the organized exchange is not an attainable institutional environment for trading foreign exchange, irrespective of whether or not it is the desired search and information system.

Admittedly, however, the only one order matching technology that could have survived technical progress in the past might have been the early merger of all major national FX markets worldwide, which were originally set up as organized exchanges. Furthermore, the answer to why this did not happen would lie in an evolutionary analysis of the FX market, were it not (fortunately) for the inferiority of order matching compared to dealing (section 2.2.2)[61].

2.2.2 Foreign Exchange Market

MONOPOLSITIC INFORMATION AND STRATEGIC BEHAVIOUR: The first of a series of arguments against organizing an exchange when there is monopolistic information was brought forward by Blume and Easley (1990). Applying a game-theoretic framework, they demonstrate that there is no incentive for 'informational monopolists' (Kyle 1985, p. 1316) to 'surrender' and reveal their private information to any other market participant unless he is compensated for this service, in other words, unless information is actually traded.

'The necessary condition for implementability [of rational expectations equilibria], nonexclusivity in information, requires that each trader's private information be perfectly predictable by an outside observer who could observe the private information of all the other traders. Put slightly differently, if the information observed by all other traders is perfectly transmitted by the market, then the contribution to social knowledge of any other trader's private information is nil. His information is redundant. When this condition is false, some trader has truly private information which he may choose to exploit. His ability to exploit this information may destroy the incentive compatibility of any equilibrium allocation' (Blume and Easley 1990, p. 210).

Translating this into institutional economic terms, there is no incentive for an FX dealing bank to organize an exchange which perfectly aggregates private information. With *every* FX dealing bank possessing private information, therefore, it is easy to see that perfect information aggregation is not attainable since it is not desirable. The argument runs along the following line.

---

[61] For details on the decline of foreign exchange dealing 'on the floor' and other issues on the history of foreign exchange dealing, see Einzig (1970). Note also that the major difference of the foreign exchange market to stock exchanges that obviously survived the technical revolutions of the last century is the traded object. The stocks that were traded on national stock exchanges differed from each other until recently. American stocks were traded in the U.S., German stocks in Germany, etc. when the telegraph first allowed for sending orders around the world. Foreign exchange, on the contrary, is and has always been the same everywhere. Starting to trade identical stocks on the major stock exchanges around the world may thus explain exactly why these exchanges have begun to merge in recent months.

Bank n's trading profit depends on bank n's information set according to equation (IV.20) above. Hence, there is a conflict of interest between each bank n and the other $N-1$ banks for each bank n having monopolistic information. On the one hand, the more information the exchange rate contains, the better it is for bank n. On the other hand, bank n certainly prefers *not* to communicate its *own* private signal to the other $N-1$ banks. Both strategies maximize profits. For self-enforcement, therefore, a search and information system must balance both party's interests. But the organized exchange was shown above to be biased towards the interest of the $N-1$ market participants. The return on information to bank n is equal to zero. Thus, it is not self-enforcing. Bank n loses from joining the exchange since it gives up the opportunity to realize the information value of its private signal. Hence, the arrangement is never mutually agreed upon.

NON-ZERO RETURN ON INFORMATION: Turning to the second argument in favour of dealing, it is again a major characteristic of the FX market that each bank is an informational monopolist. Due to customer trading, each market participant faces trading partners that are uninformed relative to himself. For exactly this case, however, Kyle (1985) demonstrates that information trading is profitable *provided* that

- the underlying search and information system is a dealing system and
- the market otherwise resembles the Walrasian auction.

Consequently, his analysis, which follows, can be interpreted such that FX dealing banks strictly prefer dealing to order matching, ceteris paribus. Dealing allows for a positive return to monopolistic information whereas order matching does not.

Intuitively, a dealer has an incentive to learn private information for not constantly quoting the 'wrong' price. In contrast to the broker above, the dealer is engaged in price discovery *and* he trades for his own account. Since, furthermore, the dealer can only learn by trading, he is prepared to pay a premium to the informed trading partners in return for their orders. In other words, a dealer is prepared to pay a price that he would not have paid had he possessed all relevant information about future exchange rates. The broker above does not have this incentive. He has no original interest in the private signals since he only matches orders. He is not prepared to pay a premium (which is exactly what forced the informational monopolist to act competitively in the previous section) (Kyle 1985, pp. 1315-17, 1333-35).

For simplicity, let Bank A receive a private signal such that he knows with certainty the realization e_2 of $\tilde{e}_2$, for $\tilde{e}_2 \rightarrow N(\bar{e}, \sigma_e^2)$. Furthermore, let a single, risk-neutral Dealer D observe the aggregate net order flow ΔUSD_1 and let him set the execution price or exchange rate e_1 accordingly. The net order flow, which is not limited, can be broken down into the informed, Bank A trade ΔUSD_1^A and the $N-1$ uniformed trades

$\Delta USD_1^{N-1} = U_1$. Neither variable can however be observed by the Dealer D. In addition, U_1 is the realization of the random variable $\tilde{U}_1$ that is normally distributed with mean zero and variance σ_U^2 [62]. The distribution of $\tilde{U}_1$ is finally known to Bank A and the Dealer D (Kyle 1985, pp. 1317-18). The trading sequence is summarized in table IV.11 below. It is clearly equivalent to the Walrasian auction example above.

TABLE IV.11: Trade Protocol of Kyle (1985)

Nature chooses e_2 and U_1.
Bank A chooses ΔUSD_1^A (step one).
Dealer D observes the net order flow $\Delta U\tilde{S}D_1^A + \tilde{U}_1$.
Dealer D determines and announces the market clearing price e_1 (step two).

Source: Kyle 1985, pp. 1317-18

Kyle (1985) suggests the following equilibrium for the described model, given that Bank A's trading profits can most generally be denoted as

(IV.33) $$\tilde{\mathrm{P}}_2^A = (\tilde{e}_2 - \tilde{e}_1)\Delta U\tilde{S}D_1^A = (\tilde{e}_2 - \tilde{e}_1)\Delta USD_1^A(\tilde{e}_2),$$

where $\Delta USD_1^A(\tilde{e}_2)$ is Bank A's order strategy. Note also that $\tilde{e}_1$ is a function of Bank A's order strategy given that $e_1(\Delta U\tilde{S}D_1^A + \tilde{U}_1)$ is the dealer's pricing rule. Hence,

(IV.34) $$\tilde{e}_1 = \tilde{e}_1\left[\Delta USD_1^A(\tilde{e}_2), e_1(\Delta U\tilde{S}D_1^A + \tilde{U}_1)\right].$$

In equilibrium, therefore, the dealer shall be expected to set the exchange rate $e_1(\Delta U\tilde{S}D_1^A + \tilde{U}_1)$ such that

[62] Following Garman (1976), for a group of market participants in the present case, the uninformed are treated as a statistical ensemble due to the fact that they share important characteristics. This is a standard modelling assumption in microstructure theory. Note also that representing the uninformed as a statistical distribution does not allow them to act strategically, e.g., by delaying trade, etc. For models that concentrate on strategic behaviour of uninformed market participants, see O'Hara (1995, chapter 5).

(IV.35) $$\tilde{e}_1\left[\Delta USD_1^A(\tilde{e}_2), e_1\left(\Delta U\tilde{S}D_1^A + \tilde{U}_1\right)\right] = E_1^D\left(\tilde{e}_2 \middle| \Delta U\tilde{S}D_1^A + \tilde{U}_1\right)^{63}.$$

In other words, in equilibrium, the market shall be expected to be efficient in processing information. The dealer rationally sets the time 1 exchange rate in step two such that it is equal to his expectation of the time 2 exchange rate, given the net order flow that he can observe[64].

Turning to Bank A, the equilibrium is determined such that the bank substitutes the yet unknown time 1 exchange rate or $\tilde{e}_1$ in equation (IV.33) above by the right-hand side of equation (IV.35) above. In other words, the informational monopolist substitutes the dealer's expected value of the time 2 exchange rate for $\tilde{e}_1$ in step one above (Kyle 1985, p. 1318). Moreover, Bank A's equilibrium order strategy must satisfy

(IV.36) $$E_1^A\left[\tilde{P}_2^A\left(\Delta USD_1^A, e_1\right) \middle| \tilde{e}_2 = e_2\right] \geq E_1^A\left[\tilde{P}_2^A\left(\Delta USD_1^{A'}, e_1\right) \middle| \tilde{e}_2 = e_2\right],$$

for each trading strategy and any realization of the time 2 exchange rate e_2. In other words, following the order strategy ΔUSD_1^A must yield expected profits at least as high as that from any other order strategy $\Delta USD_1^{A'}$ for being the equilibrium order strategy. Finally, Bank A must take into account the dealer's price setting rule e_1 for maximizing expected profits. The effect that Bank A's trade has on the market clearing price is sufficiently taken into account in this case only. More importantly, it is exactly how Bank A exploits its monopoly position (Kyle 1985, p. 1318).

Following the definition of equilibrium, Kyle (1985) subsequently demonstrates that the optimal strategies for Bank A and the Dealer D are given as

(IV.37) $$\Delta USD_1^A(\tilde{e}_2) = \beta(\tilde{e}_2 - \bar{e})$$

and

[63] Without loss of generality, the analysis is again carried out for continuous instead of discrete variables.

[64] 'This model is not quite a game theoretic one because the market makers do not explicitly maximize any particular objective. We could, however, replace the market efficiency condition in step two with an explicit Bertrand auction between at least two risk neutral bidders ... The result of this explicit auction procedure would [however] be our market efficiency condition' (Kyle 1985, p. 1318). The efficiency condition is, thus, a reasonable simplification.

(IV.38) $$e_1\left(\Delta U\tilde{S}D_1^A + \tilde{U}_1\right) = \bar{e} + \lambda\left(\Delta U\tilde{S}D_1^A + \tilde{U}_1\right),$$

where $\beta = \left(\frac{\sigma_U^2}{\sigma_e^2}\right)^{\frac{1}{2}}$ and $\lambda = \frac{1}{2}\left(\frac{\sigma_U^2}{\sigma_e^2}\right)^{-\frac{1}{2}}$ (Kyle 1985, pp. 1319-20).

In equilibrium, therefore, the execution price in equation (IV.38) above always differs from the mean of the time 2 exchange rate which Bank A bases its decision on according to equation (IV.37). This expresses the fact that Bank A cannot observe the market clearing price whereas the dealer can by definition. More importantly, however, Bank A's expected profits are given as

(IV.39) $$E_1^A\left(\tilde{P}_2^A\right) = \frac{1}{2}\left(\sigma_U^2\sigma_e^2\right)^{\frac{1}{2}} > 0$$

in equilibrium (Kyle 1985, p. 1320). Hence, Kyle (1985) demonstrates that, ceteris paribus, informational monopolists prefer dealing to order matching since they form their expectations rationally[65].

Leaving the formal analysis behind, the return on information clearly depends on the uninformed market participants' order flow. For illustration, imagine the variance of the uninformed order flow to be equal to zero. The optimal strategy for Bank A is then not to trade for the simple reason that the dealer can immediately identify the informed player's order and learn the private information that Bank A has. The bank cannot trade profitably. It cannot 'hide' its trade from the broker behind the uninformed order flow (O'Hara 1995, p. 93).

'What price comes to be depends on the actual net order flow. An unexpectedly large uninformed buy imbalance could overwhelm the informed trader's sell order, causing the market maker to set a high price even though the full-information value is low' (O'Hara 1995, p. 98).

Clearly, the same argument of not being able to hide its trade from the dealer induces Bank A *not* to agree to open trading instead of sealed trading. Could the dealer observe the net order flow *and* each deal individually, the return to Bank A's information would again be equal to zero. At this stage, the results of sections 2.2.1 and 2.2.2 can therefore be summarized as follows (table IV.12).

[65] Kyle's (1985) results are more recently and most prominently confirmed in Rochet and Vila (1994).

TABLE IV.12: Return on Information to Sealed Trading, Open Trading, Order Matching, and/or Dealing

	Open Trading	**Sealed Trading**
FWB/ Order Matching (section 2.2.1)	zero (open-outcry auction, regret-free)	zero (Walrasian auction, not regret-free)
Kyle (1985)/ Dealing (section 2.2.2)	zero (regret-free)	$E_1^A\left(\widetilde{P}_2^A\right)=\frac{1}{2}\left(\sigma_U^2\sigma_e^2\right)^{1/2}$ (stochastic, regret-free)

Similar to the second-price sealed-bid auction, the Kyle (1985) model has useful theoretical properties. Most importantly, it provides a framework for discussing the key issue of dealing versus order matching in isolation. In particular, the model can immediately be compared with the Walrasian auction above. Furthermore, equation (IV.39) indirectly reconfirms the results that were derived by Blume and Easley (1990).

Unfortunately, however, the trade protocol in table IV.11 does not find its expression in any of the alternative search and information systems and their real world equivalents. Most importantly, trading is periodic although the market is a dealing system. Furthermore, the dealer is a monopolist. Finally, the orders are market orders although limit orders were said to be the more appropriate order type for the above trade protocol, etc. In other words, the market structure that Kyle (1985) investigates is highly artificial and very abstract in nature[66].

The abstract nature of the Kyle (1985) model is due to the fact that it belongs to the class of rational expectations models, as his definition of equilibrium demonstrates. According to the above mentioned, however, rational expectations is not a neutral modelling assumption with respect to the underlying market structure. On the contrary, the rational expectations approach is limited to organized exchanges and some Kyle (1985)-type markets. But it is not appropriate for modelling decentralized markets such as the foreign exchange market (O'Hara 1995, pp. 89-90)[67].

[66] The assumption that the dealer cannot observe individual orders is not as critical as it may seem when comparing the trade protocol with real world equivalents. On the FX market, e.g., the market makers do generally not know whether their counterparty is an information trader, a liquidity trader, or whether he is hedging an open position. The assumption of not being able to distinguish information traders from other traders thus may well be justified on these grounds.

[67] The presentation above ignores the dealer. So does Kyle (1985). But in another paper, he demonstrates that the expected return to the dealer is non-zero. Although he loses from the deals

NON-ZERO RETURN ON INFORMATION REVISITED: Sequential trade models such as Glosten and Milgrom (1985) or Easley and O'Hara (1987) can be interpreted as decentralized markets and vice versa. Ignoring rational expectations for the above reasons, therefore, they can more appropriately be referred to when addressing the efficiency of the FX market organization with respect to information trading. Anticipating the non-existence of fully revealing rational expectations equilibria for monopolistic information and overcoming the problems that Kyle (1985) was facing, the sequential trade models ignore *information aggregation* of the above kind altogether. Alternatively, they focus on learning and *information transmission* among traders. Most recently, it is Perraudin and Vitale (1996) who formalize the problem of information trading, most conveniently, with special emphasis on the FX market. By its very nature, their model comes closest to the current market practice, at the same time, establishing the efficiency of dealing and sealed trading. The return on information trading is positive. Finally, they also provide an explanation for reciprocal trading (although not in the strong sense of membership). Their analysis is again based on the uncertainty case of the basic asset demand model above. For the complexity of their calculations due to dynamic optimization, however, only the most essential elements of Perraudin and Vitale (1996) are repeated formally.

Imagine n risk neutral banks to deal on the customer market as well as on the interbank market such that

- at time 1, each bank n quotes a price to a non-bank customer who arrives with probability $1/n$ at bank n,
- at time 2, the banks trade among themselves if they wish, and
- at time 3, each bank n again trades with a non-bank customer with probability $1/n$.

The exchange rate at time $T = 4$ shall realize as 1 or -1 with probabilities q and $(1-q)$, respectively. Furthermore, a customer buy order will indicate that $\widetilde{e}_4$ becomes 1 with probability α whereas it does not indicate anything with probability $(1-\alpha)$. The same holds with respect to a sell order and $\widetilde{e}_4$ being -1 (Perraudin and Vitale 1996, pp. 75-77). Finally, there is no order flow information available (Perraudin and Vitale 1996, p. 79).

Given that each market maker trades three times, therefore,

'he may be able to use the information that he has gained from period 0 [time 1] trades. The information is potentially valuable, first, because, in his own period 2 [time 3] trading, it may permit him to quote a bid-ask spread that yields higher expected profits. Second, he may be able to 'sell' the information to other dealers in that they may be willing to trade with him at

with informed traders, he gains from trading with the other $N-1$ uninformed banks at the same time (Kyle 1984).

advantageous terms in the interbank market in order to learn about his order flow' (Perraudin and Vitale 1996, p. 78).

Perraudin and Vitale (1996), furthermore, demonstrate that this is indeed the case.

Let Bank A be the bank that receives a customer buy order at time 1. In this case, 'news of a buy order increases total expected profits in period two [at time 3]' (Perraudin and Vitale 1996, p. 82).

(IV.40) $E_1^A\left(\widetilde{\mathrm{P}}_4^A(q_b)\right) > E_1^A\left(\widetilde{\mathrm{P}}_4^A(q)\right)$ (Perraudin and Vitale 1996, pp. 79-80, 90).

At the same time, of course, the expected profit of a bank that did *not* receive the customer order at time 1, let it be Bank B, increases equivalently when 'buying' the news on the interbank market from Bank A at time 2. Due to updating the private belief q about the time 4 exchange rate, Bank B can also adjust the own price quote at time 3 to its advantage. Hence,

(IV.41) $E_1^B\left(\widetilde{\mathrm{P}}_4^B(q_b)\right) > E_1^B\left(\widetilde{\mathrm{P}}_4^B(q)\right)$.

Bank A is finally willing to 'sell' his information because both banks can bargain over Bank B's expected return to the *additional* information which is equivalent to

(IV.42) $E_1^B\left(\widetilde{\mathrm{P}}_4^B(q_b)\right) - E_1^B\left(\widetilde{\mathrm{P}}_4^B\left(e_3^B(q) \mid q_b\right)\right) > 0$.

This is the expected return to Bank B from being able to adjust its quotes at time 3. More precisely, it is the expected profit of knowing q_b *and* adjusting the time 3 exchange rate minus the expected profit of knowing q_b but *not* adjusting the time 3 exchange rate. This is the case because the additional return to knowing q_b but not adjusting the time 3 exchange rate compared to not knowing q_b at all cannot be subject to bargaining. Bank B is not prepared to pay for information if it cannot exploit it by adjusting the own price quote (Perraudin and Vitale 1996, p. 80).

Translated into institutional economic terms, the above results clearly depend on the search and information system being a dealing system that operates according to the rule of sealed trading.

- For a broker, there is no incentive for paying a premium since his profits are not affected by knowing private information or not.

- ‘Buying’ information is rational if and only if it can be exploited later on during the trading process. But this is the case if and only if the information does not become common knowledge. In other words, buying information is rational if and only if trading is sealed[68].

Table IV.12 above is thus reconfirmed as follows (table IV.13), leaving to the appendix the surprising coexistence of open trading and dealing as found on the London Stock Exchange. But first, let us demonstrate, for the sake of completeness, that it is an inefficient arrangement for governing foreign exchange dealing (section 2.2.3). Let us conclude this section, finally, by briefly reviewing a second proposition that can be found in Perraudin and Vitale (1996).

TABLE IV.13: Return on Information at FWB and on the FX Market

	Return on Information
FWB **(Rational Expectations)**	zero
FX Market **(Sequential Learning)**	$E_1^{A,B}\left(\widetilde{P}_4^{A,B}(q_b)\right) - E_1^{A,B}\left(\widetilde{P}_4^{A,B}(q)\right)$

The more market makers Bank A can sell his information to, the stronger is the incentive to do so. Moreover, the stronger the incentive to sell information is, the more market makers want to buy it. In the limit, therefore, the decentralized market is the efficient arrangement for all dealers, the ‘buyers’ and the ‘sellers’ of information, if there are sufficient trading opportunities (Perraudin and Vitale 1996, p. 84). If, however,

‘dealers can transact with only a fraction of other marketmakers, the advantage of better incentives will be reduced as it will then not be possible to capture the feedback rent associated with information [the return on information]. In addition, the decentralized market will suffer from the fact that dealers who do not receive interdealer trades will be unable to update their probabilities in response to period 0 [time 1] order flow’ (Perraudin and Vitale 1996, p. 84) which may want them to switch to other market structures.

68 ‘In standard, dynamic microstructure models such as those of Glosten and Milgrom (1985) or Easley and O’Hara (1987), this particular link between trading in different periods is broken by the fact that order flow information is assumed to be public knowledge’ (Perraudin and Vitale 1996, p. 79). Hence, there is no information trading in their models, simply because trading is open by assumption.

In other words, information trading is beneficial for the informational monopolist *and* the uninformed banks if and only if there are maximum trading opportunities on the interbank market. It is only then that both parties, the informed and the uninformed, benefit from information trading. A mechanism that can finally ensure maximum trading opportunities from an institutional economic perspective is reciprocal trading. In addition to establishing the efficiency of dealing and sealed trading, therefore, Perraudin and Vitale (1996) also provide an explanation for reciprocal trading (although they do not exactly provide an explanation for membership which requires reciprocal trading on the bilateral rather than the multilateral level).

2.2.3 London Stock Exchange

Open trading destroys the incentives that drive information trading. Compared to the current market practice, therefore, the LSE provides an inappropriate search and information system in this respect. As with the arguments above, the return on information is equal to zero (table IV.14; proposition 2).

TABLE IV.14: Return on Information at FWB, on the FX Market, and at LSE

	Return on Information
FWB	zero
FX Market	$E_1^{A,B}\left(\widetilde{\mathrm{P}}_4^{A,B}(q_b)\right) - E_1^{A,B}\left(\widetilde{\mathrm{P}}_4^{A,B}(q)\right)$
LSE	zero

PROPOSITION 2: Each FX dealing bank has monopolistic information. When designing the search and information system, each bank's objective is, therefore, to take full advantage of this monopoly position subject to the constraint that it is also uninformed relative to the trading partners at the same time. The conflict of interest that arises from the distribution of information is best resolved by trading information among each other which is equivalent to implementing a dealing system combined with sealed trading. In this case, the incentive to reveal information is greatest since the return on information is greatest. So is the incentive to pay for additional information since it can be exploited further. The efficiency of information trading increases for intensifying interbank trading which can be achieved by introducing reciprocal trading. Complementing this outcome, there is finally no incentive to join any of the two organized exchanges given that each market participant has monopolistic information. They do better by trading information exclusively rather than perfectly aggregating it. This hypothesis can leave aside the fact that any FWB- or LSE-like search and information system is not attainable in the absence of law.

3. Market Risk Exposure and the Efficiency of Market Making and Membership

3.1 Costs of Delay

Market risk is again the risk of adverse price movements. It is what turns a bank's open currency position into a risky asset. For risk averse banks, therefore, customer trading repeatedly disturbs their optimal portfolio. Hence, there is a constant desire for trading foreign exchange on the interbank market. Apart from the reallocation of inventory (section 4), the reallocation of market risk or 'inventory risk' (Stoll 1992, p. 82) is an important trading motive for FX dealing banks.

'[The market maker] now seeks to restore its own equilibrium by going to another marketmaker or the broker market for a two-way price. ... It is this search process for a counterparty who is willing to accept a new currency position that accounts for a good deal of the volume in the foreign exchange market' (Burnham 1991, p. 135).

For the reallocation of market risk, banks unambiguously prefer immediacy to any kind of delay, ceteris paribus. The alternative search and information systems above must therefore be compared with respect to the time that is required for searching potential trading partners. Clearly, the corresponding analysis must centre around the issue of continuous trading and market making versus periodic trading and order matching. In other words, it must focus on the current FX market practice compared to the one of FWB. In contrast to the previous section, however, the London Stock Exchange is analytically equivalent to the FX market this time. Deriving a formal expression for the search costs, which obviously result in costs of delay, is postponed to the comparative analysis below. For the applied framework, they are again not independent of the implemented market structure.

3.2 Comparative Analysis

3.2.1 Frankfurter Wertpapierbörse

Imagine the asset demand model with return uncertainty above. Also imagine the time horizon to be $T = 3$. Each identical bank n's terminal portfolio is then given as

(IV.43) $$P_3 = EUR_0 + (\tilde{e}_3 - \tilde{e}_1)\Delta USD_1 + (\tilde{e}_3 - \tilde{e}_2)\Delta USD_2 + \tilde{e}_3 USD_0 .$$

Furthermore, let each bank n be risk averse, equally informed, and not endowed with US dollars. For a standard, negative exponential utility function with a expressing the degree of risk aversion or

$$\text{(IV.44)} \qquad U(\mathrm{P}) = -e^{-a\mathrm{P}},$$

maximizing expected terminal wealth $EU_0(\mathrm{P}_3)$, therefore, requires that

$$\text{(IV.45)} \qquad USD_1 = \frac{E_1\tilde{e}_3 - e_1}{a \cdot \operatorname{var}_1(E_2\tilde{e}_3)}$$

and

$$\text{(IV.46)} \qquad USD_2 = \frac{E_2\tilde{e}_3 - e_2}{a \cdot \operatorname{var}_2 \tilde{e}_3}$$

for all n (Grossman and Miller 1988, pp. 622-25)[69].

Equations (IV.45) and (IV.46) express the optimal USD position at each time. Equation (IV.45), furthermore, expresses the excess demand for US dollars at time 1 given that the initial endowment was assumed to be equal to zero. Hence,

- bank n's optimal USD position at each time 1,2 is non-zero for any non-zero expected change in price,
- the more risk averse bank n is, the lower the optimal USD position and vice versa, and
- the more volatile the exchange rate is, the lower the optimal USD position and vice versa.

These results are familiar from standard microeconomic analysis of risk averse agents. But let the banks now be exposed to exogenous liquidity shocks stemming from customer trading. Furthermore, let customer trading take place *one time ahead* of interbank trading, in other words, when $t = 0,1$[70]. For simplicity, let the shocks be given as

---

[69] Note that USD_t is required to be a continuous variable which can be assumed without loss of generality.

[70] Grossman and Miller (1988) assume that customer trading and interbank trading take place *at the same time*. Altering this assumption does not affect the outcome. However, it is believed to contribute to a better understanding of the model.

(IV.47) $s_0^A = s,$ for a single Bank A at time $t = 0$

and

(IV.48) $s_1^B = -s,$ for another Bank B at time $t = 1$

such that

(IV.49) $USD_0^A = s.$

For the remaining $N-2$ banks, finally, optimal portfolio balance is assumed for all t. For identical, equally informed banks, the optimal USD position is given as

(IV.50) $USD_0^n = USD_1^n = USD_2^n = 0,$

since

(IV.51) $E_1\tilde{e}_3 - e_1 = E_2\tilde{e}_3 - e_2 = 0,$ for all $n \in (N-2)$

(Grossman and Miller 1988, pp. 622-25).

In this setting, therefore, trade can only find a motive in Bank A's and Bank B's desire to rebalance their portfolios due to market risk. There is no difference in private beliefs on future exchange rates which would generate trade nor does any bank face ruin due to customer trading which is the driving force behind FX dealing in section 4 below. Hence, Grossman and Miller (1988) describe a situation that is analytically equivalent to the one that the present section wants to focus on.

Moreover, the nature of the liquidity shocks

(IV.52) $s_0^A = -s_1^B$

allows for concentrating on Bank A's demand for immediacy. Provided that Bank A wants to reallocate market risk, Grossman and Miller (1988) investigate if and when Bank A is prepared to wait for one period to square out its USD position by trading with Bank B compared to if and when Bank A is not prepared to do so (Grossman and Miller

1988, p. 618). But, ultimately, this implies that Grossman and Miller (1988) investigate Bank A's preference for market making compared to order matching. On the one hand, market makers implementing a dealing system would immediately 'offset this temporary imbalance by taking trading positions [at time 1] that they hold until date 2' (Grossman and Miller 1988, p. 622). For a matching system, on the other hand, Bank A would have to hold the imbalanced position itself until a corresponding order arrives. Hence, Grossman and Miller (1988) again provide a useful model for the present analysis. This is even more true given that equations (IV.47) and (IV.48) are assumed to be common knowledge, thus, isolating information-related problems.

Bank A's preference for the market making system is intuitively straightforward. Market making enables Bank A to hold constantly the optimal portfolio. The order matching system does not have the same property for the absence of continuous trading. Formally, this result can be derived as follows. Given the liquidity shock s at time 0, Bank A's 'effective' USD position at time 1 is given as the optimal USD position of equation (IV.45) above adjusted by the anticipated liquidity shock s.

(IV.53) $$USD^A_{1,effective} = USD^A_1 - s.$$

The time 2 USD position deviates from the optimal time 2 position accordingly.

(IV.54) $$USD^A_{2,effective} = USD^A_2 - s.$$

For Bank B, a similar result holds with respect to the time 2 position.

(IV.55) $$USD^B_{2,effective} = USD^B_2 + s.$$

Since, however,

(IV.56)

$$EU^A_0\left(USD^A_{1,effective}, USD^A_{2,effectve}\right) < EU^A_0\left(USD^A_{1,effective}, USD^A_2\right) < EU^A_0\left(USD^A_1, USD^A_2\right)$$

and

(IV.57) $$EU^B_0\left(USD^B_1, USD^B_{2,effective}\right) < EU^B_0\left(USD^B_1, USD^B_2\right),$$

Bank A and Bank B, both un-surprisingly prefer interbank dealing to not trading. Additionally, Bank A prefers continuous trading and market making to order matching and periodic trading. The costs of delay would otherwise be given as

(IV.58) $$C_D = EU_0^A\left(USD_1^A, USD_2^A\right) - EU_0^A\left(USD_{1,effective}^A, USD_2^A\right)$$ (table IV.15).

In other words, Bank A optimally wants to supply s units of USD at time 1 to a yet unknown market maker. Its excess demand at time 2 is equal to zero at the same time. Simultaneously, Bank B optimally wants to purchase these s units from the same market maker at time 2.

TABLE IV.15: Costs of Delay Related to FWB and the FX Market

	Costs of Delay
FWB	$EU_0^A\left(USD_1^A, USD_2^A\right) - EU_0^A\left(USD_{1,effective}^A, USD_2^A\right)$
FX Market	zero

3.2.2 Foreign Exchange Market

Having argued in favour of dealing for the reallocation of market risk, the 'supply' of market making services was again left aside. The previous section turned from Kyle (1985) to Perraudin and Vitale (1996) such that a separate analysis of an arbitrary dealer and how he profitably redistributes wealth from the uninformed to the informed became useless. Perraudin and Vitale (1996) demonstrate that information trading is profitable for both sides of the market such that *all* market participants engage in purchasing and selling information as long as the market has the appropriate structure. A similar argument is clearly needed for the supply of insurance opportunities among identical banks. But

'it is efficient for dealers to perform the insurance role only if they are sufficiently less risk-averse than their customers. In particular, the dealership market is superior if dealers are risk-neutral and customers are risk-averse (Pagano and Roell 1990, p. 85).

Hence, this standard result from insurance theory would obviously pose substantial problems to *identical* FX dealing banks if it was not for the following.

Returning to Grossman and Miller (1988), the interbank market clears at time 2 if and only if

(IV.59) $$\frac{E_2\tilde{e}_3 - e_2}{a \cdot \mathrm{var}_2\,\tilde{e}_3} - s + \frac{E_2\tilde{e}_3 - e_2}{a \cdot \mathrm{var}_2\,\tilde{e}_3} + s + (N-2)\frac{E_2\tilde{e}_3 - e_2}{a \cdot \mathrm{var}_2\,\tilde{e}_3} = 0.$$

Not surprisingly, this is the case if and only if $E_2\tilde{e}_3 - e_2 = 0$, which is the terminal condition.

At time 1, the market analogously clears whenever

(IV.60) $$\frac{E_1\tilde{e}_3 - e_1}{a \cdot \mathrm{var}_1\left(E_2\tilde{e}_3\right)} - s + (N-1)\frac{E_1\tilde{e}_3 - e_1}{a \cdot \mathrm{var}_1\left(E_2\tilde{e}_3\right)} = 0.$$

This, in turn, is the case if and only if

(IV.61) $$\frac{E_1\tilde{e}_3 - e_1}{a \cdot \mathrm{var}_1\left(E_2\tilde{e}_3\right)} = \frac{s}{N}.$$

Equation (IV.61), therefore, implies that during the first trading session, the market clears *and* each bank ends up with its optimal portfolio if and only if $E_1\tilde{e}_3 > e_1$. In other words, if and only if Bank A is willing to accept a discount such that the execution price is less than the expected final-period exchange rate, *all* market participants end up with their optimal USD position *and* the market clears. At the same time, *each* of the $N-1$ banks that were not subject to a liquidity shock at time 0 provide the market making service to Bank A. They exclusively satisfy Bank A's demand for immediacy for

(IV.62) $$e_1 = E_1\tilde{e}_3 - \frac{s\left[a \cdot \mathrm{var}_1\left(E_2\tilde{e}_3\right)\right]}{N},$$

where $\frac{s\left[a \cdot \mathrm{var}_1\left(E_2\tilde{e}_3\right)\right]}{N}$ is the risk premium that Bank A must pay to each market participant

for reallocating market risk. The risk premium primarily depends on the exchange rate volatility and the number of market participants. The demand for US dollars is non-zero for each bank according to equation (IV.45) above (Grossman and Miller 1988, pp. 624-26).

Leaving the quantities to the following paragraphs, however, Grossman and Miller (1988) finally demonstrate that Bank A is prepared to pay the above risk premium since it is less than or equal to the costs of delay of having to wait for Bank B or equation (IV.58) above. Furthermore, they show that market making is profitable for the remaining $N-1$ banks, including Bank B. They gain from selling their shares of the liquidity shock s to Bank B at the exchange rate $e_2 = E_2\tilde{e}_3 > e_1$ at time 2 (Grossman and Miller 1988, pp. 624-26).

Summarizing, the problem that the insurer must generally be less risk averse than the insuree for efficiently reallocating market risk is resolved to the satisfaction of all banks by *sharing* the risk. Risk sharing is the efficient solution to reallocating market risk among identical market participants.

- The costs of immediacy, more precisely, the liquidity costs in the form of a discount for continuous trading opportunities overcompensate the costs of delay that would be non-zero otherwise.
- It is optimal for all market participants not only to demand immediacy - i.e., market making activities - but also to supply them.

It is thus the pool of all N banks in contrast to each individual bank that can effectively address the imperfection of market risk exposure (table IV.16). Pagano and Roell (1990) thus qualify their above statement accordingly.

'The hypothesis that dealers as a group may behave as if they were less risk-averse than their customers is not far-fetched: this can happen if they divide orders among themselves so as to share the riskiness of the implied inventories' (Pagano and Roell 1990, p. 85).

TABLE IV.16: Search Costs Related to Hedging on FWB and the FX Market

	Search Costs	
	Costs of Delay	**Liquidity Costs (Discount)**
FWB	$EU_0^A\left(USD_1^A, USD_2^A\right) - EU_0^A\left(USD_{1,effective}^A, USD_2^A\right)$	zero
FX Market	zero	$s\left[a \cdot \mathrm{var}_1\left(E_2\tilde{e}_3\right)\right] \leq C_D$

3.2.3 Free Entry Foreign Exchange Market

Surprisingly, the analysis of market risk exposure cannot be left at table IV.16 above. On the contrary, the following paragraphs demonstrate that membership is critical for a smooth operation of risk sharing arrangements. Continuing with Grossman and Miller (1988), for this purpose, equation (IV.61) states that each bank, including Bank A, optimally holds s/N units of US dollars. The excess supply of US dollars at time 1 is thus spread among *all* market participants. More importantly, it is *equally* spread among all market participants for *identical* discounts. Consequently, there is a remarkable 'solidarity' among FX dealing banks in the Grossman and Miller (1988) model. The efficient solution to reallocating market risk is characterized by extremely harmonious behaviour on behalf of all market participants. This is, however, not set as a theme; rather, it is simply based on a set of assumptions, most prominently,

- identical banks and
- a high degree of transparency

such that cheating is impossible. It is immediately detected.

With the first assumption reflecting the reality on the FX market, it is cooperative behaviour that is the key to the efficiency of risk sharing among all market makers since the second assumption is not reasonable. Information is imperfect on the FX market. Hence, whether or not cooperation is self-enforcing in the absence of law remains to be seen. Moreover, it can be expected that in the absence of any institutional safe-guards, cooperative behaviour is rather unlikely. If and only if the search and information system of the current FX market practice can be demonstrated to suppress strategic behaviour, therefore, is it efficient with respect to the reallocation of market risk.

As opposed to Grossman and Miller (1988), the information on the liquidity shock s is private information to Bank A in the real world. Ceteris paribus, cooperative behaviour is thus not a reasonable assumption. Private information on s enables Bank A to profit systematically (more) from interbank liquidity trading than its partners. The bank could, for example, split s into small units, contact many dealers simultaneously, and pretend that the demand for immediacy is actually low. This is advantageous since the discount in equation (IV.62) above is a function of s. Furthermore, since Bank A itself is a market maker, it could subsequently protect its own optimal USD position by quoting much higher prices *after* s has already been sold and the trading partners have eventually learned the size of it. But apart from extremely high risk premia, the described behaviour may actually result in market failure.

Replacing the ceteris paribus-assumption by membership in the strong form of reciprocal trading on the bilateral level, however, honest behaviour and, hence, efficient risk sharing is guaranteed. As soon as trade is required to be reciprocal, Bank A knows with certainty that if it ever wants to trade again, it necessarily has to take an equal share of the 'excess supply' of USD in the market, thus, reporting the correct value of s to the trading partners. If it did not, parts of the original deals would certainly be reversed. If Bank A wants to stay in business, the trading partners acquire exactly this right whenever Bank A sells a share of s to them.

Trying to protect its own USD position by quoting 'off the market' is also prevented by reciprocal trading. If Bank A did so, the trading partners would behave accordingly whenever they are subject to a liquidity shock themselves. The credible threat to Bank A, if it then rejects a quote, is the termination of the business relationship. Similar to section 2, therefore, membership makes the efficient solution to market risk exposure self-enforcing or incentive compatible provided that Bank A wants to stay in business.

Concluding the discussion of Grossman and Miller (1988), a second argument in favour of membership relies on the fact that market making is costly. Bank A prefers N to tend to infinity according to equation (IV.62) above. In this case, the discount tends to zero. At the same time, however, the expected profit to the suppliers of immediacy, the market makers, tends to zero. It is a positive increasing function of the discount. If market making is costly, therefore, the discount is bounded below. But for given exchange rate volatility, risk aversion, and liquidity shocks, this implies that the number of market makers is at the same time bounded above. For too many market makers, the supply of immediacy is no longer profitable. The market for reallocating market risk collapses (Grossman and Miller 1988, pp. 626-27). Splitting s equally among all market participants finally results in what is known as the game of hot potato which is outlined below, following proposition 3.

PROPOSITION 3: Foreign exchange positions are subject to adverse price movements. When designing the search and information system, therefore, each bank's objective is to ensure hedging opportunities. For this purpose, it is optimal for all market participants to implement a market maker system. It efficiently provides the desired immediacy for the reallocation of market risk. Market making is reciprocal in the weak sense since it is a profitable activity. In other words, all market participants are market makers. Since it is finally efficient to share equally market risk among identical banks, membership in the form of reciprocal trading is the necessary condition for preventing the exploitation of private information. It furthermore guarantees the existence of the market since market making is costly. The current FX market practice is thus the appropriate arrangement for efficiently addressing the exposure to market risk (table IV.17).

TABLE IV.17: Search Costs Related to Hedging on FWB, the FX Market, or the Free Entry FX Market

	Search Costs	
	Costs of Delay	**Liquidity Costs (Discount)**
FWB	$EU_0^A\left(USD_1^A, USD_2^A\right) - EU_0^A\left(USD_{1,effective}^A, USD_2^A\right)$	zero
FX Market	zero	$s\left[a \cdot \mathrm{var}_1\left(E_2\tilde{e}_3\right)\right] \leq C_D$
Free Entry FX Market	fails	

THE GAME OF HOT POTATO: The liquidity shock is not known with certainty. Moreover, Bank A's trading partners do not know whether Bank A's trading motive is only hedging instead of also being information trading. Hence, each of Bank A's trading partners interprets a deal according to its own information set. Self-enforced by reciprocal trading, more precisely, they calculate the expected share of the dealing amount that they have to hold in their portfolio given the likelihood that the deal was insurance-motivated. They then forward the remaining currency units to the next bank, etc.

Giving Lyons (1996) the final remark on the game of hot potato, section 3 shall thus be concluded here by pointing to the most important, non-institutional economic models of the foreign exchange market in the sense that they have information-induced or insurance-motivated trading as a theme. Although not including all components simultaneously, the interbank FX market is best represented in Flood (1992, 1996), Lyons (1995, 1996, 1997) and Kirman (1995, 1996).

'The metaphor of the hot potato offers a link between ... liquidity trading and foreign exchange trading. Foreign exchange dealers use the metaphor in referring to the repeated passage of idiosyncratic inventory imbalances from dealer to dealer following an innovation in customer order flow. ... To clarify the hot potato process, consider the following crude but not unrealistic example. (Keep in mind that roughly 85 percent of foreign exchange trading is interdealer, a much higher share than in other multiple-dealer markets.) Suppose that there are ten dealers, all of whom are risk averse, and each currently with a zero net position. A customer sale of \$ 10 million worth of deutsche marks is accommodated by one of the dealers. Not wanting to carry the open position, the dealer calculates his share of this inventory imbalance - or one-tenth of $ 10 million - calls another dealer and unloads $ 9 million worth of deutsche marks. The dealer receiving this trade then calculates his share of this inventory imbalance - or one-tenth of $ 9 million - calls another dealer, and unloads $ 8.1 million worth of deutsche marks. The hot potato process continues. In the limit, the total interdealer volume generated from the $ 10 million customer trade is $ 9 million / (1-0.9) = $ 90 million. Thus, the example produces an interdealer share of 90 percent, roughly matching the empirical share' (Lyons 1996, p. 184).

4. Position Risk Exposure and the Efficiency of Continuous Trading and Standard Dealing Amounts

4.1 Liquidity Costs

Commercial banks deal foreign exchange with their non-bank customers continuously and for their own account. Similar to gamblers who randomly win and lose money, therefore, they are subject to unknown inflows and outflows of different currencies. Furthermore, supply and demand is almost surely imbalanced whenever trade occurs. Ceteris paribus, this imbalance creates inventory problems for the banks and execution problems for the non-bank customers. In the worst case, a bank has to turn down customer deals since it runs out of stock of one or more currencies.

Against this background, section 4 analyzes the banks' exposure to position risk or the so called gambler's ruin problem. In other words, the present section analyzes whether or not the current practice of interbank foreign exchange dealing reallocates inventory efficiently among identical banks, given that a shortage in one currency always implies an 'excess supply' in the second currency of a particular currency pair.

4.1.1 Foregone Commissions

It was Garman (1976) who first described a dealer for financial assets as a gambler in the sense that he faces similar constraints. Ceteris paribus, his inventory position or endowment is an exogenous, random variable and he is 'out of the game' if the position ever realizes at zero value, which is a positive likelihood. The application of the gambler's ruin problem to FX dealing banks is straightforward. A bank receives customer orders that are unknown to it in time, size, and direction. At the same time, they determine the bank's currency positions. The only difference to gambling is that, 'per shot', foreign exchange dealing affects *two* positions instead of only one.

Imagine a single bank, let it be Bank A from section 3 above, to be endowed with EUR_t units of Euros and USD_t units of US dollars subject to

(IV.63) $EUR_t, USD_t \geq 0$, for all t[71].

Furthermore, denote $a(t)$ as the cumulative units of USD that non-bank customers *asked* from Bank A up to time t and $b(t)$ as the cumulative units of USD that they *bid* from the same bank during the same time period. In other words, denote $a(t)$ as the cumulative units of USD that non-bank customers purchased from Bank A up to time t and $b(t)$ as the cumulative units of USD that they sold to it up to time t. Bank A's USD and EUR positions at time t are then given as

(IV.64) $USD_t = USD_0 + b(t) - a(t)$

and

(IV.65) $EUR_t = EUR_0 + e_t a(t) - e_t b(t)$,

respectively. The dealing amount is again assumed to be standardized at one US dollar. The exchange rate is assumed to be determined exogenously (Garman 1976, pp. 262-64)[72].

Turning from Bank A to the non-bank customers, the key to Garman's (1976) results is to model the customer buy and sell orders as independent stochastic processes. More precisely, let them be given as Poisson distributed random variables with the order arrival being stationary. Stationarity implies that the aggregate customer supply and demand per time t can be represented algebraically as the arrival rate functions $\lambda_b(t)$ and $\lambda_a(t)$, respectively (Garman 1976, p. 263)[73].

[71] For a single Bank A, the superscript can again be ignored for simplicity. Note also that the analysis leaves behind the framework of the basic asset demand model of Chapter III, section 5. Chapter V, section 1, however, returns to the standard framework.

[72] Note that in the original version of the presented model, the exchange rate e_t is not exogenous but only constant over time. Furthermore, the order arrival rates $\lambda_{a,b}$ below are not only functions of time but also the exchange rate. Since the importance of the gambler's ruin problem with respect to the search and information system can be highlighted by ignoring the exchange rate, however, the bank's price setting behaviour is left aside. It is subject of Chapter V, section 3 below. Reference is then made to the original version of Garman's (1976) model, providing a possible explanation for the bid-ask spread.

[73] For a detailed discussion on the advantages of the Poisson distribution, see Garman (1976, pp. 259-62).

Finally, suppose that $\eta_{\overline{EUR}}(t)$ denotes the probability that $EUR = \overline{EUR}$ at time *t*. In other words, suppose that $\eta_{\overline{EUR}}(t)$ denotes the probability that Bank A's Euro position is equal to the amount $\overline{EUR}$ at time *t*. $\mu_{\overline{USD}}(t)$ shall express the same likelihood with respect to Bank A's USD position (Garman 1976, p. 264).

In this case, the probability of running out of Euros, in other words, the probability that $EUR_t = EUR = 0$, for $t \to \infty$, is approximately given as

$$\text{(IV.66)} \qquad \lim_{t\to\infty} \eta_0(t) \begin{cases} \approx \left(\dfrac{\lambda_b(t)}{\lambda_a(t)}\right)^{EUR_0/e_t} & if \qquad \lambda_a(t) > \lambda_b(t) \\ = 1 & otherwise \end{cases},$$

with the probability of running out of US dollars being equivalent to

$$\text{(IV.67)} \qquad \lim_{t\to\infty} \mu_0(t) \begin{cases} \approx \left(\dfrac{\lambda_a(t)}{\lambda_b(t)}\right)^{USD_0} & if \qquad \lambda_a(t) < \lambda_b(t) \\ = 1 & otherwise \end{cases}$$

(Garman 1976, p. 264).

Most importantly, equations (IV.66) and (IV.67) indicate that

- the probability of running out of USD and/or EUR is non-zero. In fact,
- the probability of running out of either currency is equal to one since $\lambda_a(t)$ can *either* be less than *or* greater than $\lambda_b(t)$. But $\lambda_a(t)$ cannot be less than *and* greater than $\lambda_b(t)$.

Ceteris paribus, therefore, Bank A has to turn down customer deals with certainty at some point in time as soon as it provides dealer services to non-bank customers over an extended period of time. This is due to the stochastic and imbalanced nature of the customer buy and sell order flow, given that the case of perfect balance is reasonably ignored. But turning down customer deals means turning down business opportunities. Hence, the costs related to the gambler's ruin problem can finally be interpreted as the costs of foregone commissions which could be charged for each customer deal otherwise.

Finally, Garman (1976) has frequently been criticized for a number of excessively restrictive assumptions (O'Hara 1995, pp. 23-24, a/o). Among others,

- he defines aggregate supply and demand as the sum of orders per unit of time and
- he assumes the cumulative order flows $a(t)$, $b(t)$ to be sole functions of $\lambda_{a,b}(t)$ such that the currency positions are random, time series variables only.

But the weaknesses of the model are at the same time its strengths.

- Isolating the asynchronous nature of the customer order flow and
- ignoring Bank A and the non-bank customers in the sense that they are not active economic agents,

the analysis can focus on the dynamics of Bank A's currency position. And this is exactly what motivates liquidity trading on the interbank FX market (section 4.1.4). Furthermore, even if the view is maintained that Garman's (1976) analysis is too stylized, later inventory control models are even less appropriate in the present context. The research that was initiated by Stoll (1978) and, most prominently, continued by Cohen, et al. (1981), Ho and Stoll (1981), and O'Hara and Oldfield (1986) exclusively abstracts from market structure issues. Compared to Garman (1976), therefore, the starting point of each of the models is too specific for the present focus.

4.1.2 Interest Payments

Instead of vanishing from the economic scene due to the gambler's ruin problem, dealing continues to be one of the oldest business activities of all. Hence, dealers must have found ways to take the edge off the ruin problem. One of these inventions is interbank lending. In the model of section 4.1.1, Bank A is not permitted to borrow. If it were, however, one could argue that access to loan facilities would prevent it from being led to the slaughter like a lamb. Bank A would regain control over the development of its currency positions by adjusting them through lending and borrowing on the international credit markets.

Unfortunately, however, if interbank credit markets existed for the adjustment of currency positions only, then they would collapse. The probability of running out of either currency is still equal to one, which induces banks not to lend to each other. According to equation (IV.67) above, Bank A runs out of US dollars for $t \rightarrow \infty$ if the demand for USD per period t is not strictly smaller than the corresponding supply. Allowing for loans would therefore postpone Bank A having to put off customer trading to a later period. But it could *not* prevent it from happening. When it comes to paying off the borrowed amount, Bank A may well be lacking the necessary funds. Since this is common knowledge, however, Bank A's request for a USD loan is always interpreted as a signal that the bank will run out of this particular currency in the long run with certainty. It will thus default on the loan with certainty, which is why it is not granted to it in the first place.

Admittedly, market failure very much relies on the rigorous modelling assumptions above.

- If there existed a situation where the probability of running out of inventory is less than one for *both* currencies, interbank lending would reduce exactly this probability. Banks would, therefore, start lending to each other.
- Banks would also lend to each other if the imbalance in the customer order flows was temporary and, thus, off-setting in the long run rather than permanent. In other words, banks would lend to each other if the arrival rate functions $\lambda_{a,b}(t)$ were non-stationary.

Leaving the first case to Chapter V, section 1, the relevant costs related to preventing the gambler's ruin in the second case can be interpreted as the interest payments on interbank loans. Let them be USD-denominated loans. Since being short in US dollars is always equivalent to being long in Euros, furthermore, these costs are partly offset by interest earnings on interbank lending denominated in EUR. They are, however, most likely non-zero.

4.1.3 Zero Costs of Foreign Exchange Trading

Due to the nature of foreign exchange, a shortage of Euros compared to Bank A's desired position results in an excess supply of US dollars and vice versa. This interdependence between USD_t and EUR_t immediately suggests a second solution to the gambler's ruin problem, apart from interbank lending. In fact, it suggests the efficient solution to the gambler's ruin problem. Banks rationally engage in interbank foreign exchange dealing for two reasons.

- Ceteris paribus, Bank A regains control over its currency positions for zero costs in terms of interest payments.
- Ceteris paribus, Bank A also regains control over its currency positions for zero costs in terms of forgone commissions.

The driving force behind the first argument is straightforward. Exploiting the interdependence of foreign exchange positions, Bank A can exchange an excess supply of US dollars for the corresponding shortage in Euros. It can do so in a *single* transactions, the foreign exchange transaction, and on a *single* market, the interbank foreign exchange market. Bank A does not have to borrow US dollars on one market and lend Euros on the other, most likely, for different interest rates.

The second efficiency argument results from the fact that foreign exchange trading turns the stochastic and exogenous nature of the cumulative order flow into a deterministic and endogenous one. The automatism that underlies the ruin scenario is effectively broken because interbank foreign exchange trading manipulates the cumulative order flow rather than the currency positions themselves, as it is the case for interbank lending.

A final argument in favour of interbank foreign exchange trading can be brought forward as follows. Credit relationships are subject to non-zero default risk, which trade relationships are not subject to by definition[74]. Empirical evidence also supports the view of zero costs of foreign exchange trading relative to interbank lending. Empirically, FX dealing banks do not lend from the interbank credit markets for closing open positions or acquiring necessary funds. On the contrary, FX positions are created, held open, and closed by specific combinations of spot and swap transaction, on the FX market only (Fischer-Erlach 1995, pp. 44-49).

'A ... trader in need of cash wants to sell ... to avoid the need to borrow money' (Stoll 1992, p. 77).

4.1.4 Order Processing Costs

Having established the trade solution to the inventory control problem, the more important question is how to design the interbank foreign exchange market efficiently. Given continuous trading on the customer market and also given that the gambler's ruin problem is not information-induced, the relevant measure is again search costs. Obviously, the problem for Bank A is to find a counterparty that is long in exactly the same currency where it is short itself and vice versa.

Search costs become the costs of delay of finding potential trading partners on the interbank market. In contrast to section 3, however, delay, in the present case, is not costly for the risk of adverse price movements. The exchange rate is exogenous by assumption. But it is costly for having to turn down customer deals when running out of foreign exchange holdings. Since a bank runs out of foreign exchange holdings if the trading frequency on the customer market differs substantially from the one on the interbank market, the costs of delay are therefore a function of the trading frequency. The higher it is on the interbank market and the higher it is on the interbank market

[74] What is referred to as default risk is equivalent to credit risk in nature. But it is different to the foreign exchange-specific credit risk that has already been discussed above. FX-specific credit risk is due to the asynchronous settlement of payment and delivery leg. It is thus a credit risk that is related to a trade relationship. But it is *not* a credit risk that is related to a standard credit relationship.

relative to the customer market, the lower the likelihood of running out of foreign exchange due to customer trading.

Furthermore, since foreign exchange deals are not subject to market risk, the problem is therefore not to find

- a trading partner at time 1 *and*
- a trading partner who carries the market risk from time 1 to time 2.

The problem is simply to find a trading partner at time 1 for being able to stay in customer business at time 2 and thereafter. In other words, the costs of delay are not determined by the choice between market making and order matching as was the case in section 3. On the contrary, they are exclusively determined by the choice between continuous trading and periodic trading.

Continuing with the costs of delay, however, they still find their expression in the liquidity costs of 'selling quickly' (Stoll 1992, p. 77) or 'the discount for the immediate opportunity to trade' (Stützel 1975, p. 2518). This is similar to the previous section. But anticipating that the costs of delay are determined by the trading frequency, the corresponding liquidity cost category shall not be referred to as the discount for immediacy. In analogy to Stoll (1992), let it rather be given as the 'order processing costs' (Stoll 1992, p. 79). Bank A's objective is, therefore, to minimize order processing costs subject to the costs of delay being equal to zero.

Turning to the order processing costs in greater detail, they find their most prominent specification in the concept of liquidity. The highest liquidity is always associated with the lowest order processing costs and vice versa. This is the case even though two different concepts of liquidity can be distinguished.

- Following Stützel (1975), the first one refers to the *asset* (definition IV.5).
- With respect to Harris (1991), the second one makes reference to the asset *market* (definition IV.6).

DEFINITION IV.5 (ASSET-RELATED LIQUIDITY): 'Ein Vermögensgegenstand, den man im eigenen Bestand hält, ist um so liquider, ... je besser seine „Abtretbarkeit" ist
(= je geringer das „Disagio wegen vorzeitiger Veräußerung" ist
= je geringer die Differenz zwischen dem Betrag, den man als Gegenwartswert des planmäßigen Veräußerungs- oder Rückzahlungserlöses in Rechnung stellt, und dem Sicherheitsäquivalent des Betrages, den man im Notfalle der vorzeitigen Veräußerung vermutlich erhalten wird)' (Stützel 1975, p. 2518).

DEFINITION IV.6 (MARKET-RELATED LIQUIDITY): 'a market is liquid if traders can quickly buy and sell large numbers of shares when they want and at low transaction costs.

Liquidity is the willingness of some traders (often but not necessarily dealers) to take the opposite side of a trade that is initiated by someone else, at low cost' (Harris 1991, p. 3).

Making recourse to either or both concepts of liquidity, finally, allows for applying the indicators that have been suggested for measuring liquidity to the comparison of the foreign exchange market practice with the relevant alternative in terms of order processing costs, namely, Sotheby's (Chapter III, appendix). More precisely, continuous trading as opposed to periodic trading can be investigated with respect to their effects on

- the price elasticity of demand or the relative marginal price effect per additional unit of foreign exchange supplied (the lower the price elasticity, the higher are the order processing costs and vice versa) (Stützel 1975, p. 2516),
- the width of the market or the order processing costs for a given order size (the wider the market, the lower are the order processing costs and vice versa) (Harris 1991, p. 3), and
- the depth of the market or the maximum order size that can be processed at given order processing costs (the deeper the market, the lower are the order processing costs and vice versa) (Harris 1991, p. 3).

4.2 Comparative Analysis

4.2.1 Sotheby's

Empirically, the width and depth of a market are measured in terms of

- the probability of no trade or the 'execution risk' (the higher the execution risk, the higher are the order processing costs) (Pagano and Roell 1990, p. 85) and
- the standard deviation of the execution price (the higher the price volatility, the higher are the expected order processing costs for a given order size and/or the lower is the order size for given expected order processing costs (Telser 1978, chapters 5 and 8; Telser 1981, p. 4, a/o).

Furthermore, it is Mendelson (1982) who formalizes the advantages of a low trading frequency over a high one in terms of execution risk and standard deviation of the execution price. In other words, it is Mendelson (1982) who can be referred to for a rigorous argument in favour of periodic trading compared to continuous trading. Using the same approach as Garman (1976), namely, treating demand and supply as independent statistical processes, Mendelson (1982) demonstrates that 'for a higher number of transactions, the behavior of the market is fairly 'smooth' and 'orderly', whereas for a significantly lower number of transactions there is a considerable loss of 'liquidity'' (Mendelson 1982, p. 1522).

Turning to his model in some detail, let

(IV.68) $$\lambda_{a,b}(t) = \lambda_{a,b}$$

be the *interbank* order arrival rates at each time t. Furthermore, let T represent the time period in between two market clearings such that

(IV.69) $$T = k \cdot t, \qquad \text{for } k = 1,2,\ldots$$ [75].

In this case,

(IV.70) $$\Gamma_{a,b} = \lambda_{a,b} T$$

is the expected number of buy and sell orders per market clearing or the order intensity of a market (Mendelson 1982, pp. 1510-11). More importantly,

- the execution risk is a decreasing function of $\Gamma_{a,b}$. The more orders are expected per clearing, the lower the probability that a particular order cannot be executed, given that orders are matched. Furthermore,
- the standard deviation of the execution price is also a decreasing function of $\Gamma_{a,b}$. The more orders expected per clearing, the higher is the trading volume, the smaller each individual order compared to the aggregate order flow. Hence, the execution price becomes less volatile (Mendelson 1982, pp. 1512-14).

Clearly, both effects are liquidity increasing in terms of width and depth. A high value of T ensures low order processing costs for a given order size and/or a high value of T allows for processing larger orders at given costs. Periodic trading is thus more efficient than continuous trading. The intuition of the law of large numbers is, furthermore, obvious.

'The market is ... liquid because the liquidity demands of buyers and sellers satisfy each other' (Harris 1991, p. 28).

---

[75] Note that $\lambda_{a,b}(t)$ referred to the *customer* order arrival rates in the previous section. The concept of time is also a different one in the present section compared to previous as well as the following ones.

In terms of Badgehot's (1971) famous remarks, the law of large numbers finds its expression in that

'the market price ... is not merely a consensus of the transactors in the market place, it is also a consensus of their mistakes ... Unless these errors are in some sense systematic across the population of investors - or, to put it the other way around, to the extent that the commission of these errors is more or less statistically independent one investor from another - market price is virtually unaffected by these errors. This is a consequence of the law of large numbers [author's notation]: because the number of individual transactors is large and because their mistakes of judgement and estimation are likely to be independent one transactor from another, the net effect of their mistakes on the equilibrium price is likely to be miniscule' (Badgehot 1971, p. 3).

Table IV.18 below, finally, summarizes the relation between trading frequency and order processing costs as it is suggested by Mendelson (1982)[76].

TABLE IV.18: Order Processing Costs at Sotheby's and on the FX Market

	Order Processing Costs
Sotheby's/ Periodic Trading	maximum liquidity in terms of width and depth/ minimum order processing costs
FX Market/ Continuous Trading	minimum liquidity in terms of width and depth/ maximum order processing costs

4.2.2 Foreign Exchange Market

'The conclusion is quickly reached that active markets are continuous ... Other things equal, investors prefer to trade immediately. As a result, most major markets are continuous markets rather than call markets' (Stoll 1992, pp. 75-76).

Stoll (1992), therefore, argues that increasing the trading frequency does not necessarily reduce the positive effects of the law of large numbers. Following Mendelson (1982), this is indeed the case as soon as frequent market clearing, in other words, a low level of T, is offset by a high value of $\lambda_{a,b}$, in other words, a large size of the market. This is due to equation (IV.70) above. The previous two sections furthermore demonstrate why the foreign exchange market may actually be exceptionally large compared to other

76 Apart from Mendelson (1982) and Harris (1991), Cohen and Schwartz (1989), Wagner (1989), Wunsch (1989), and Pagano and Roell (1990) also bring forward decreasing price volatility due to increasing order intensity when they argue in favour of periodic trading.

markets such that continuous trading may actually not be more costly than periodic trading in terms of order processing costs. Information trading and the game of hot potato result in substantial trading volume such that FX dealing banks may be prepared to engage in continuous trading.

Leaving the narrow framework of Mendelson (1982), however, the following arguments may be brought forward in favour of continuous trading for the efficient reallocation of inventory.

- There is a trade-off between minimizing the liquidity costs in the sense of section 3 (the discount for immediacy) and minimizing the liquidity costs in terms of the present section (the order processing costs).
- The execution risk is zero when turning from an order matching system to market making and membership in the sense of reciprocal trading. Mendelson's (1982) results, therefore, apply to order matching systems only.
- There is a trade-off between minimizing the costs of delay and minimizing the liquidity costs in the form of order processing costs when choosing the optimal trading frequency. The higher is the trading frequency on the customer market compared to the interbank market, the more serious the gambler's ruin problem at each time t and hence, the more expensive is delay. But Mendelson (1982) only focuses on order processing costs.

For the significance of the first two arguments, the final argument suggests that the optimal solution to reallocating inventory is given as approximately identical trading frequencies on the customer and the interbank market.

(IV.71) $$T_{customer} \approx T_{interbank}.$$

If Mendelson's (1982) view is *not* the correct view, therefore, FX dealing banks are in favour of continuous trading. If it is, they are, however, not. Hence, the issue of how to reallocate inventory efficiently cannot unambiguously be resolved on theoretical grounds.

The empirical results that are reported in Amihud and Mendelson (1987, 1991), Stoll and Whaley (1990), and Lauterbach and Meyer (1997), however, suggest that Mendelson's (1982) propositions are *not* correct. They support the view that price volatility is actually lower for continuous trading. Lauterbach and Meyer (1997), in particular, demonstrate that in switching from periodic trading to a continuous market structure, the price volatility at the Tel Aviv Stock Exchange decreased significantly (Lauterbach and Meyer 1997, pp. 39, 42-46).

Following Lauterbach and Meyer (1997), therefore, the issue of how to reallocate inventory efficiently is resolved in favour of continuous trading (proposition 4). This outcome would finally be in line with the results of the previous sections, sections 1-3 above. It would thus support the (surprising?) efficiency of the search and information system of the foreign exchange market (Chapter VII).

PROPOSITION 4: Continuous trading reduces the costs of delay. For

(IV.72) $$\Gamma_{continuous} \geq \Gamma_{periodic},$$

therefore, banks always prefer continuous trading to periodic trading. But for

(IV.73) $$\Gamma_{periodic} < \Gamma_{continuous},$$

there is a trade-off between minimizing the costs of delay, on the one hand, while minimizing the order processing costs in terms of a wider and deeper market on the other. Whether equation (IV.72) holds or whether it is equation (IV.73) instead is a matter of current debate. On the basis of empirical observations, however, it is expected that the trading frequency on the interbank market should be equal approximately to the trading frequency on the customer market for not running out of foreign exchange.

4.2.3 Foreign Exchange Market Revisited

Stützel's (1975) asset-related definition of liquidity has been ignored until now. Furthermore, the price elasticity of demand does not seem to have anything to do with market structure issues. Nevertheless, let equation (IV.74) below repeat the standard definition of the price elasticity of demand for discrete variables. X denotes the quantity held of an arbitrary object. X, thus, denotes the initial endowment or inventory position. P expresses the corresponding purchase price.

(IV.74) $$\varepsilon(X) = \frac{P}{X}\frac{\Delta X}{\Delta P}.$$

In this case, the price elasticity of demand for US dollars at each time t is given as

(IV.75) $$\varepsilon(USD) = \frac{e}{USD}\frac{\Delta USD}{\Delta e}.$$

Furthermore, let Bank A have the desire to sell US dollars immediately. Finally, note that

$$\text{(IV.76)} \qquad \frac{\Delta e(\Delta USD)}{\Delta USD} < \frac{\Delta e(\Delta USD+1)}{\Delta USD+1}, \qquad \text{for all } \Delta USD,$$

if the buyers of US dollars are risk averse such that

$$\text{(IV.77)} \qquad \frac{\Delta USD}{\Delta e(\Delta USD)} > \frac{\Delta USD+1}{\Delta e(\Delta USD+1)}.$$

If, therefore, Δe is interpreted as the discount that Bank A has to pay for the immediate sale of ΔUSD units of USD, the discount for large dealing amounts is greater than the one for small ones according to equation (IV.76) above. The buyers value each additional unit of USD that they purchase less than the one before. A relatively small dealing amount, therefore, guarantees foreign exchange to be a marketable, liquid asset in the sense of Stützel (1975). According to equation (IV.77), it ensures a greater price elasticity of demand. For small dealing amounts, the buyers react 'more quickly' to a small change in price.

Most importantly, the described interpretation of the price elasticity of demand implies that the size of the dealing amounts affects search costs. For given costs of delay, the liquidity costs can be reduced if the dealing amounts are small relative to the trading volume. Hence, the described interpretation of the price elasticity of demand provides an argument for introducing standard dealing amounts as in the case of the FX market.

But the above interpretation also provides an argument in favour of continuous trading. If dealing amounts are restricted to a level where they are small enough to ensure a high enough order arrival rate $\lambda_{a,b}$ such that $\Gamma_{a,b}$ is constant, even for a high trading frequency, FX dealing banks are indifferent between continuous trading and periodic trading. More generally, introducing dealing limits always increases the marketability of the traded object and, thus, supports continuous trading. As it is common practice on the interbank FX market, finally, large customer orders must then be split apart, increasing the expected order arrival rate further. Hence, standard dealing amounts are even self-reinforcing[77].

[77] Note that the search costs are also affected by the *level* of inventory. Hence, the more efficient the trade solution to the reallocation of inventory is, the lower the inventory can be and the more elastic the demand which increases liquidity. In this sense, efficient market design is also self-reinforcing.

Appendix: Search and Information Acquisition on the London Stock Exchange

Instead of leaving behind the issue of sealed versus open trading, sections 2.2.1-2.2.3 above may point to two possible answers to the interesting question why *stock* traders sometimes implement a dealing system combined with open trading, as the case on the London Stock Exchange.

A major difference of the stock market compared to the foreign exchange market is that, on the stock market, not every market participant is an informational monopolist in the above sense.

- Monopoly power is not evenly distributed. In fact, it is not even randomly distributed. On the contrary, most market participants are systematically excluded from private information on future stock prices due to the nature of this information. They are not insiders because they are not 'close enough' to the listed corporation (this may actually be the reason why private information on stocks is generally referred to as insider information, which is rarely the case for private information on foreign exchange).
- The private information on future stock prices does not differ from stock trader to stock trader as much as it does for the private information on future exchange rates. On the contrary, on the stock market, each insider has, strictly speaking, the same private information (let it be information on an envisaged merger, a major loss, or an excellent business year, a/o).
- There is a consensus view on how the stock price is determined. In other words, it is generally agreed upon that the stock price is the discounted value of all future dividends. Hence, there are no differences in opinion as such.

For all three reasons combined, the conflict of interest between the informed and the uninformed cannot be resolved by allowing for information trading. On the contrary, any 'market for information' would most likely fail due to adverse selection of the Akerlof (1970)-type. An agreement always points to a loss because, on the stock market, the uninformed market participants are 'truly' uninformed in the sense of the standard microstructure literature[78].

For the adverse selection problem related to information trading, therefore, the collapse of the secondary market for stocks can only be prevented by following the strategy of information aggregation rather than information trading, provided that private

[78] For an excellent overview, see again O'Hara (1995, chapters 4 and 5).

information matters at all. Open trading is, thus, the only arrangement that can be mutually agreed upon. In other words, one reason for implementing open trading, although the market is a dealing system, could be the different nature of information imperfections when it comes to stocks. This interpretation would also explain why the market maker function is restricted to a few market participants only. The more market makers there are, the less effectively could information be aggregated.

The second line of arguments in favour of dealing combined with open trading for trading stocks relates to the unique nature of stocks compared to foreign exchange. Stocks are common-value objects. But they are not money. Hence, they cannot be exchanged for a domestic currency as easily as can be a foreign currency. But this implies that market makers may actually not be willing to implement reciprocal trading for trading stocks. They may prefer *not* to stand ready for a deal at any time since it would be too risky. In other words, trading stocks in a dealing system may require dealing to be restricted to a small number of market makers who then receive a sufficient number of buy and sell orders in order to be prepared to stand ready for a deal at any time. In a sense, they would be compensated for standing ready for a deal at any time by having a certain degree of market power[79].

Restricting the number of market makers due to the nature of stocks however does not yet explain why trading should be open. But referring to Perraudin and Vitale (1996) above, the efficiency of dealing combined with sealed trading is a function of the number of dealers. As it has already been discussed above, more precisely, the efficiency decreases with the number of market makers.

'If dealers are able to transact with all other market makers in the interval between customer trades, ... a decentralized market is fully efficient. ... [If this is not the case], however, total expected dealer profits are higher in a centralized market than a decentralized market' (Perraudin and Vitale 1996, p. 84).

Consequently, stock traders may prefer open trading to sealed trading, for a given, small number of market makers. The market makers themselves would again be compensated for the costs that are related to open trading in the form of foregone returns on information by positive returns to market power.

After a close look at the actual rules and regulations of the London Stock Exchange (Chapter III, sections 2.2.1 and 2.2.2), it seems that the number of market makers is a

79 The argument is closely related to the ones that are presented in section 4 below on liquidity trading. Essentially, it is suggested that stocks are not as liquid, in the sense of marketable, as foreign exchange is.

decreasing function of the degree of transparency of a market structure. In other words, the degree of centralization seems to be an increasing function of the degree of transparency. There is more than one market maker at LSE but less than there are on the FX market. At the same time, it is the midspread price and not the bid-ask spread that is actually published at LSE. The LSE rules, therefore, preserve the privacy of the bid-ask spread for a small number of market makers, where the FX market preserves the privacy of the execution price for a large number of market makers, where other markets do not preserve any private information and, thus, switch to a monopolistic broker and no market maker.

CHAPTER V

The Optimal Pricing System

> 'In an undeveloped community, where opportunities for the profitable employment of time are strictly limited, it may be worth while for a seller (of labour or of goods) to spend some time 'higgling and bargaining' to get as good a price as he can. ... But as economic activity increases, haggling over small sums becomes a more and more uneconomic way of spending time' (Hicks 1932, p. 64).

At first sight, modern bargaining theory suggests otherwise. Delay, which is always inefficient ex post, may be rational when taking the ex ante view of the bargaining partners. For example, enduring a strike may be the only way for a firm to convince its employees that it is unable to pay higher wages. In doing so, the firm credibly signals that the costs related to lost production are smaller than the ruinous costs induced by a wage increase (Kennan and Wilson 1993, p. 45-46).

'The substance of this hypothesis is that bargaining is substantially a process of communication necessitated by initial differences in information known to the parties separately. Thus, delay may be required to convey private information credibly. ... The costly process of bargaining can be an efficient way of establishing a common informational basis for an agreement' (Kennan and Wilson 1993, p. 46).

According to this view, the bargaining game or pricing system of any market organization is determined by

- the nature and the degree of information asymmetries, if there are any, and
- the need for conveying private information credibly provided that the communication of private signals increases efficiency[80].

[80] It is at least since Akerlof (1970), that the *credible* communication of private information requires separate attention.

Consequently, Hicks (1932) above may well be right when classifying delay as costly. But, at the same time, asymmetric information may be the source of more serious inefficiencies (Kennan and Wilson 1993, pp. 46-47).

Assessing bargaining games in the light of private information points to a possible explanation of the large variety of pricing systems that can be observed empirically (Chapter III, section 3). More importantly, it points to the line of arguments that establishes the optimal pricing system of the foreign exchange market, given the initial condition of imperfect information. Sections 1 and 2 below explain the superiority of the first-price sealed-bid auction over all other bargaining arrangements and auction games on these grounds. The first-price sealed-bid auction is the optimal pricing system for liquidity trading (section 1) *and* information trading (section 2) because the trading partners are imperfectly informed in both cases.

- For liquidity trading, the information on each bank's reservation price is private, which challenges the bargaining partners.
- For information trading, the problem is essentially the same. In this case, however, the pricing system must also ensure incentive compatible outcomes. Given that the execution price communicates monopolistic information on future exchange rate movements, the inference that the buyer of information makes from each deal must point to the information that the seller actually has. In other words, it must ensure truthful reporting on behalf of the informational monopolist. It must not be misleading in order to make information trading worthwhile.

Hedging, furthermore, does not require separate attention with respect to the pricing system. The characteristics of the bargaining game are essentially the same as the ones when the banks are liquidity traders. Hence, section 3 does not turn to hedging, as it may seem. On the contrary, the final paragraphs of Chapter V reconsider liquidity trading. But they leave behind bargaining and auction theory. Returning to Garman (1976), more precisely, section 3 establishes the efficiency of the bid-ask spread. It does so by lifting the assumption of exogenous exchange rates[81].

Concluding these preliminary remarks, a market maker system was, finally, demonstrated above to be the search and information cost minimizing market structure for hedging, liquidity trading, and information trading. Hence, on the interbank FX market, a periodic 'desire to trade' (Stoll 1992, p. 79) faces a continuous opportunity to trade. Ceteris paribus, therefore, it can reasonably be assumed that it is always search cost minimizing when the desire to trade is signalled by

[81] For details on the effects of risk aversion on bidding behaviour, see Holt (1980), Riley and Samuelson (1981), and Matthews (1987). See also McAfee and McMillan (1987, pp. 718-20) for a summary.

- the banks that want to sell monopolistic information,
- the banks that demand insurance services, and/or
- the banks that demand liquidity services.

In other words, it is assumed throughout the following that the 'information supplier', the insuree, or the 'liquidity demander' is the *asking* bank and *not* the quoting bank.

A second argument in favour of this assumption is based on the observation that avoiding arbitrage generally leads to quotes that do not contain any information for normal market conditions. If they did, they would necessarily deviate from all other quotes in the market. Avoiding arbitrage, therefore, equalizes the market makers' quotes such that any asking bank cannot extract any information from a deal with the quoting bank which however does not hold vice versa. Furthermore, the asking bank could always and costlessly step back from trading if the quote did contain information. But this would obviously give rise to free-riding[82].

1. Position Risk Exposure and the Efficiency of Competition and the First-Price Sealed-Bid Auction

Imagine Bank A to attach a value of EUR 1.2025 to one US dollar. An arbitrary Bank B's reservation price shall furthermore be given as 1.2045. Also assume that each bank's valuation is private information. Finally, remember that foreign exchange is a common-value object which implies that the revelation of reservation prices always provides useful information to any other bank with access to this information.

When negotiating the execution price, Bank A and Bank B face a complicated coordination problem in the above setting. It is not only that there are 19 possible solutions to any bargaining game (1.2026, 1.2027, ..., 1.2044). But imperfect information also allows for a twentieth alternative which is given as 'failure to agree'. Prior to actually concluding a contract, Bank A and Bank B do not know with certainty whether a deal with the respective trading partner can be profitable in the first place. Furthermore, Bank B does not know whether Bank A refuses a sales offer because its reservation price is lower than Bank B's quote or whether Bank A refuses a sales offer because it tries to extract a greater profit from trade. The same holds for buy offers, provided that a second round of bargaining is permitted[83].

---

82 For more details on arbitrage trading, see Fischer-Erlach (1995, pp. 40-44).

83 Standard dealing amounts are assumed throughout the following. Hence, it is only the exchange rate and the order type that is actually negotiated.

Many more of this kind of problem can be seen as depending on the structure of the bargaining game. Section 1, therefore, starts with a more systematic description of the bargaining problem, at the same time providing a definition of bargaining costs (section 1.1). Similar to the previous chapter, however, starting the analysis with a close-to-reality set of assumptions makes the search for the transaction cost minimizing pricing system an almost intractable assignment. The comparative analysis of section 1.2, therefore, initiates the discussion by assuming foreign exchange to be an independent-private-values object. Most generally, this implies that conveying reservation prices is of no significance for the trading partners. Their posterior beliefs are still identical to their prior ones. For this simplification, section 1.2 then demonstrates that auctions outperform any bargaining arrangement (section 1.2.1). More precisely, the first-price sealed-bid auction is demonstrated to be equivalent to any other auction mechanism but better than any bargaining arrangement (section 1.2.2). This result is most important because the simplifying, independent-private-values assumption correctly specifies the nature of foreign exchange when it is traded for liquidity reasons.

1.1 Bargaining Costs

Imagine the asking Bank A to evaluate one USD in terms of EUR such that $v_T^A = 1.2025$ as above. Furthermore, let the market making Bank B again attach the value of EUR 1.2045 to one USD. At any time t, therefore, Bank A is willing to sell USD to Bank B if the exchange rate e_t is greater than 1.2025. The reverse holds for Bank B. Assuming that price changes are discrete and restricted to ± 5 basic points, Bank A would, thus, sell USD to Bank B at time t if and only if

(V.1) $$e_t = 1.2030, 1.2035, 1.2040\,.$$

The related pay-offs to both banks are given in table V.1 below. Let them be zero if Bank A and Bank B do not agree on a single price for whatever reason.

TABLE V.1: A Standard Bargaining Problem

Bank A \ Bank B	**30**	**35**	**40**
30	5 , 15	0 , 0	0 , 0
35	0 , 0	10 , 10	0 , 0
40	0 , 0	0 , 0	15 , 5

Hence, the question for Bank A and Bank B is how to split the pie of 20 basic points between each other given that there are three Nash equilibria in pure strategies of which the two banks have to select one as soon as they have recognized each other as potential trading partners. In other words, Bank A's and Bank B's problem is one of pure coordination[84]. The most prominent solution to this class of games was suggested by Schelling (1960). The parties should agree on what he calls a 'focal point' (Schelling 1960, pp. 54-58). It would be an even split in the present case or the solution 1.2035.

Whereas the standard bargaining problem describes the basic notion of how to split a pie, however, Bank A and Bank B face a much more complex environment on the FX market.

- Foreign exchange is a common-value object.
- The interdependent reservation prices $v_{A,B}$ are private information to each bank.
- Trading may have two different motives for risk neutral banks, that is, three different motives for risk averse banks.
- The trading motive is private information to the asking Bank A, which is the first mover.
- The order type is unknown when initiating price negotiations.
- There is a finite number of banks $N-M$ similar to Bank B. Hence, there is a finite number of banks $N-M$ that stand ready for a deal.
- There is a finite number of banks M similar to Bank A. Hence, there is a finite number of banks M that request a deal.

In other words, information is extremely incomplete and asymmetrically distributed on the FX market prior to starting price negotiations (for the sake of simplicity, however, the banks shall be assumed to be risk neutral and M as well as N shall be assumed to be common knowledge).

The bargaining costs can finally be defined as any form of inefficiency that results from the described imperfections in the distribution of information. More precisely, let them be given as

- any foregone trading profits due to a failure to agree although there would be a profitable trading opportunity,
- any foregone trading profits due to a failure to realize the maximum trading profits, in other words, any foregone trading profits due to not selling to the potential trading partner with the highest reservation price or buying from the potential trading partner with the lowest reservation price, and
- any (remaining) costs of delay (Kennan and Wilson 1993, pp. 45-46).

---

[84] A game of pure coordination is a normal form game with more than two Nash equilibria in pure strategies that cannot be Pareto ranked (Rasmusen 1994, pp. 26-28).

The costs of delay in the sense of bargaining costs, more precisely, differ from the costs of delay as search costs, although they result from market risk and/or the depreciation of private information, as well. Bargaining costs realize when the set of potential trading partners is already known. In other words, the costs of delay as bargaining costs depend on the number of rounds that are needed for selecting the counterparty to a transaction from the set of potential trading partners. The costs of delay as search costs, on the contrary, depend on the number of rounds that are needed to *identify* a set of potential trading partners. Pricing follows search. Furthermore, the likelihood of the failure to agree on a profitable deal differs from the probability of not finding a trading partner in the same respect. Finally, there is, of course, no failure to realize maximum trading profits with respect to *one and the same* potential trading partner. Table V.1 above shows that the trading profit is constant and equal to 20 basic points for all solutions. But there is a positive likelihood of not trading with the 'optimal' counterparty for *many* potential trading partners (Kennan and Wilson, pp. 45-46).

1.2 Comparative Analysis

1.2.1 Bargaining Arrangements

Why is the auction a frequently chosen bargaining process?

'One answer is, perhaps, that some products have no standard value. For example, the price of any catch of fish (at least of fish destined for the fresh fish market) depends on the demand and supply conditions at a specific moment of time, influenced possibly by prospective market developments. For manuscripts and antiques, too, prices must be remade for each transaction. For example, how can one discover the worth of an original copy of Lincoln's Gettysburg Address except by auction method?' (Cassady 1967, p. 20).

This intuition in favour of auctions for pricing independent-private-values objects (definition V.1) can be confirmed as follows. Most conveniently, the presented arguments simultaneously establish the optimality of auctions for liquidity trading.

DEFINITION V.1 (INDEPENDENT-PRIVATE-VALUES OBJECT): for independent-private-values objects, any' differences among the bidders' evaluations reflect actual differences in their tastes [only]. ... Any one bidder's valuation is statistically independent from any other bidder's valuation' (McAfee and McMillan 1987, p. 705).

Imagine a single, risk neutral seller of one USD, Bank A, meeting a finite number of risk neutral, potential buyers, banks $N-M$, at time $t<T$. Furthermore, let it be common

knowledge that Bank A, the first mover, is a liquidity trader with a reservation price v^A. It shall also be known that banks $N-M$ do not have private information on e_T. Moreover, their reservation prices per unit of USD shall be given as $v^{N-M} > v^A$. But whereas v^A is commonly known, let v^{N-M} be private information to banks $N-M$ (Kennan and Wilson, pp. 67-69).

Before turning to the optimal pricing system for this particular bargaining problem, however, note the difference to the foreign exchange market. This is important because the outcome of bargaining games is very sensitive to the set of underlying assumptions.

- Most generally, Bank A is in a weak position compared to the market makers when it enters trade for rebalancing its USD position. But the described bargaining game is, nevertheless, a reasonable starting point. It would reflect the reality on the foreign exchange market as soon as the market makers knew Bank A to be a liquidity trader, which underlies the approach of separating section 1 (liquidity trading) from section 2 (information trading) anyway. Furthermore, the assumption that v^A is common knowledge turns out below to be of limited significance for the general outcome.
- Foreign exchange is an independent-private-values object. The most important consequence of the independent-private-values assumption is that v^{N-M} can simply be assumed to differ from v^A, at the same time, not having to explain *why* this is the case. This is crucial because, on the one hand, it is only a non-zero difference between v^{N-M} and v^A that motivates trade. On the other hand, this difference is zero for risk neutral banks, for perfect information on future exchange rates, and for the common-value assumption unless search costs in the sense of Chapter IV, section 4 are introduced into the model. But incorporating search costs complicates the analysis for no immediate reason. Hence, the independent-private-values assumption is a simplifying assumption if trading is liquidity trading and liquidity trading only.
- *M* is equal to one. The bargaining game that is optimal for the liquidity trader Bank A is optimal for all other liquidity traders at the same time, assuming that there is no conflict of interest among liquidity traders. The other liquidity traders can and will thus be ignored for simplicity.
- The order type is common knowledge. This assumption, finally, ignores market making in the sense of participating in a double auction (bidding for a sale *and* a purchase). But whether Bank A is a seller or a buyer is of no significance for the following given that, 'from a theoretical point of view, monopsony is essentially the same as monopoly apart from reversal of the signs of some variables' (McAfee and McMillan 1987, p. 701).

Turning from the set-up of the bargaining game that reasonably anticipates liquidity trading to the outcome, 'any outcome between all of the gains from trade going to the buyer and all of the gains going to the seller was seen as possible [in classical economics]' (McAfee and McMillan 1987, p. 703),

if information is complete. Modern bargaining theory, however, revises this view by showing that strategic behaviour always implies a last-mover-advantage. All trading profits always go to either the buyer or the seller depending on who makes the final offer. For non-zero costs of delay, therefore, it is always optimal for whoever has the bargaining power to make a take-it-or-leave-it offer and capture all profits from trade. Furthermore, it is always optimal for the other party to agree to this procedure (Rasmusen 1994, pp. 279-81, a/o). Finally, however, none of the described solutions is valid for the above game with private information, neither the 'classical' one nor the 'strategic' one.

A DUOPOLISTIC, ONE-SHOT BARGAINING GAME: The reservation prices v^{N-M} are private information as opposed to v^A which is commonly known. Furthermore, it is a standard result in bargaining theory that Bank $B \in N - M$ always misrepresents its valuation in a one-shot bargaining game if $N = A, B$ only. More precisely, Bank B always offers v^A if it makes the one and only price offer. All trading profits go to Bank B in this case (Kennan and Wilson 1993, p. 49).

If, on the contrary, Bank A makes the price offer, the bank always risks a failure to agree although trade could be profitable. In other words, there is a non-zero probability that Bank A suggests a price higher than v^B such that Bank B would reject the offer. Minimizing bargaining costs, therefore, Bank A always offers a price 'close enough' to its own reservation price v^A. This strategy minimizes the likelihood of the failure to agree given that the costs of delay are zero for a one-shot game. So is the likelihood not to realize maximum trading profits for being a duopolistic game. Hence, trading profits always go to Bank B in a duopolistic, one-shot bargaining game (Rasmusen 1994, pp. 284-89).

A DUOPOLISTIC, REPEATED BARGAINING GAME: Theory suggests that there is a trade-off between the costs of delay and the costs of misrepresenting private information in a repeated bargaining game. On the one hand, Bank B repeatedly rejects Bank A's price offers greater than v^A if and only if the costs of delay related to the bargaining game are smaller than the entire trading profits. In other words, Bank B repeatedly rejects Bank A's offer if and only if

(V.2) $$C_D < v^B - v^A .$$

In all other cases, Bank B prefers to accept a less favourable offer than v^A at an early stage in the bargaining process (Kennan and Wilson 1993, p. 49).

On the other hand, the liquidity trader Bank A faces the same if not higher costs of delay compared to Bank B which is generally ignored in standard bargaining theory. Bank A's threat to delay an agreement is thus not credible. Hence, repeated play does not increase the trading profits to Bank A above zero.

A COMPETITIVE, ONE-SHOT BARGAINING GAME: On the FX market, each liquidity trading Bank A faces more than one market making bank. Furthermore, Bank A's bargaining costs are highest for any duopolistic bargaining game. Trading profits are equal to zero in this case. Hence,

PROPOSITION 5: it is optimal for Bank A to grant the right to submit quotes to each of the market makers $N - M$. In other words, it is optimal for Bank A to price the US dollars that are for sale by auction method. Bank A, the auctioneer, invites $N - M$ banks, the bidders, to compete for a standard dealing amount.

Taking into account the above mentioned, the reasons are the following.

- The likelihood of failing to agree although trade would be profitable is equal to zero. This is due to the fact that Bank A can exclusively base its decision on its own reservation price v^A. Given that the market makers' valuations are unknown to Bank A, it can replace the unknown v^{N-M} by the corresponding quotations.
- Bank A can exploit the competition among market making banks. Competition limits the potential for strategic behaviour. More precisely, if Bank B quotes exactly v^A, Bank $C \in N - M$ can offer a price to Bank A that is slightly higher than Bank B's quote, etc. However, since this is anticipated by Bank B, the price is actually driven up to the point where each market maker quotes at least 'close to' its reservation price. The trading profit to Bank A is, thus, no longer equal to zero.
- The likelihood of not realizing maximum trading profits is equal to zero for the same reason as Bank A's trading profits are non-zero. The market makers quote close to their reservation prices such that the one bank with the highest reservation price is most likely going to be Bank A's counterparty for the transaction.
- The costs of delay are equal to zero for a one-shot game.

Summarizing, the optimality of the pricing system for Bank A depends on giving up the right to quote. Moreover, it depends on competition among market making banks, in other words, on a number of market makers greater than one. Competition ensures that each market maker's bid is such that Bank A does not systematically lose due to the imperfect distribution of information, which otherwise would give rise to strategic behaviour on behalf of the market makers. Furthermore, it is obvious that repeated play cannot increase the efficiency of the pricing system. Repeated play only increases the costs of delay else being equal. It is, moreover, auction theory and the theory of optimal mechanism design that confirm proposition 5 above, which came from the assessment of the broader perspective of bargaining theory.

- Holt (1979) and Harris and Raviv (1981) demonstrate that the expected trading profits are zero for the bidders if the object that is for sale is sold by auction method.
- Laffont and Maskin (1980), Myerson (1981), Milgrom (1985), and Engelbrecht-Wiggans (1986), a/o come to the same conclusion.

The present section 1.2.1 shall, finally, be concluded with the following remarks.

- The trading profits to the bidders is zero whether or not v^A is known to them. Hence, the significance of assuming asymmetric information on each other's reservation prices above is clearly limited.
- According to Harris and Raviv (1981), Myerson (1981), and Riley and Samuelson (1981), the profitability of selling by auction method can be increased by Bank A announcing a reserve price, in other words, by announcing a minimum price offer. But this is the case if and only if Bank A is a monopolist. For more than one liquidity trader and/or competitive behaviour as it was assumed above, on the contrary, competition again redirects the outcome towards the original level (McAfee and McMillan 1987, p. 713).
- Avoiding arbitrage trading may explain why market makers actually participate in FX dealing by auction method given that Bank A does not agree on any duopolistic bargaining game. It allows for bids 'close to' but not equal to their own reservation prices. In other words, it allows market makers to profit from trade.
- Membership allows for non-zero trading profits for the market makers since competition is not perfect for the number of market participants being strictly limited above (Harris and Raviv 1981, p. 1492).
- For the final two arguments, the auction method is self-enforcing, which duopolistic bargaining arrangements are not[85].

---

[85] Methodologically, Chapter V stands on its own compared to the analysis of the search and information system in Chapter IV above. The discussion on competition in the present context, for example, differs significantly from the one on competitive behaviour in Chapter IV, section 2 above. Re-evaluating open-bid auctions below is, furthermore, in sharp contrast to having established sealed trading as an integral part of the efficient search and information system, etc. Since, however, Chapter V comes to conclusions that are perfectly compatible with the ones of Chapter IV above, this approach reinforces the efficiency hypothesis with respect to the organization of the foreign exchange market rather than weakening it (the only institution that is, admittedly, carried over from the previous chapter is dealing such that the pricing system is a bargaining game in nature rather than a matching algorithm).

1.2.2 Auctions

According to bargaining theory, the auction is the optimal pricing system for liquidity trading. But auctions can differ in two important respects.

- They may be first-price or second-price auctions. At the same time,
- they may be sealed-bid or open-bid auctions (Chapter III, section 3.2.1).

For symmetric bidders, however, auction theory derives the following, powerful result.

PROPOSITION 6: Any of the four auction mechanisms is the optimal bargaining game for liquidity trading since they all yield the same exchange rate on average.

Proposition 6 is known as the revenue equivalence theorem. Relying on the assumption of symmetric bidders, auction theory conveniently dissolves the information imperfections of the previous section when establishing this theorem. In other words, all banks N are correctly assumed to be identical, by the very nature of auction theory and in contrast to bargaining theory. Throughout the following, therefore, each bank n only knows its own reservation price with certainty (McAfee and McMillan 1987, p. 714).

Starting with the Dutch auction, a first result can be established as follows. The Dutch auction is analytically equivalent to the first-price sealed-bid auction. In other words, the bidders face the same decision problem in each of the two settings.

- They have to choose their quotes without knowing any other market maker's quote.
- The winner always pays as much as his own quote.

On average, therefore, the resulting exchange rate is the same although it is not yet clear what the optimal bid actually is (Vickrey 1961, pp. 20-23; McAfee and McMillan 1987, p. 707).

Based on this first result, the answer to the revenue equivalence of all auctions lies in the fact that the bidders act differently in the remaining three auctions such that, in the end, all auctions yield the same outcome on average (McAfee and McMillan 1987, p. 707).

THE ENGLISH AUCTION: Starting with the English auction, the successful bidder is always the one with the highest reservation price paying a price that is slightly above the second-highest reservation price (McAfee and McMillan 1987, p. 707). But this implies that each bidder optimally submits a bid that is equal to the its reservation price.

- There is no return to bidding higher. On the contrary, the bidder risks to pay a price that is actually above his reservation price if he turns out not to be the bidder with the highest reservation price in the population. The exchange rate may be below his bid but above his actual reservation price. Furthermore, he pays the second-highest reservation price in any case if he is the bidder with the highest reservation price.

- There is no return to bidding lower. On the contrary, the bidder risks losing a profitable trading opportunity to a bidder with a lower reservation price if he bids 'too low'. The bidder with the second-highest reservation price may then actually profit from a deal with Bank A (Vickrey 1961, pp. 20-21).

The average return to the winning bank to following the optimal strategy is finally given as the expected difference between the winning bank's reservation price and the second-highest reservation price. Hence, the expected payment to Bank A is, by definition, the expected value of the winning bidder's reservation price minus the expected value of the same bidder's trading profit. More precisely, it is given as

$$\text{(V.3)} \qquad \tilde{v}_{winner} - E\left(\tilde{v}_{winner} - \tilde{v}_{second-highest}\right)$$

(McAfee and McMillan 1987, pp. 707-708).

THE SECOND-PRICE SEALED-BID AUCTION: Turning to the second-price sealed-bid auction, the optimal strategy for each bidder is again to submit a bid that corresponds to its own reservation price. The average return to the market makers as well as Bank A are thus again determined by expression (V.3) above. For the second-price sealed-bid auction, this is the case because it is a second-price auction.

'The bidder's choice of bid determines only whether or not he wins; the amount he pays if he wins is beyond his control' (McAfee and McMillan 1987, p. 708).

But this is equivalent to the English auction above. There, the execution price is also beyond the control of each bidder. In this sense, therefore, the second-price sealed-bid auction is analytically equivalent to the English auction, thus, yielding the same exchange rate on average, for the same reasons as above. In terms of McAfee and McMillan (1987), both reasons are repeated below.

'Suppose the bidder considers lowering his bid below his valuation. The only case in which this changes the outcome occurs when this lowering of his bid results in his bid now being lower than someone else's and as a result this bidder now does not receive the item. Because he would have earned non-negative rents if he won, lowering his bid below his valuation cannot make him better off. Conversely, suppose he considers raising his bid above his valuation. The only case in which this changes the outcome occurs when some other bidder has submitted a bid higher than the first bidder's valuation but lower than his new bid. Thus raising the bid causes this bidder to win, but he must pay more for the item than it is worth to him; raising his bid above his valuation cannot make him better off' (McAfee and McMillan 1987, p. 708).

THE FIRST-PRICE SEALED-BID AUCTION: In a first-price sealed-bid auction, finally, the winning bidder is always the one with the highest bid as it is the case in the English auction as well as the second-price sealed-bid auction. But, in the present case, the payment is equal to his *own* rather than the second-highest bid. Clearly, this is in contrast to both auctions above. Most importantly, each bidder can therefore influence the payment that he has to make to Bank A. But this also implies that each bank must have a conjecture on all other bidders' valuations. On the one hand, he wants the payment to be as low as possible. On the other hand, the lower his bid is, the higher the risk that some other bidder bids higher even though he himself may be the bidder with the highest reservation price (McAfee and McMillan 1987, pp. 709-710).

The following bidding strategy can be demonstrated to be a Nash equilibrium strategy in a first-price sealed-bid auction[86].

- Each bidder chooses his bid assuming that his reservation price is highest since the assumption of having the highest reservation is costless if incorrect.
- Conditional upon the assumption that its own reservation price is the highest one, the other bidders' decision is optimally conjectured as bidding the expected second-highest reservation price.
- The bidder then submits a bid that is equivalent to the expected second-highest reservation price (McAfee and McMillan 1987, p. 710).

In other words,

> 'the bidder estimates how far below the own valuation the next valuation is on average, and then submits a bid that is this amount below his own valuation' (McAfee and McMillan 1987, p. 710).

Clearly, this strategy results in the same expected payment to Bank A on average as the English auction and the second-price sealed bid auction since the winning bidder is again the bidder with the highest reservation price. Proposition 6 above is, thus, confirmed and the first-price sealed-bid auction is the optimal pricing system for liquidity trading, given proposition 5 above[87].

---

86 The optimal bidding strategies above are dominant strategies instead (McAfee and McMillan 1987, p. 708).

87 For more details on the revenue equivalence theorem, see Vickrey (1961), Holt (1980), Harris and Raviv (1981), Myerson (1981), and Riley and Samuelson (1981). Furthermore, Stark and Rothkopf (1979), Engelbrecht-Wiggans (1980), and Milgrom (1985, 1986) provide excellent surveys of the literature on auction theory apart from McAfee and McMillan (1987).

2. Dispersed Information and the Efficiency of Competition and the First-Price Sealed-Bid Auction

Section 2 very much follows the same reasoning as section 1. The first half of the comparative analysis below establishes an auction mechanism as the optimal pricing system (section 2.2.1) whereas the second half specifically identifies the efficiency the first-price sealed-bid auction (section 2.2.2). In the present context of information trading, however, the first-price sealed-bid auction is the *only* efficient bargaining game which is due to returning to the common-value assumption. Since the present section as well as section 1 above lead to compatible outcomes, furthermore, there is no trade-off between choosing one or the other pricing system for different trading motives. Fortunately, therefore, the common knowledge assumption concerning the trading motive, which most prominently (and most critically) underlies the present chapter, turns out to be harmless.

2.1 Bargaining Costs Revisited

Turning from the more general, standard bargaining theory above to the more specific mechanism design literature below, let the relevant bargaining costs be adjusted to this alternative approach to market design issues as follows. Provided that FX dealing is information trading, the most important criteria for the efficiency of a pricing system is clearly the truthful communication of monopolistic information among banks. Information trading obviously collapses otherwise. Hence, let the first criteria for the optimality of a pricing system be the incentive compatibility of the corresponding rules. Since, however, any bank participates in information trading if and only if this activity is expected to be profitable, let the second criteria again be given as the individual rationality of a pricing system. The bargaining game must ensure non-zero expected trading profits. Finally, the mechanism design literature also suggests efficiency as the third criteria (Myerson 1985, pp. 115-16).

2.2 Comparative Analysis

2.2.1 Bargaining Arrangements

Adopting a more formal approach to selecting the optimal pricing system for information trading, imagine the following bargaining game which is drawn from Myerson (1985). A single, risk neutral potential seller of one unit of foreign exchange, Bank A, meets a single, risk neutral potential buyer, Bank B, at time $t < T$. It is common knowledge that Bank A has private information on the final period exchange rate e_T. The private information is given as the realization of the random variable $\tilde{v}^A$, Bank A's reservation price. It is also known that Bank B has no private information on e_T. But Bank B knows the probability distribution of $\tilde{v}^A$. In technical terms, Bank B knows

(V.4) $$F(v^A) = \Pr ob(\tilde{v}^A \leq v^A)$$

and

(V.5) $$f(v^A) = F'(v^A) > 0, \qquad \text{for } 0 \leq v^A \leq V.$$

Bank B's reservation price is thus given as

(V.6) $$v^B = g(\tilde{v}^A),$$

where $g:[0,V] \to \Re$ is a continuous function. g is furthermore known to Bank A (Myerson 1985, pp. 130-31).

In economic terms, Myerson's (1985) model clearly describes the situation prior to negotiating the exchange rate of an information-induced FX deal. Bank A, the asking bank, receives a signal from its customer business, technical or financial analysts, a/o, which it translated into the reservation price v^A. Bank B does not receive this signal. For simplicity, it does not receive any signal. Hence, Bank B's reservation price v^B exclusively depends on the realization of $\tilde{v}^A$, thus, returning to the common-value assumption with respect to foreign exchange.

The solution to the described bargaining game is, most generally, given as the following set of 'outcome functions' (Myerson 1985, p. 116).

(V.7) $$p:[0,V] \to [0,1]$$

and

(V.8) $$e:[0,V] \to \Re.$$

In other words, the solution to the described bargaining game is given as

(V.9) $p = p(v^A, v^B)$

and

(V.10) $e = e(v^A, v^B)$.

Equation (V.9) expresses the probability p of trade to occur between Bank A and Bank B, given both banks' reservation prices v^A and v^B. Equation (V.10), furthermore, expresses the expected revenue to Bank A, in other words, the agreed upon exchange rate e, again, given v^A and v^B (Myerson 1985, p. 131).

The optimal solution to the price negotiations, thus, consists of the exchange rate *and* the probability of concluding a deal rather than the exchange rate only. This is due to price changes having two opposite effects. On the one hand, Bank A's revenues rise with the exchange rate. On the other hand, the probability of concluding a deal falls simultaneously and vice versa. A solution, therefore, consists of a combination of the two variables exchange rate and trading probability. Each bank's equilibrium strategy must take into account the counterparty's reaction[88].

Turning from the outcome of the bargaining game to the procedural rules that lead to the optimal bargaining solution (p, e), the mechanism design literature suggests that a bargaining game is optimal if and only if it ensures the bargaining solution (p, e) to be

- individually rational,
- incentive compatible, and
- efficient,

as it has already been suggested above.
If the bargaining process is individually rational and incentive compatible only, it is furthermore referred to as feasible instead (Myerson 1985, p. 131).

INDIVIDUAL RATIONALITY: (p, e) is individually rational if and only if the expected trading profit, the difference between the reservation price and the execution price, is non-negative for both banks. Consequently, the optimal pricing system must satisfy

(V.11) $\mathrm{P}^A(v^A, p, e) \geq 0$

[88] The equilibrium concept of the mechanism design literature incorporates the bargaining costs in the 'standard' sense above.

and

(V.12) $\mathrm{P}^B\left(v^B, p, e\right) \geq 0$ (Myerson 1985, p. 117).

Prior to turning to incentive compatibility, however, equation (V.12) needs further emphasis. For a common-value object and for perfect information, more precisely, v^A and v^B would be identical. This implies, however, that for the present case of imperfect information, Bank B must always lose whenever trade occurs. It is common knowledge that Bank A has valuable private information on the future exchange rate. Bank A, therefore, is known to have a strategic advantage over Bank B.

This outcome is obviously not compatible with the individual rationality constraint above. Hence, trade should never occur. This is the familiar adverse selection problem, most prominently studied in Akerlof (1970). Nevertheless, the FX market is an extremely active market and equation (V.12) above must therefore be satisfied, in one way or the other.

It is finally Chapter IV, section 2 that embodies the answer to this dilemma. Bank B expects to sell profitably the information that it purchases from Bank A 'at a loss' to other market participants at a later stage. The individual rationality constraint is thus still binding since Bank B rationally accounts for the expected profits from future trade.

Formally, this can be expressed such that $g\left(v^A\right)$ is always strictly greater than v^A, thus reflecting the expected profit from trade in future periods. For simplicity, let $g\left(v^A\right)$ be given as a linear function of v^A such that

(V.13) $$g\left(v^A\right) = \begin{cases} v^A + \alpha & \textit{if} \quad v^A + \alpha < V \\ V & \textit{otherwise} \end{cases},$$

for α being an arbitrary constant greater than zero (Myerson 1985, p. 137).

INCENTIVE COMPATIBILITY: It would be easiest for both banks if Bank A simply reported its private information to Bank B in return for an agreed upon fee, less than or equal to α. But it has also turned out on various occasions that strategic behaviour prevents such a solution. On the one hand, Bank B cannot verify Bank A's so called virtual valuation (in other words, the reservation price that Bank A reports to Bank B). On the other hand, Bank B can free-ride on Bank A communicating his reservation price truthfully. It can simply step back from trading.

Ignoring direct reporting, therefore, trade is profitable for Bank B if and only if the inference that it can make from the agreed upon exchange rate points to Bank A's reservation price v^A and not to some other valuation w^A. Applying the revelation principle of definition V.2 below, furthermore, this is the case if and only if the profit to Bank A is highest when reporting v^A instead of w^A to a fictitious broker. Formally, this is the case if and only if (p,e) satisfies

(V.14) $$\mathrm{P}^A\left(v^A, p, e\right) \geq \mathrm{P}^A\left(w^A, p, e\right),$$

for all v^A and w^A in the interval $[0,V]$. The pricing system is finally incentive-compatible in this case. (Myerson 1985, p. 117).

DEFINITION V.2 (REVELATION PRINCIPLE): 'for any Bayesian equilibrium of any bargaining game, there is an equivalent incentive-compatible direct mechanism that always yields the same outcomes (when the honest equilibrium is played). This result, which is well known and very general, is called the revelation principle. The essential idea is that, given any equilibrium of any bargaining game, we can construct an equivalent incentive-compatible direct mechanism as follows. First, we ask the buyer and seller each to confidentially report his valuation. Then, we compute what each would have done in the given equilibrium strategies with these valuations. Finally, we implement the outcome (i.e., transfers of money and the object) as in the given game for this computed behavior. If either individual had any incentive to lie to us in this direct mechanism, then he would have had an incentive to lie to himself in the original game, which is a contradiction of the premise that he was in equilibrium in the original game' (Myerson 1985, pp. 116-17)[89].

EFFICIENCY: Completing the set of constraints on possible pricing systems, any incentive compatible pricing system is efficient if and only if there exists no other incentive compatible pricing system that yields higher expected profits. In other words,

(V.15) $$\mathrm{P}^A\left(v^A, p, e\right) > \mathrm{P}^A\left(v^A, \hat{p}, \hat{e}\right)$$

and

(V.16) $$\mathrm{P}^B\left(v^B, p, e\right) > \mathrm{P}^B\left(v^B, \hat{p}, \hat{e}\right),$$

for all $(\hat{p}, \hat{e})$ other than the equilibrium values (p,e) (Myerson 1985, p. 120).

---

[89] For details on the revelation principle, see also Myerson (1979) and Harris and Townsend (1985).

Unfortunately, the efficiency constraints of equations (V.15) and (V.16) above induce substantial computational problems. Hence, it is general practice in the mechanism design literature to assume that, ceteris paribus, any complicated bargaining game induces higher bargaining costs than a so called 'simple mechanism' (definition V.3).

DEFINITION V.3 (SIMPLE MECHANISM): any mechanism that has only the following two possible outcomes is a simple mechanism. Either foreign exchange is sold for the exchange rate s, for $s=(0,V)$ and $v^A \leq s$, or it is not sold at all. More formally, any mechanism is a simple mechanism if and only if

(V.17) $$p^{(s)}\left(v^A\right)=\begin{cases}1 & if \quad v^A \leq s \\ 0 & if \quad v^A > s\end{cases}$$

and

(V.18) $$e^{(s)}\left(v^A\right)=\begin{cases}s & if \quad v^A \leq s \\ 0 & if \quad v^A > s\end{cases}$$ (Myerson 1985, pp. 132-33).

Hence, Myerson (1985) also focuses his attention on simple mechanisms only. The efficiency constraints can therefore be specified as follows.

EFFICIENCY REVISITED: Let (p,e) be the outcome of any incentive compatible, simple pricing system in the sense of definition V.3 above. Then, (p,e) is efficient if and only if p satisfies the following three conditions.

(V.19) $$p(v^A=0)=1,$$

(V.20) $$p(V-\alpha \leq v^A \leq V)=0, \text{ and}$$

(V.21) $$p\left(0<v^A<V-\alpha\right)=const. \text{ (Myerson 1985, p. 137).}$$

Starting with equation (V.19), a simple pricing system is efficient if and only if the probability of trade is one whenever Bank A's reservation price is equal to zero. This must be the case because Bank B's reservation is always greater than Bank A's according to equation (V.13) above. Hence, Bank B's reservation price is greater than zero when Bank A's is equal to zero.

Furthermore, a simple pricing system is efficient if and only if the probability of trade is zero whenever Bank A attaches such a high value to its foreign exchange position that Bank B's expected trading profit is equal to zero. Intuitively, this is the case because Bank B then learns (more) from *not* trading rather than from trading with Bank A. Formally, it is the case because v^B is rationally bounded above according to equation (V.13).

Finally, a simple pricing system is efficient if and only if the probability of trade is constant for all other v^A. According to equations (V.17) and (V.18), more precisely, it must be either zero or one, depending on the exchange rate. If the equilibrium exchange rate is above v^A and below v^B, the probability of trade must be one for the pricing system to be efficient. It must be zero otherwise since both banks would gain from adjusting the exchange rate upward if it were below v^A and downward if it were above v^B.

EXAMPLE: Let $V = 1$, $F(v^A) = v^A$, and $v^B = g(v^A) = v^A + \alpha$. In other words, let the EUR/USD exchange rate lie between zero and one with each realization being equally likely since the assumption $F(v^A) = v^A$ implies that $f(v^A) = const. = 1$. Furthermore, Bank B's valuation is greater than Bank A's reservation price by a constant amount α since it expects to trade profitably on the information from Bank A in the future.

For this case, Myerson (1985) demonstrates that, in equilibrium, a feasible and efficient pricing system must satisfy

(V.22) $$s \leq 2\alpha$$

and

(V.23) $$p(v^A) = 1,$$

for every v^A such that $0 \leq v^A < \alpha$ (Myerson 1985, pp. 136-37).

Most importantly, equation (V.22) ensures that Bank B's expected profit is non-negative. More precisely, $\mathrm{P}^B(s) \geq 0$ if and only if $s \leq 2\alpha$. Hence, 2α also determines the maximum exchange rate. Equation (V.23), on the contrary, expresses the fact that for any v^A lower than Bank B's minimum valuation α trade is profitable for both banks with certainty and should thus occur. Finally, note that Bank B's profit is at its maximum and Bank A's at its minimum when $s = \alpha$. α, thus, specifies the minimum exchange rate such that $\alpha \leq e \leq 2\alpha$ (Myerson 1985, pp. 137-38). END OF EXAMPLE

Having established the optimality conditions for simple pricing systems, any pricing system that yields the described outcome is an optimal pricing system. In other words, if auctions can be demonstrated to yield this outcome, they are sufficiently demonstrated to be an optimal pricing system, irrespective of whether or not there are other optimal pricing systems. Let the discussion of auctions, however, be preceded by a review of the assumptions that underlie Myerson's (1985) analysis and that are critical with respect to the FX market.

- Bank A has private information whereas Bank B does not have any information. As in Chapter IV, section 2, however, the assumption simplifies the analysis without loss of generality.
- The number of buyers and sellers is restricted to one each. The assumption is relaxed below.
- Bank A knows α with certainty. The assumption is also relaxed below.

Any other simplifying assumptions have already been addressed in the previous section.

Turning from pure theory to the optimality of real-world pricing systems, finally, it is surprisingly straightforward to establish the feasibility and efficiency of auctions. More precisely, if α in the above example is equal to 0.4,

'the best feasible mechanism for the buyer [Bank B] is the simple mechanism $\left(p^{(0.4)}, e^{(0.4)}\right)$. That is, if the buyer can control the negotiations, he wants to make a nonnegotiable first-and-final offer to buy the object for a price of .4' (Myerson 1985, p. 137).

The described pricing system is also the efficient mechanism since $\left(p^{(0.4)}, e^{(0.4)}\right)$ satisfies equations (V.22) and (V.23) above. The exchange rate is less than or equal to 2α and Bank A accepts Bank B's offer with certainty since the trading profit is non-negative (Myerson 1985, p. 138).

On the other hand, the full amount of trading profits goes to Bank B for $s = \alpha$. Hence, this outcome is not entirely satisfactory for Bank A. The expected return on information is equal to zero which is why Bank A may actually refuse to sell it to Bank B. Furthermore, the pricing system cannot yet be described as an auction. But two assumptions from the set of critical assumption above seriously restrict a fruitful discussion of Myerson's (1985) important result.

- Bank A faces only one Bank B.
- Bank A knows α with certainty.

BANK A KNOWS α WITH CERTAINTY: 'If the seller were able to observe bidders' valuations, he could offer the item to the bidder who values it the most at a price slightly below this bidder's valuation, threatening to refuse to sell it if this offer is rejected. Given that the seller has so committed himself, it is in the bidder's interest to accept this take-it-or-leave-it offer; the commitment makes the threat credible' (McAfee and McMillan 1987, p. 704).

Hence, Bank A would actually realize maximum trading profits instead of minimum ones if it really did know α. Assuming Bank B to control the negotiations is thus not reasonable for Bank A knowing α.

Relaxing the assumption of common knowledge of α for moving closer to reality, however, 'the seller's ability to extract surplus is more limited' (McAfee and McMillan 1987, p. 704). More precisely, Bank A can be assumed to transfer the right to quote to the market making Bank B if the associated rise in p above overcompensates the diminishing return on information. It ensures that trade is more likely, ceteris paribus. In terms of standard bargaining costs above, the probability of a failure to agree falls to zero for transferring the right to quote to the market maker.

Should it be rational for Bank A to transfer the right to quote to the market maker, finally, Bank A and Bank B would agree on an auction mechanism given that it corresponds to the optimal pricing system suggested by Myerson (1985) above. In other words, the auction would then be individually rational, incentive-compatible, and efficient for Bank A and Bank B, given that both banks want to trade information.

BANK A FACES ONLY ONE BANK B: Requiring the reduction in bargaining costs to exceed the reduction in the return on information is a strong requirement for Bank A to agree to selling by auction. For a single Bank B, in fact, the return on information even falls to zero. Howver, given that quoting α is also Bank B's best policy in a competitive environment (section 1.2),

'the seller can [again] exploit competition among the bidders to drive up the price' (McAfee and McMillan 1987, p. 704),

as it has already been discussed above (section 1.2). Hence, his return on information does not fall to zero, although he transfers the right to quote to the market makers[90]. For the real-world case, therefore, competition safeguards the transfer of the right to quote from the informational monopolist to the market makers such that Bank A can be expected to agree on trading by auction. So can be the market makers for buying valuable information

[90] The underlying assumption is, of course, that market makers differ with respect to α.

Since, furthermore,

'the seller will not be able to drive the price up so far as to equal the valuation of the bidder who values the item most, because the seller does not know what this valuation is' (McAfee and McMillan 1987, p. 704)[91],

the hurdle for choosing an auction mechanism is actually not as high as it originally seemed to be. The market makers can, again, be expected to regard the auction as the optimal pricing system. Proposition 5 above is, again, reconfirmed.

2.2.2 Auctions

In section 2.2.1, differences in the market makers' valuations were assumed to arise from access to different information and not from differences in taste. In other words, foreign exchange was correctly assumed to be a common-value object. Unfortunately, however, the revenue equivalence theorem, which drove proposition 6 above, only holds for independent-private-values objects. It is only for independent-private-value objects that learning other market makers' quotes and/or their deals is of no relevance to the determination of a bank's own reservation price. The degree of transparency, which clearly distinguishes open-bid from sealed-bid auctions, does not matter in this case only. It is, however, more so in all other cases (McAfee and McMillan 1987, p. 705). Intuitively, the revenue equivalence theorem breaks down because there is no return on information to Bank A as soon as the bidding is open. α is equal to zero since Bank B cannot further exploit the information that it purchases from Bank A, which is why it does not buy the information in the first place. Yet, this is not the case when the bidding is sealed. Hence, the revenue cannot be the same for both auction types.

BANK A: Turning to Bank A in detail, imagine the market for antiques. Furthermore, let the pricing be organized as an auction. If the bidders are consumers, in this case, each one of them attaches a certain value to each object. This reservation price is determined by his taste only. More importantly, the potential buyers are not going to revise their reservation prices according to the bids that others are prepared to submit. If, however, the bidders are antiques dealers who purchase an object for resale, other bidders' valuations are important information. They reflect the market participants' expectations of the trade price that they can achieve on the customer market in the future. Dropping out of an auction early, which is known in an open-bid but not a sealed-bid auction, therefore, implies that the dealer's own expectation of future prices must have been 'wrong' in the sense of 'too low'. For an open-bid auction, this information induces the

[91] Once again, arbitrage may also be the reason for not being able to drive the price up to the limit.

dealer to revise his price expectation upwards. But for a sealed-bid auction, the information is not available to him and he drops out indeed. This, finally, implies that the execution price should be higher for an open-bid auction than it would be for a sealed-bid auction. In other words, the expected return on information should be highest for Bank A if the bidding were open provided, of course, that Bank B does not rationally reject bidding at all (McAfee and McMillan 1987, pp. 720-23).

It is Milgrom and Weber (1982) who confirm this view. They formally demonstrate that, on average,

- the English auction yields the highest revenue to the seller of a common-value object,
- the second-price sealed-bid auction yields the second highest revenue, and
- the first-price sealed-bid and Dutch auction, both yield the lowest expected revenue (Milgrom and Weber 1982, pp. 1090-1111).

Hence, the choice of auction should be straightforward from Bank A's perspective.

The generality of Milgrom and Weber's (1982) result is, however, severely restricted.

- Their analysis is again based on the assumption that Bank A is a monopolist.
- Bank A is assumed to decide on the auction type by himself. Bank B's approval is not required.
- Bank A's reservation price is assumed to be common knowledge which, most importantly, contradicts the basic idea of information trading (Milgrom and Weber 1982, p. 1097-1100).

BANK B: Starting with the conflict of interest between Bank A and Bank B when choosing the auction type, it is Engelbrecht-Wiggans, et al. (1983), Milgrom (1981), and, again, Milgrom and Weber (1982) who demonstrate that the expected profit to any Bank B to concluding a deal with Bank A is equal to zero as soon as Bank B's quote is known to at least one other bidder (Milgrom and Weber 1982, pp. 1090-1111). Following McAfee and McMillan (1987), in other words, they demonstrate that

'it is more important to a bidder that his information be private than that it be precise' (McAfee and McMillan 1987, p. 722)

for information trading to be profitable.

The above intuition that information trading requires sealed bidding is thus formally confirmed. Bank B always and strictly prefers a sealed-bid auction to an open-bid auction for information trading. α is positive in this case only. The purchase of information is pointless otherwise. Hence, the choice is between the first-price sealed-bid and the second-price sealed-bid auction, given that the pricing system must be mutually agreed upon among all FX dealing banks. Instead of immediately turning to this choice problem, however, a second argument in favour of sealed bidding can be derived as follows.

BANK A REVISITED: The conflict of interest between Bank A and Bank B that seems to emerge when designing the pricing system dissolves when relaxing the remaining two critical assumptions that underlie Milgrom and Weber (1982) above, namely, that Bank A is a monopolist and that Bank A's valuation is common knowledge. More precisely, Wilson (1985b) shows that for sufficiently many buyers and sellers, there is no other bargaining game than the sealed-bid double auction that would increase some traders' expected profits from trade not adversely affecting other traders' expected profits from trade' (Wilson 1985b, pp. 1101-14).

'That is, the sealed-bid double auction would survive any attempt to get the traders to agree unanimously to change the trading institution' (McAfee and McMillan 1987, p. 726).

It is the effect of competition and imperfect information that drives this result.

- Bank B prefers the double auction because, quoting a bid *and* an ask rate, Bank B is able to extract more information from the deal with Bank A. Knowing that Bank A refuses a buy offer in a single price auction is 'less information' than knowing that it refuses a buy *and* a sell offer in a double auction. The additional information in the double auction compared to the single-price auction is that there must be bidders in the market that submit more favourable bids than Bank B itself did. In the single-price auction, however, Bank A could *either* be a buyer *or* other bidders submitted a higher bid.
- Bank A prefers the double auction to the single-price auction because it can *always* gain from trade as long as its reservation price differs from any bidder's quote.
- The positive effects of competition have already been addressed on various occasions.

Hence, the sealed-bid double auction is the efficient arrangement. The move towards open bidding would increase Bank A's expected trading profits but, at the same time, reduce Bank B's expected trading profits. The move towards single-price auctions would reduce Bank A's and Bank B's expected trading profits simultaneously.

BANK A AND BANK B: The remaining question is, therefore, whether FX dealing banks agree on the second-price or the first-price sealed-bid auction, as it has already been suggested above. But Bank A cannot credibly commit itself to report truthfully the second-highest bid to the bidder who wins the auction which is however necessary given that the second-highest bid determines the execution price. As long as the execution price that it charges the winning bank is slightly below this bank's quote, Bank A can always argue that this was the second-highest bid although the actual second-highest bid that it received was actually less. A documentation of each auction would thus be required in order to enable Bank B to verify Bank A's information. For frequent trading, the related operational costs are higher than turning to the first-price auction which does not require monitoring at all. Hence,

PROPOSITION 7: the first-price sealed-bid auction is the optimal pricing system for information trading.

- The first-price sealed-bid auction allows for non-zero returns on information being sealed.
- It avoids agency problems for being first-price.
- It determines the return on information such that it can be mutually agreed upon as being an auction. Safeguarded by competition among the bidders, the transfer of the right to quote to the buyers of information, in other words, market making is individually efficient, incentive compatible, and efficient.

Finally, since the first-price sealed-bid auction is also the optimal pricing system for liquidity trading, it is the optimal pricing system for foreign exchange dealing as a whole.

3. Position Risk Exposure and the Efficiency of the Bid-Ask Spread

Chapter IV, section 4 above introduced the gambler's ruin problem. Ignoring the exchange rate, the outcome of running out of foreign exchange was based on the dynamics of each bank's currency positions due to customer trading. The interbank market was finally said to return the control over their inventories to the FX dealing banks.

Given that the optimal pricing system is a first-price sealed-bid (double) auction, however, the exchange rate is also an effective control variable for currency positions. In other words, the assumption of exogenous exchange rates above is obviously inappropriate. Hence, let us reinvestigate Garman's (1976) model for endogenous exchange rates.

Let Bank n be a market maker who determines the exchange rate e_t once and for all at time $t = 0$.

(V.24) $$e_t = e, \qquad \text{for all } t.$$

Furthermore, let the bank have an infinite horizon such that $t \to \infty$. In other words, let the exchange rate be endogenously determined but fixed[92].

Most importantly, in this case, $\lambda_{a,b}$, the arrival rate functions above, are given as

(V.25) $$\lambda_{a,b} = \lambda_{a,b}(e,t)$$

instead of being functions of time only. Hence, the ultimate failure probabilities in equations (IV.66) and (IV.67) above turn out as

(V.26) $$\lim_{t\to\infty} \eta_0(t) \begin{cases} \approx \left(\dfrac{e\lambda_b(e)}{e\lambda_a(e)}\right)^{EUR_0/e} & if \quad e\lambda_a(e) > e\lambda_b(e) \\ = 1 & otherwise \end{cases},$$

for the Euro position, respectively,

(V.27) $$\lim_{t\to\infty} \mu_0(t) \begin{cases} \approx \left(\dfrac{\lambda_a(e)}{\lambda_b(e)}\right)^{USD_0} & if \quad \lambda_a(e) < \lambda_b(e) \\ = 1 & otherwise \end{cases},$$

for the US dollar position.

At first sight, therefore, they are still equivalent to equations (IV.66) and (IV.67) above. Endogeneity of the exchange rate seems to have no effects with respect to the gambler's ruin problem. Bank n runs out of either currency with certainty.

92 Although the assumption of fixed exchange rates is extremely restrictive, it highlights the problem of 'staying alive' (O'Hara 1995, p. 16). For a short horizon T, it would furthermore anticipate competition and avoiding arbitrage trading. Both factors limit each market maker's discretion in the short run.

But the optimal pricing system is a double auction. Hence, bank n may as well quote two *different* prices, one for buying foreign exchange and one for selling it. Let the exchange rate, therefore, be given as a bid-ask spread such that

(V.28) $$e = e_a,$$

if the counterparty sells foreign exchange to bank n and

(V.29) $$e = e_b,$$

if he buys it from bank n instead.

In this case, the ultimate failure probabilities are given as

(V.30) $$\lim_{t\to\infty} \eta_0(t) \begin{cases} \approx \left(\dfrac{e_b\lambda_b(e_b)}{e_a\lambda_a(e_a)}\right)^{EUR_0/\bar{e}} & \text{if} \quad e_a\lambda_a(e_a) > e_b\lambda_b(e_b) \\ = 1 & \text{otherwise} \end{cases},$$

for the Euro position, respectively,

(V.31) $$\lim_{t\to\infty} \mu_0(t) \begin{cases} \approx \left(\dfrac{\lambda_a(e_a)}{\lambda_b(e_b)}\right)^{USD_0} & \text{if} \quad \lambda_a(e_a) < \lambda_b(e_b) \\ = 1 & \text{otherwise} \end{cases},$$

for the US dollar position. $\bar{e}$ is chosen such that $e_b < \bar{e} < e_a$ (Garman 1976, pp. 264-66).

Hence, Bank n's optimal pricing policy for not running out of either US dollars and/or Euros must satisfy

(V.32) $$e_a\lambda_a(e_a) > e_b\lambda_b(e_b)$$

and

(V.33) $\lambda_a(e_a) < \lambda_b(e_b)$.

For endogenous exchange rates, furthermore, this can easily be achieved by setting e_b such that it is not equal to e_a. More precisely, it is optimal for bank n to quote a bid-ask spread such that

(V.34) $e_b < e_a$

because, in this case, equations (V.32) and (V.33) above can hold simultaneously. The spread, furthermore, widens until this is the case with certainty. Hence,

PROPOSITION 8: it is optimal for a dealer (on the customer as well as the interbank market), to quote a non-zero bid-ask spread in order to minimize position risk exposure.

It is again competition that limits bank n's ability to extract monopolistic rents from the bid-ask spread. Finally, reciprocal trading also finds a source in the bid-ask spread. For a non-zero difference between buy and sell offers, it is always optimal for each FX dealing bank to deal on its own quote. Hence, reciprocal trading guarantees an 'even' distribution of the return to the spread among all market participants.

CHAPTER VI

The Optimal Settlement System

> 'Well-designed multi-currency services such as multi-currency settlement mechanisms and bilateral and multilateral obligation netting arrangements could greatly enhance the efforts of individual banks to reduce their FX settlement exposures' (Bank for International Settlements 1996, p. 2).

Chapter III, section 4 above introduced credit risk, liquidity risk, and systemic risk as the imperfections which the settlement system of the foreign exchange market must take into account. Compared to the current market practice (single-currency, bilateral, and gross settlement), it furthermore outlined four alternative ways for organizing cross-border funds transfers. Bilateral and multilateral netting schemes were presented along with two 'private sector clearing house arrangements' (Marquardt 1994, p. 138), most prominently, the CLS Bank. The efficiency of the foreign exchange market structure is now reviewed within this framework. Given that the settlement of FX transactions is subject to major changes, however, it should not be surprising that the current practice cannot be established as the transaction cost-minimizing alternative. On the contrary,

- netting arrangements are shown to dominate gross settlement if liquidity risk and/or systemic risk are significant (sections 2 and 3), and
- multi-currency settlement are shown to dominate single-currency settlement if credit risk is significant (section 1).

1. Credit Risk Exposure, Credit Limits, and the Efficiency of Multi-Currency Settlement

1.1 Agency Costs Revisited

Whether or not the settlement of foreign exchange transactions is subject to credit risk of the moral hazard-type depends on whether or not the search and information system effectively separates reliable from unreliable banks. It is only unreliable banks that fail half-way through the settlement process.

If the search and information system does not effectively separate reliable from unreliable banks, the insufficiency of self-selection finds its formal expression in $\rho_t^n > 0$, for all *n, t*, which implies that π^n is also non-zero. Hence, credit risk matters with respect to the design of the settlement system. The game tree in figure III.6 above has not successfully been reduced to the 'Bank A is reliable'-branch only.

Assuming that self-selection is insufficient (the validity of this assumption is addressed shortly), the settlement system can only respond to the exposure to credit risk by restricting the loss that would result from a counterparty's insolvency. By definition, settlement systems cannot affect the likelihood of insolvency as such.

- The FX market lacks a contract enforcement system due to the absence of law.
- The settlement of the two legs of a foreign exchange transaction cannot be monitored due to asynchronous settlement.
- Incentive contracts cannot be written for spot transactions and equally entitled agents.

Consequently, the settlement system can only limit credit.

But limiting credit restricts trade. The agency costs of the moral hazard component of credit risk, therefore, are equal to the opportunity costs of foregone trading profits or

$$\text{(VI.1)} \qquad \left|v_T^n - e_t\right|$$

per US dollar that a risk neutral bank *n* cannot trade at time *t*. More precisely, they turn out for Bank A as

$$\text{(VI.2)} \qquad \sum_{t=1}^{T-1}\left(USD^* - USD_{\lim it}^A\right)\left|v_T^A - e_t\right|,$$

where USD^* is equivalent to the optimal level of a long or short US dollar position and $USD_{\lim it}^A$ expresses the corresponding credit limit such that

$$\text{(VI.3)} \qquad \left|USD_{\lim it}^A\right| < \left|USD^*\right|$$

for normal market conditions. For non-zero interest rates, the opportunity costs of foregone trading profits increase by the opportunity costs of foregone interest earnings or

(VI.4) $$\sum_{t=1}^{T-1}\left(USD^{*}-USD^{A}_{\lim it}\right)\left(v^{A}_{T}-e_{t}\right)\left(i_{T}-i_{t}\right)$$ [93].

Continuing with the assumption of insufficient self-selection, $USD^{A}_{\lim it}$ varies with respect to the underlying search and information system.

- For a decentralized market, the size of $USD^{A}_{\lim it}$ depends on the market participants' beliefs about Bank A's reliability. It is therefore not the same for each bank *n*. More importantly, however, $USD^{A}_{\lim it}$ varies with respect to time due to learning. Equation (VI.2) above turns into equation (VI.5) below.

(VI.5) $$\sum_{t=1}^{T-1}\left(USD^{*}-USD^{A}_{\lim it,t}\right)\left|v^{A}_{T}-e_{t}\right|.$$

The higher is Bank A's reputation, the higher is its credit limit, the lower is its deviation from the optimal USD position, and the lower is its opportunity costs of foregone trading profits.

From a different perspective, the fact that the credit limit is a positive increasing function of the risk premium can be interpreted such that there is a trade-off between the size of the risk premium and the size of the credit limit. For high risk premia, the credit limits are high, at the same time, reducing the opportunity costs of foregone trading profits. If it was not for the adverse selection effect of non-zero credit risk, a decision on the optimal combination of risk premium and credit limit would in fact be

[93] Chapter VI necessarily leaves behind the more stylized framework that was adopted in Chapter IV. There, the entire analysis was carried out for the repeated trade of one US dollar per period in which case credit limits cannot be analyzed. Since they could only be equal to zero or one, they would either restrict trade altogether or they would not have any consequence in terms of a change in transaction costs. This is due to ignoring ΔUSD_t, the dealing amount, above by setting it equal to one. Most importantly, particularly for any empirical research, the different approaches to the agency costs imply that the two cost components, the adverse selection component and the moral hazard component, cannot simply be added in order to determine the overall agency costs.
Furthermore Chapter III, section 5 outlined that US dollar credit limits automatically result in credit limits for each bank's Euro position. Hence, the opportunity costs of deviating from the optimal long US dollar position are identical to the opportunity costs of deviating from the corresponding short Euro position and vice versa. Any proposition that can be derived for one currency, therefore, applies more generally. Moreover, the comparative approach even allows for restricting the focus on the limit for *either* the long *or* the short position.
Finally, USD^{*} does not tend to infinity though the banks are risk neutral. The dealing amounts are standardized and the maximum number of deals that can be concluded per period is certainly less than infinity in the real world. But, in any case, the absolute level of USD^{*} is of no significance for the following.

based on comparing the unfavourable increase in the execution price with the additional trading profits related to an increase in the credit limit and vice versa.

- For the organized exchange, USD^{A}_{limit} is constant with respect to time. Equation (VI.2), therefore, correctly specifies the opportunity costs of foregone trading profits. But furthermore, a trade-off also exists. USD^{A}_{limit} is equivalent to the collateral c^{A} that Bank A has to deposit with the organized exchange above. Hence, the opportunity costs of foregone trading profits or

(VI.6) $$\sum_{t=1}^{T-1}\left(USD^{*}-c^{A}\right)\left|v_{T}^{A}-e_{t}\right|$$

have to be weighed against the opportunity costs of foregone interest earnings, namely,

(VI.7) $$c^{A}\cdot i_{T-1}$$

in order to determine the optimal level of c^{A}.

Without loss of generality, the comparative analysis of the following section relies on equation (VI.5) and the corresponding expression for the opportunity costs of foregone interest earnings. It, thus, relies on the decentralized market as the relevant search and information system.

Addressing the assumption of insufficient self-selection, finally, the various examples of failing banks above demonstrated that it is a reasonable one. The fact that credit limits apply universally to all market participants in each of the alternative single-currency settlement systems above provides further empirical support. Contract performance must obviously be the optimal strategy for some unreliable banks, at least for some time[94]. And even if the underlying search and information system were the organized exchange, the insufficiency of self-selection must be interpreted in a similar sense. Delivery is ensured up to the level of c^{A} *irrespective* of Bank A's type. But dealing beyond the limit is not at all restricted to reliable banks. Hence, self-selection is insufficient. In other words, credit risk does not matter for a dealing amount smaller than the level of collateral *because* there is a limitation to trade. But it would matter all the more for a dealing amount greater than the collateral for exactly the same reason. Organizing an exchange does not perfectly select reliable banks since it restricts learning.

94 Contract performance is the optimal strategy for unreliable banks if and only if the condition for self-enforcement above holds.

1.2 Comparative Analysis

1.2.1 Single-Currency Settlement

GROSS SETTLEMENT: As a reference for the following, the agency costs C_A related to the FX market practice are given as

$$C_A = \sum_{t=1}^{T-1}\left(USD^* - USD^A_{\lim it,t}\right)\left|v^A_T - e_t\right| + \sum_{t=1}^{T-1}\left(USD^* - USD^A_{\lim it,t}\right)\left|\left(v^A_T - e_t\right)\left(i_T - i_t\right)\right| \qquad \text{(VI.8)}$$

$USD^A_{\lim it,t}$ expresses the sum of Bank A's bilateral credit limits that each of the other N-1 banks imposes on it[95].

BILATERAL NETTING: Surprisingly, bilateral netting does not affect equation (VI.8) as it may seem at first sight. This is the case because, even for gross settlement, credit limits always apply to Bank A's net debit position with the other banks at settlement time t (Fischer-Erlach 1995, p. 132). It is only the net debit position that is subject to credit risk. More precisely, it is only the net debit position that is subject to the 'time zone problem' which results from using national payments systems that is subject to credit risk. In the sense that an early purchase of US dollars can be offset by a resale later during the *same* time period $(t-1,t)$, Bank A has unlimited credit *during* the trading session and regardless of the nature of the settlement system. The outgoing USD payment is neutralized by an incoming USD payment *at the same settlement time t* and within the *same* time zone[96].

MULTILATERAL NETTING: If it were for multilateral netting only, ECHO would finally not affect C_A either for the same reason given above. All three single-currency settlement systems would incur identical specific costs. Since, however, ECHO provides a settlement guarantee, the situation is more complicated.

---

95 The problem of how to determine the optimal level of the credit limits $USD^n_{\lim it}$ is ignored. It is of no significance for the present analysis. One possible approach can be found in Schoenmaker (1995, pp. 7-9).

96 The underlying view is of course the one that has already determined Chapter III. Any imperfection that is not exclusive to FX transactions is ignored. One of these problems is default risk which is minimized by real-time gross settlement. But for details on the broader issue of how to design national payments systems, see Summers (1994).

Providing a settlement guarantee has external effects on the search and information system. More precisely, for providing settlement guarantees, ECHO is not only a settlement system but also analytically equivalent to the collateral solution to the prisoners' dilemma. But participating in a clearing house that guarantees settlement *and*, at the same time, relying on reputation and transaction-specific investments for the selection of reliable banks is therefore inefficient since it is costly and unnecessary. The 'spirit' of ECHO is at odds with a decentralized market. It fulfills additional functions that are original to the search and information system.

Should, therefore, ECHO be more costly than the FX market practice in terms of foregone trading profits, in other words, should the ECHO settlement guarantees be less than the bilateral credit limits of the current FX market practice, the service of guaranteeing settlement must have its origin in one of the other imperfections. This assumes, of course, that it is an efficient arrangement and that it can be attributed to the problem of cross-border funds transfer.

More formally, this argument can be repeated as follows. If c^A_{ECHO} is given such that, ceteris paribus,

(VI.9) $$\sum_{t=1}^{T-1}\left(USD*-c^A_{ECHO}\right)\left|v^A_T-e_t\right|>\sum_{t=1}^{T-1}\left(USD*-USD^A_{\lim it,t}\right)\left|v^A_T-e_t\right|,$$

ECHO can only be efficient for some reason other than credit risk exposure, given that the underlying search and information system is the decentralized market. The costs of collateralizing settlement guarantees must be overcompensated by additional gains such that the overall transaction costs are minimized. Again, $USD^A_{\lim it,t}$ must have reached a level that is well above the level of c^A_{ECHO}.

Based on various discussions with ECHO member banks, this second view can be taken here and section 3.2.2 below provides an explanation for the settlement guarantee which does not have its origins in credit risk exposure. Hence, the agency costs related to single-currency settlement can be summarized as follows (table VI.1).

TABLE VI.1: Agency Costs of Single-Currency Settlement

	FX Market	Bilateral Netting	ECHO
Agency Costs	$\sum_{t=1}^{T-1}\left(USD^{*}-USD^{A}_{\text{limit},t}\right)\left\|v^{A}_{T}-e_{t}\right\| + \sum_{t=1}^{T-1}\left(USD^{*}-USD^{A}_{\text{limit},t}\right)\left\|\left(v^{A}_{T}-e_{t}\right)\left(i_{T}-i_{t}\right)\right\|$		

1.2.2 Multi-Currency Settlement

Since netting has just been demonstrated to have no effects on agency costs, the discussion of multi-currency arrangements can be restricted to the CLS Bank. The CLS Bank is in effect a payments system for the settlement of foreign exchange transactions only. The distinct feature compared to all single-currency arrangements is thus the fact that the settlement agent has simultaneous access to all nostro accounts denominated in all participating currencies. The foremost important consequence of this institutional characteristic is that the settlement of the two legs of a foreign exchange transaction can and will be synchronous. Funds are transferred from the buyer's account to the seller's account and vice versa if and only if the necessary balance is available on *both* accounts. For the first time in the history of foreign exchange dealing, therefore[97], non-cash settlement will take place as payment-versus-payment. Consequently, the CLS Bank strikes credit risk at its root. More precisely, it eradicates credit risk altogether. The agency costs are equal to zero since, ceteris paribus, all FX dealing banks set ρ_t^A and π^A equal to zero and trade is not restricted by limiting credit (the obvious external effects of zero credit risk on the design of the search and information system are discussed in Chapter VII below).

2. Liquidity Risk Exposure and the Efficiency of Multilateral and Net Settlement

2.1 Costs of Making Payments

Let Bank A be sound and risk neutral.

- Bank A's temporary ability to pay is then a positive increasing function of the bank's payment reserves c^A. The higher the reserves in terms of daylight overdrafts and/or

[97] For the history of foreign exchange dealing, see Einzig (1970).

The following functional form meets this criteria as well as the standard assumptions with respect to a normal cost structure. Since $\frac{1}{v^A} - \frac{1}{v*}$ measures the costs of delay per unit of account only, the expression is multiplied by the payment flow f^A.

(VI.12) $$C_D^A = \frac{1}{2} f^A \left(\frac{1}{v^A} - \frac{1}{v*} \right)^2 .$$

According to equation (VI.12), the obvious solution to minimizing the costs of delay is to hold high enough payment reserves compared to the payment flow.

But holding payment reserves is costly. With a few exceptions that are discussed below, daylight overdrafts are subject to the already familiar opportunity costs of holding collateral or interest costs given as

(VI.13) $$C_C = c^A \cdot i .$$

Bank A's objective is therefore not only to minimize the costs of delay but to minimize the costs of making payments

(VI.14) $$C_C + C_D = c^A \cdot i + \frac{1}{2} f^A \left(\frac{1}{v^A} - \frac{1}{v*} \right)^2 .$$

The first-order condition finally requires

(VI.15) $$c_{Min}^A = f_{Min}^A \left(\frac{1}{v*} - i \right)$$

which is equivalent to

(VI.16) $$\frac{1}{v_{Min}^A} = \frac{1}{v*} - i$$ (Schoenmaker 1995, pp. 1-14).

According to equation (VI.16), Bank A's optimal turnover ratio, not surprisingly, differs from the zero cost ratio. For non-zero interest rates, the costs of delay are also non-zero since payment reserves are subject to opportunity costs. The higher the interest rate, furthermore, the more the optimal ratio differs from the zero cost ratio due to the increasing costs of holding payment reserves.

Non-zero costs of delay, finally, imply that the likelihood of settlement failures is also non-zero. Hence, the intuition of liquidity risk exposure is, first of all, confirmed. The customer order flow and/or a counterparty's default both adversely affect Bank A's temporary ability to pay. All market participants reasonably expect themselves as well as their counterparties not to be sufficiently endowed with foreign exchange at all times. In terms of Shen (1997),

> 'there is a trade-off between minimizing liquidity risk and minimizing liquidity cost. As a result, from a bank's perspective, it is usually too costly to totally eliminate liquidity risk' (Shen 1997, p. 52).

But rather than confirming the intuition of liquidity risk only, the model, secondly, provides the basis for comparing the alternative settlement systems with respect to their specific costs.

2.2 Comparative Analysis

2.2.1 Single-Currency Settlement

For a given institutional environment, the payment flow is determined by Bank A's customer business, its market making activities, the default of counterparties, etc. f^A can thus reasonably be assumed to be exogenous for each of the alternative settlement systems. In this case, the payment reserves c^A are the bank's only decision variable such that, according to equation (VI.15),

(VI.17) $$c^A_{Min} = \overline{f^A}\left(\frac{1}{v^*} - i\right).$$

c^A_{Min} is therefore the transaction cost-minimizing response to the size of Bank A's FX business.

Across different institutional environments, exogeneity of the payment flow however cannot be assumed. On the contrary, the effects of alternative settlement procedures on the size of the payment flow are at the heart of the following discussion. But instead of focusing on payment reserves *and* payment flows, c^A is alternatively assumed to be fixed at the level of $c^A_{FX,Min}$. The comparison of the alternative settlement systems is thus reduced to a comparison of the costs of delay[100].

FX MARKET: For the current FX market practice, Bank A's costs of delay when using a US-based payments system for the settlement of the US dollar denominated leg of a foreign exchange transaction are given as

(VI.18) $$C_{D,FX} = \frac{1}{2} f^A_{FX} \left(\frac{1}{v^A_{FX}} - \frac{1}{v^*} \right)^2 .$$

In contrast to equation (VI.18), however, the costs of delay are equal to zero for some payments systems, most importantly, the Europe-based settlement system TARGET (Trans-European Automated Real-Time Gross-Settlement Express Transfer). Positive working balances that are held with the European Central Bank, which is the settlement agent of TARGET, are interest-bearing. Thus, there is no trade-off between liquidity risk and liquidity costs. v^A_{FX} is always equal to v^* since banks are prepared to hold voluntarily any level of working balances that ensures prompt payment[101].

BILATERAL NETTING: Leaving the foreign exchange market practice behind, imagine Bank A and Bank B next to settle their USD net debit positions with one another in regular intervals. This arrangement of bilateral netting clearly reduces the payment flow that each bank has to channel through the US-based payments system. Table VI.5 below illustrates the point. So does table VI.2 below. The settlement flow of USD 344 billion that was subject to bilateral netting in 1997 was reduced by USD 173 billion. In other words, USD 171 billion were actually settled for a volume of trade that was as high as USD 344 billion.

A reduced payment flow, however, increases the efficiency of the settlement of FX transactions. For given payment reserves $c^A_{FX,Min}$, the costs of delay fall. According to equation (VI.12), therefore,

(VI.19) $$C_{D,Net}\left(f^A_{Net}\right) < C_{D,FX}\left(f^A_{FX}\right), \quad \text{since } f^A_{Net} < f^A_{FX} .$$

---

[100] In this respect, the analysis departs from Schoenmaker (1995). For details, see Schoenmaker (1995, p. 6).

TABLE VI.2: Effect of Netting*

	Bilateral Netting		**Multilateral Netting**	
	1997 survey	1996 survey	1997 survey	1996 survey
A: value of settlement flows subject to netting (% of gross flows)	USD 344bn (29%)	USD 277bn (24%)	USD 14bn (1.2%)	USD 9bn (1.0%)
B: reduction in settlement flows due to netting (% of gross flows)	USD 173bn (15%)	USD 123bn (13%)	USD 10bn (0.8%)	USD 6bn (0.7%)
Memo[#]: strength of netting (B÷A)	50%	54%	71%	67%

* This table is based on the average of the settlement amounts paid by banks and those received (the difference between the two across all currencies being insignificant). # Effect of netting on the portion of the gross flows to which it was applied.
Source: Bank for International Settlements (1998, p. 16, table 6)

MULTILATERAL NETTING: It is a straightforward argument to extend this to multilateral netting. But, since more than two banks net their obligations with one another, ECHO furthermore increases the effectiveness of netting arrangements. Table VI.2 again illustrates the point. Whereas bilateral netting reduced the payment flow by 50 per cent in 1997, ECHO did so by 71 per cent. For the same reason as above, therefore,

$$C_{D,ECHO}\left(f_{ECHO}^{A}\right) < C_{D,Net}\left(f_{Net}^{A}\right) < C_{D,FX}\left(f_{FX}^{A}\right) \qquad \text{(VI.20)}$$

and multilateral netting is the efficient response to the exposure to liquidity risk provided that the settlement is single-currency.

2.2.2 Multi-Currency Settlement

A comparison of the CLS Bank with the netting variant of continuously linked settlement is straightforward. Netting provides maximum efficiency since it minimizes the payment flow. Yet a comparison of both multi-currency settlement arrangements with single-currency settlement is more complicated. By its very nature, multi-currency settlement must be compared with the sum of all national payments systems as well as for the costs of making payments instead of just the costs of delay.

[101] For details on TARGET, see European Monetary Institute (1995, 1996, 1997, a/o).

CLS BANK: Starting with the CLS Bank, multi-currency, gross settlement is less efficient than the FX market practice.

- Although the payment flows in each national payments system decrease significantly as soon as the CLS Bank is operational (payment flows are shifted from national systems to the new bank), the potential gains are at least compensated for by the costs of making payments related to the new system. More precisely, if the payment reserves held with national payments systems can be adjusted to the reduced payment flow, the costs of making payments are identical to the ones given as equation (VI.18) above. f_{CLS}^{A} is exactly equal to the difference between the two payment flows before and after the settlement of FX transactions is separated from the settlement of other domestic and cross-border transactions - as it is the case with Bank A's payment reserves c_{CLS}^{A}.
- The potential gains of moving away from national payments systems are overcompensated since, on the one hand, the payment reserves with the CLS Bank are not interest-bearing. The opportunity costs of collateral increase for each transaction that Bank A no longer settles with TARGET but with the CLS Bank. On the other hand, they are overcompensated because some of the national payments systems are netting systems whereas the CLS Bank is not. Since netting has transaction cost-reducing effects on the size of the order flow, however, moving to gross settlement is inefficient.

Hence, it is expected that

(VI.21) $$\sum_{\substack{National\\Payments\\Systems}} \Delta\left(C_{C,FX} + C_{D,FX}\right) < C_{C,CLS} + C_{D,CLS}\,.$$

MULTI-CURRENCY NETTING: An unambiguous classification of multi-currency netting in relation to single-currency settlement arrangements is ultimately not possible on theoretical grounds. Multi-currency netting may or may not be more efficient than the current FX market practice, bilateral netting, or ECHO. This depends on the size of the transaction cost-increasing effects of multi-currency settlement compared to the transaction cost-reducing effects of netting, given that most national payments systems are gross settlement systems. But this is an empirical question in nature. Consequently, table VI.3 above summarizes the current state of affairs after discussing credit risk exposure and liquidity risk exposure accordingly.

TABLE VI.3: Agency Costs and Costs of Making Payments of Alternative Settlement Systems

	Single-Currency Settlement (SC)			Multi-Currency Settlement (MC)		Efficient Arrangement
	FX Market	**Bilateral Netting**	**ECHO**	**CLS Bank**	**Multi-Currency Netting (MN)**	
Agency Costs	$\sum_{t=1}^{T-1}\left(USD^{*}-USD_{\text{limit},t}^{A}\right)\left\|v_T^A - e_t\right\| + \sum_{t=1}^{T-1}\left(USD^{*}-USD_{\text{limit},t}^{A}\right)\left\|\left(v_T^A - e_t\right)\left(i_T - i_t\right)\right\|$			zero	zero	CLS Bank or Multi-Currency Netting
Costs of Making Payments	$\frac{1}{2} f_{FX}^{A}\left(\frac{1}{v_{FX}^{A}}-\frac{1}{v^{*}}\right)^{2}$	$C_{D,Net} < C_{D,FX}$	$C_{D,ECHO} < C_{D,Net}$	$C_{D,SC} + C_{C,SC} < C_{D,CLS} + C_{C,CLS}$	$C_{D,MN} + C_{C,MN} < C_{D,CLS} + C_{C,CLS}$	ECHO or Multi-Currency Netting
	for $C_{C,FX} = C_{C,Net} = C_{C,ECHO}$ and $C_{C,TARGET} = 0$			for $C_{C,TARGET} = 0$		

3. Systemic Risk Exposure and the Efficiency of Net Settlement

3.1 Social Costs

Starting with gross settlement, the following - already quite familiar - example demonstrates that it is the spill-over effects of one bank failing to deliver which can turn a liquidity shortage into a systemic crisis. Systemic risk arises because a single settlement failure potentially triggers a chain reaction which can result in the cancellation of all payment flows[102].

EXAMPLE: Assume that the four payment obligations below enter a gross settlement system in exactly this order.

Transaction 1:	Bank C pays Bank A USD 20 million.
Transaction 2:	Bank A pays Bank B USD 15 million.
Transaction 3:	Bank B pays Bank A USD 10 million.
Transaction 4:	Bank A pays Bank C USD 10 million.

Also imagine that between concluding a contract and instructing the payment there is a delay and that Bank A and Bank B hold zero payment reserves. Referring to table VI.4 below, therefore, Bank A could agree on transaction 2 *prior* to the settlement of transaction 1, anticipating a payment of USD 20 million from Bank C. Consequently, Bank B could agree on transaction 3 and Bank A on transaction 4 for the same reason. If Bank C fails to deliver, however, none of transactions 2-4 can be settled subsequently. The system collapses (Shen 1997, p. 52). END OF EXAMPLE

Given the settlement delay, the systemic crisis clearly arises because Bank A and Bank B do not hold sufficient payment reserves. Formally, therefore, systemic risk can be defined as a function of the aggregate level of payment reserves of *all* banks R relative to the aggregate payment flow of *all* banks F (differences among individual banks with respect to their contribution to systemic risk are ignored). In analogy to section 2, the likelihood of a systemic crisis is thus a function of V, the turnover ratio of the payments system, or

$$V = \frac{F}{R}. \tag{VI.22}$$

102 In contrast to Schoenmaker (1995, pp. 7-9, 14), systemic risk is assumed to result from non-zero liquidity risk only. Credit risk shall be ignored for keeping the analysis simple. Chapter VII discusses details on systemic risk *and* credit risk.

TABLE VI.4: Systemic Risk in Gross Settlement Systems
(amounts in USD million)

Payer\Payee	Bank A	Bank B	Bank C	Total Debit
Bank A		15 (2)	10 (4)	25
Bank B	10 (3)			10
Bank C	20 (1)			20
Total Credit	30	15	10	55

Source: Shen (1997, p. 48, table 1)

Assuming that the collapse of the payments system is actually prevented by filling the lack of funds (as was also the case in section 2), the related costs are again a function of the turnover ratio such that

$$C_S = \begin{cases} \frac{1}{2}F\left(\frac{1}{V}-\frac{1}{V^*}\right)^2 & \text{if} \quad V \geq V^* \\ 0 & \text{otherwise} \end{cases} \qquad \text{(VI.23)}$$

Equation (VI.23) is referred to as the social costs (of delay) because, ceteris paribus, they are not individually accounted for by the participants of a gross settlement system. Rationally, no payer considers the costs that his own failure to deliver entails for the payee in terms of also having to delay his payments (Schoenmaker 1995, pp. 6, 12-13). Furthermore, equation (VI.23) is non-zero, ceteris paribus.

'Because an individual bank does not bear the entire cost of potential chain reactions caused by its liquidity shortage, it will choose a level of liquidity that is less than what is collectively desirable' (Shen 1997, p. 55).

Finally, the social costs find their addressee, even in the absence of law. As with the organizer of exchanges, the settlement agent replaces the missing regulatory authority such that he must cover the social costs for any $V > V^*$.

Since, however, the settlement agent is not the focus of the present analysis, meaningful statements concerning Bank A's settlement costs require a reasonable restriction on the costs that the settlement agent is prepared to cover. In this case, any excess costs or benefits resulting from the costs falling short of this limit are rolled over to the FX market participants by the very design of the settlement system itself. Social costs do not affect Bank A otherwise. Since, furthermore, any move away from the FX market practice should be one towards more efficiency, the settlement agents of each of the alternative settlement systems shall be assumed to cover social costs of a level less than or equal to the social costs of the foreign exchange market practice. But prior to turning to the comparative analysis, it is again TARGET as well as netting that need special emphasis.

TARGET is not only a gross settlement system but also a *real-time* gross settlement system. Consequently, there is no settlement delay. Bank A's liquidity management with respect to its Euro payment reserves cannot rely on anticipated incoming payments by definition. This is, however, the necessary precondition for a crisis scenario as it was outlined above. Hence, real-time settlement systems such as TARGET are not exposed to systemic risk.

For analogous reasons, netting systems are always exposed to systemic risk. There is always a settlement delay since the settlement is not payment-versus-payment by definition. Turning from gross settlement to multilateral netting arrangements, furthermore, a systemic crisis results from the need to unwind (definition VI.1) payment obligations that were originally set off against each other. The following example illustrates the difference in a crisis scenario in a gross settlement system although the social costs are still given as equation (VI.23) above. The need to unwind still results from insufficient aggregate payment reserves R relative to the aggregate payment flow F.

DEFINITION VI.1 (UNWINDING): 'a procedure followed in certain clearing and settlement systems in which transfers of securities or funds are settled on a net basis, at the end of the processing cycle, with all transfers provisional until all participants have discharged their settlement obligations. If a participant fails to settle, some or all of the provisional transfers involving that participant are deleted from the system and the settlement obligations from the remaining transfers are then recalculated. Such a procedure has the effect of transferring liquidity pressures and possibly losses from the failure to settle to other participants, and may result in significant and unpredictable systemic risk' (Bank for International Settlements 1993, p. 545).

EXAMPLE: Imagine the four payment obligations presented in table VI.5 below to be settled at the end of the day using a netting system. For a smooth operation, payment reserves of USD 10 million on Bank C's nostro account with the settlement agent is sufficient.

If Bank C fails to deliver, however, the payments system has to let Bank C unwind. But Bank C leaving the system creates problems for Bank A as table VI.6 below demonstrates. Expecting a net credit position of USD 5 million, Bank A suddenly finds itself in a net debit position of the same size. For zero payment reserves, therefore, the system collapses (Shen 1997, pp. 51-52). END OF EXAMPLE

TABLE VI.5: Net Settlement Revisited
(amounts in USD million)

Payer\Payee	Bank A	Bank B	Bank C	Total Debit
Bank A		15	10	25
Bank B	10			10
Bank C	20			20
Total Credit	30	15	10	55
Total Debit	25	10	20	
Net Receipt (**Net Payment**)	5	5	(10)	

Source: Shen (1997, p. 48, table 1)

3.2 Comparative Analysis

3.2.1 Gross Settlement

FX MARKET: Starting with the FX market practice, the social costs related to each national payments system are given such that

$$C_{S,FX} = \frac{1}{2} F_{FX} \left(\frac{1}{V_{FX}} - \frac{1}{V^*} \right)^2 . \quad \text{(VI.24)}$$

Furthermore, the settlement agent is the national central bank.

Determining $C_{S,FX}$, the reference level for the following comparison, the central bank can force FX dealing banks to hold a minimum level of aggregate payment reserves $R_{FX,Min}$ such that $V_{FX} = V^*$ for a given payment flow F_{FX}. Since, however, the optimal level of aggregate payment reserves is not equal to the sum of the individually desirable ones, minimizing the social costs would come at some expense. Dictating the level of payment reserves would result in the FX dealing banks adjusting the payment flow downward according to equation (VI.14) above. For the absence of any alternative settlement system, the volume of foreign exchange dealing would be reduced. It could be channelled through the alternative system otherwise.

Given, however, that central banks can 'create money' and, thus, provide without cost the necessary funds for preventing a systemic crisis, they may alternatively rely on covering the social costs, or at least a significant portion.

- Reviewing the payments systems in the G-10 countries, there is strong empirical support for the view that they actually do so. All central banks are prepared to guarantee settlement if a liquidity shortage turns into a crisis situation (Bank for International Settlements 1993).
- Since it turns out shortly that no settlement agent other than the central bank can insure against systemic risk, there is no alternative settlement system that FX dealing banks can turn to should the central bank choose $C_{S,FX} = 0$. Hence, trade would be severely restricted. However, it is strongly expected that the inefficiencies related to restricted trade clearly overcompensate the drop in social costs.

For both reasons, let the central bank choose $C_{S,FX} > 0$, the actual level being arbitrary[103].

TABLE VI.6: Systemic Risk in Net Settlement Systems

Payer\Payee	Bank A	Bank B		Total Debit
Bank A		15		15
Bank B	10			10
Total Credit	10	15		25
Total Debit	15	10		
Net Receipt **(Net Payment)**	 (5)	5		

Source: Shen (1997, p. 52, table 2)

CLS BANK: Continuing with the CLS Bank, each currency-specific fraction of the system shall be compared with the corresponding national payments system[104]. The social costs are then given as

[103] Agency problems that result from the lender of last resort function of central banks are ignored.
[104] Section 2, alternatively, relied on comparing the multi-currency settlement systems with the sum of all national payments systems.

(VI.25) $$C_{S,CLS} = \frac{1}{2} F_{CLS} \left(\frac{1}{V_{CLS}} - \frac{1}{V^*} \right)^2$$

in analogy to equation (VI.24) above.

But the CLS Bank is not a central bank. Since it cannot create money, therefore, the attempt to cover the social costs is always more expensive for the CLS Bank than it is for central banks. More precisely, the CLS Bank must, in one way or the other, rely on sufficient payment reserves of its member banks for insuring against systemic risk. Hence, for the above mentioned constraint

(VI.26) $$C_{C,CLS} + C_{S,CLS} = C_{S,FX},$$

the CLS Bank is always second-best from Bank A's perspective.

- For constant overall costs, Bank A gets less insurance against systemic risk when joining the CLS Bank.
- For the same insurance, Bank A faces higher overall costs due to non-zero costs of collateral when joining the CLS Bank.

Consequently, Bank A cannot be expected to shift the settlement of its FX transactions from national payments systems to the CLS Bank. The CLS Bank, thus, would not be commercially viable should it try to insure against systemic risk.

The implication is straightforward. In order to survive, the CLS Bank does not cover social costs. On the contrary, it relies on the national central banks instead. Institutionally, the CLS Bank does so by restricting its settlement services to the times when each member bank has access to sufficient central bank refinancing. This is the case if and only if the settlement of each currency pair takes place during the overlapping operation times of the corresponding national payments systems. In other words, the CLS Bank provides payments services for each currency pair whenever there is a window-of-opportunity and only then. It does not settle in real-time, as it has already been outlined above (Chapter III, section 4.2.2). As in the previous section, therefore, the social costs are identical for the CLS Bank and the FX market practice, ignoring the effects of netting.

TABLE VI.7: Agency Costs, Costs of Making Payments, and Social Costs of Alternative Settlement Systems

	Single-Currency Settlement (SC)			**Multi-Currency Settlement (MC)**		**Efficient Arrangement**
	FX Market	**Bilateral Netting**	**ECHO**	**CLS Bank**	**Multi-Currency Netting (MN)**	
Agency Costs	$\sum_{t=1}^{T-1}\left(USD^* - USD_{\text{limit},t}^{A}\right)\left\lvert v_T^A - e_t\right\rvert + \sum_{t=1}^{T-1}\left(USD^* - USD_{\text{limit},t}^{A}\right)\left\lvert\left(v_T^A - e_t\right)\left(i_T - i_t\right)\right\rvert$			zero	zero	CLS Bank or Multi-Currency Netting
Costs of Making Payments	$\frac{1}{2} f_{FX}^{A}\left(\frac{1}{v_{FX}^{A}} - \frac{1}{v^*}\right)^2$	$C_{D,Net} < C_{D,FX}$	$C_{D,ECHO} < C_{D,Net}$	$C_{D,SC} + C_{C,SC} < C_{D,CLS} + C_{C,CLS}$	$C_{D,MN} + C_{C,MN} < C_{D,CLS} + C_{C,CLS}$	ECHO or Multi-Currency Netting
	for $C_{C,FX} = C_{C,Net} = C_{C,ECHO}$ and $C_{C,TARGET} = 0$			for $C_{C,TARGET} = 0$		
Social Costs (Opportunity Costs)	$\frac{1}{2} F_{FX}\left(\frac{1}{V_{FX}} - \frac{1}{V^*}\right)^2$	$C_{S,Net} < C_{S,FX}$	$C_{S,ECHO} < C_{S,Net}$ $(C_{C,ECHO} > 0)$	$C_{S,CLS} \geq C_{S,FX}$	$C_{S,MN} < C_{S,CLS}$	Bilateral Netting, ECHO, or Multi-Currency Netting
	for $C_{S,TARGET} = 0$					

3.2.2 Net Settlement

The effect of bilateral netting on the social costs are immediately apparent. Settling net debit positions reduces the payment flow such that, ceteris paribus, the social costs decrease.

(VI.27) $$C_{S,Net} < C_{S,FX}.$$

Hence, Bank A prefers bilateral netting to the FX market practice since the central bank reduces R_{FX} to a level $R_{Net} < R_{FX}$ that is individually more desirable (according to the underlying assumption that each bank benefits from reductions in social costs). For the same reason, multi-currency netting is preferred to the CLS Bank and the move from a netting system to gross settlement is a move towards less efficiency.

The same argument could be extended to ECHO if the clearing house were the settlement agent, preferably, a central bank. Since it is not, however, netting payment orders *prior* to entering a payments system entails additional costs apart from the social costs. They result from the upcoming risk of unwinding and they are thus costs of delay in nature. Furthermore, they must be accounted for by the member banks. The clearing house cannot cover these costs for the same reason that the CLS Bank cannot cover social costs. In contrast to the CLS Bank, a gross settlement system, however, ECHO can be commercially viable compared to the FX market practice since multilateral netting increases the efficiency of settlement according to equation (VI.27) above. The efficiency gains in terms of lower payment reserves can in other words offset the costs of potential unwinding, at least in principle. It is an empirical question whether they do so, although the costs of unwinding can be specified further.

Turning to the costs of unwinding, unwinding is first of all not observed empirically (Humphrey 1986, p. 100). Instead of focusing on the costs of unwinding themselves, therefore, let the analysis turn to the costs of *preventing* the need to unwind transactions. ECHO, furthermore, prevents unwinding such that it guarantees settlement based on collateral that the member banks are required to deposit with the clearing house. The costs of preventing the need to unwind are therefore analytically equivalent to the opportunity costs of collateral or

(VI.28) $$C_{C,ECHO} = c_{ECHO}^{A} \cdot i.$$

The settlement guarantee for preventing unwinding finally explains the inconsistency of the decentralized market and ECHO that section 1 above referred to. Thus, $c_{ECHO}^{A} > 0$ is *not* an organizational inefficiency. On the contrary, it finds its explanation in the present context. Furthermore, it is the only reason why the outcome of the present section differs from that of section 2 with respect to the optimal settlement system. Whereas above the choice between single-currency settlement and multi-currency settlement needed to be left to empirical research, there is now also the choice between bilateral and multilateral netting. Net settlement itself is again established as the institutional alternative with the lowest specific costs when it comes to systemic risk. Table VI.7 above may thus serve as the illustration of the following proposition 9 which summarizes and concludes Chapter VI concerning the optimal settlement system.

PROPOSITION 9:

- Settlement according to the payment-versus-payment rule eliminates credit risk. For significant credit risk, therefore, multi-currency settlement is the optimal settlement system since multi-currency settlement can follow the payment-versus-payment rule.
- Netting reduces the payment flow. A decreasing payment flow, furthermore, reduces liquidity risk. For significant liquidity risk, therefore, multilateral netting is the optimal settlement system since it reduces the payment flow to the absolute minimum. Whether or not multilateral netting should be single-currency or multi-currency is an empirical question since the opportunity costs of collateral are zero for some national payments systems, such as TARGET, which they are not for multi-currency netting (as it was assumed).
- Netting reduces the payment flow. For significant systemic risk, therefore, netting is the optimal settlement system since systemic risk is a positive increasing function of the payment flow. Whether or not netting should be single-currency or multi-currency is an empirical question for the same reason as above. Finally, however, whether or not netting should be multilateral is also an empirical question this time. The costs of preventing the need to unwind may or may not outweigh the efficiency gains in terms of reduced social costs due a lower payment flow.

CHAPTER VII

Summary and Conclusion

The inability to enforce contracts across national borders challenges international trade and finance. Transactions across national borders are subject to the absence of law. If, therefore, they are also subject to transaction-specific imperfections, any attempt to remove the related inefficiencies must be self-enforcing, if successful. In theoretical terms, legal centralism is not the appropriate view of things since international trade and finance is lacking a contract enforcement system by nature.

Lacking a contract enforcement system moves the world of international trade and finance closest to the world of the economic theory of institutions. This is particularly true for interbank foreign exchange dealing. History (Einzig 1970) and the recurrent debate on regulating international financial markets (most recently, in the aftermath of the Asian crisis[105]) demonstrate that international policy coordination has repeatedly left out the regulation of the foreign exchange market. Hence, any economic analysis of the foreign exchange market structure can immediately rely on the wealth maximizing behaviour of private economic agents. More precisely, it can rely on the institutional economic theory of markets.

Relying on the institutional economic theory of markets, the structure of the foreign exchange market should reflect the market participants' efforts to restrain any disturbances of foreign exchange dealing that result from transaction-specific imperfections. Most importantly, it should do so efficiently in the sense of minimizing transaction costs. In terms of Hayek (1978), the FX market should be the successful output of the work of the invisible hand. It should be the output of a successful trial-and-error process when referring to Menger (1883) instead.

Based on Chapter III, chapters IV-VI above provided the corresponding theory in the sense of trying to derive a theory of the efficiency of the foreign exchange market.

---

[105] For details, see, most recently, Institute of International Finance (1999a, 1999b) and International Monetary Fund (1999).

Starting with Chapter IV, more precisely, sections 1-4 analyzed the search and information system of the foreign exchange market. In reverse order, they established

- the efficiency of continuous trading *and* standard dealing amounts for the purpose of liquidity trading,
- the efficiency of market making *and* membership for the purpose of hedging,
- the efficiency of sealed trading *and* dealing for the purpose of information trading, and
- the efficiency of formal membership *or* informal membership together with partner-specific trading and sealed trading for self-selecting the most reliable trading partners (table VII.1).

TABLE VII.1: Efficiency of Institutions 1-5

Imperfection	Transaction Costs	Efficient Arrangement
Position Risk Exposure	Liquidity Costs	Institution 3 (Continuous Trading) Institution 4 (Standard Dealing Amounts)
Market Risk Exposure	Costs of Delay	Institution 4 (Market Making) Institution 5 (Membership)
Dispersed Information	Forgone Return on Information	Institution 2 (Sealed Trading) Institution 4 (Dealing)
Credit Risk Exposure	Agency Costs	Institution 1 (Partner-Specific Trading) Institution 2 (Sealed Trading) and/or Institution 5 (Membership)

Chapter IV established the efficiency of certain combinations of institutions 1-5 starting with each of a number of imperfections separately. Hence, Chapter IV fell short of discussing the problem that a *single* search and information system must serve liquidity traders, insurees, insurers, information traders, *and* reliable banks at the same time. In other words, sections 1-4 above established the efficiency of institutions 1-5 for each of the underlying imperfections *in isolation*. But it fell short of deriving a *joint* efficiency hypothesis. Hence, let the final paragraphs on the search and information system bring together the results of propositions 1-4 above.

THE JOINT EFFICIENCY OF INSTITUTIONS 1-5: Liquidity trading is the most fundamental of all three trading motives. Running out of foreign exchange holdings suspends a bank's foreign exchange business. Hedging follows closely since the exposure to market risk is still associated with an expected loss in the form of non-zero costs of delay. Consequently, information trading can be regarded as the least fundamental trading motive given that minimizing the exposure to credit risk does not motivate trade at all. On the one hand, a market structure that does not allow for information trading is costly in the sense of foregoing a positive return on information 'only'. Information trading is thus desired but not essential. On the other hand, the problem of discriminating among trading partners simply dissolves as soon as there is no foreign exchange trading any longer.

Reviewing table VII.1 on the basis of this classification, the hypothesis of the joint efficiency of institutions 1-5, in other words, the efficiency hypothesis with respect to the current search and information system can easily be deduced. Simultaneously, the statics of the search and information system of the foreign exchange market appears suddenly.

- Taking *continuous trading* and *standard dealing amounts* as the minimum requirements on the search and information system of the foreign exchange market, the implementation of market making and membership does not give rise to a trade-off situation. On the contrary, market making is the provision of continuous trading opportunities by definition. Furthermore, continuous trading and standard dealing amounts are independent of membership.
- Taking *continuous trading*, *standard dealing amounts*, *market making*, and *membership* as given, the implementation of sealed trading and dealing does not give rise to a trade-off situation either. On the contrary, market making is dealing by definition. Furthermore, market making can either be open or sealed.
- Taking *continuous trading, standard dealing amounts, dealing and market making, membership*, and *sealed trading* as given, the implementation of *partner-specific trading*, finally, does not give rise to a trade-off situation. On the contrary, partner-specific trading can only be sealed trading.

If, therefore, the above suggested classification of imperfections is valid,

PROPOSITION 10: the current search and information system of the foreign exchange market cannot be outperformed by any other arrangement in terms of minimizing search and information costs. It is efficient. The statics of the search and information system of the foreign exchange market is, furthermore, given as the following pyramid (figure VII.1).

This first of a number of results that are still to come is based on two assumptions (in addition to the one of classifying the imperfections as above).

- Formal membership is expected to be second-best compared to informal membership for the selection of reliable banks since the search and information system has a low degree of transparency combined with a low degree of centralization for other reasons than credit risk exposure.
- Free entry is expected to be second-best compared to membership although there is a trade-off between free entry and membership since information trading is optimal for an infinite number of dealers whereas hedging requires the number of market makers

to be limited above (Chapter IV, sections 2 and 3). But hedging is the more fundamental trading motive compared to information trading and minimizing the exposure to credit risk necessarily requires membership in one way or the other.

FIGURE VII.1: Statics and Efficiency of the Search and Information System of the Foreign Exchange Market

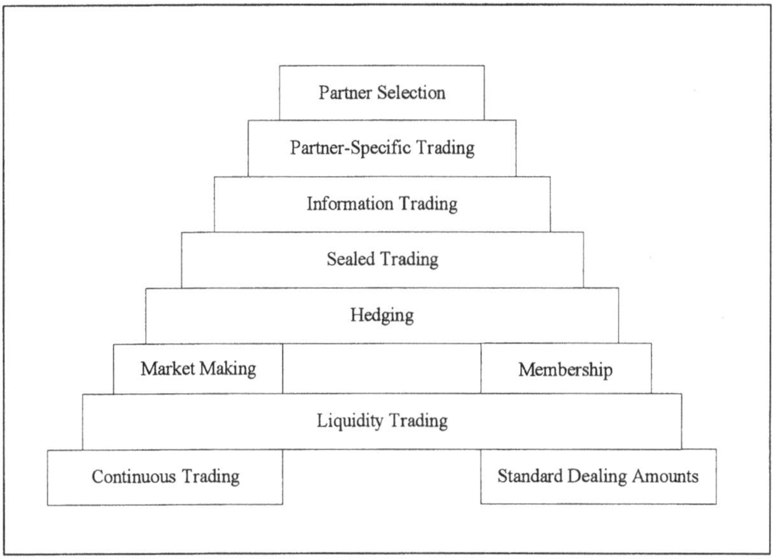

Should empirical research confirm both views, finally, this would clearly point to the fact that, on the foreign exchange market, the number of market participants is balanced very carefully. In other words, the foreign exchange market should be very sensitive to any policy measures or external shocks that affect the number of market participants. The entry barriers (partner-specific investments and reciprocal trading) seem to be chosen such that they are just low enough for the *optimal* number of market participants to enter the foreign exchange market but not any more.

From a different perspective, the problem of determining the optimal number of market participants, furthermore, provides a useful argument in favour of informal membership compared to formal membership, given the trade-off between membership and free entry. Informal arrangements are more flexible than formal ones should there be a need to adjust the number of market participants to a new environment.

THE JOINT EFFICIENCY OF INSTITUTIONS 6 AND 7: Turning from the search and information system of Chapter IV to the pricing system of Chapter V instead, the joint efficiency of the *bid-ask spread*, the *first-price sealed-bid auction*, and *competition* is a straightforward result of sections 1 and 2 above. Propositions 5-7 are compatible hypotheses such that

PROPOSITION 11: simultaneously, the first-price sealed-bid auction is the optimal pricing system for information trading, hedging, and liquidity trading. A two-tier price in the form of the bid-ask spread does not contradict this outcome for being analytically independent of the design of the bargaining game as such. The pricing system of the current foreign exchange market practice is, thus, efficient. The architecture of the pricing system may find its virtual expression in the following, defence wall-like design (figure VII.2).

FIGURE VII.2: Statics and Efficiency of the Pricing System of the Foreign Exchange Market

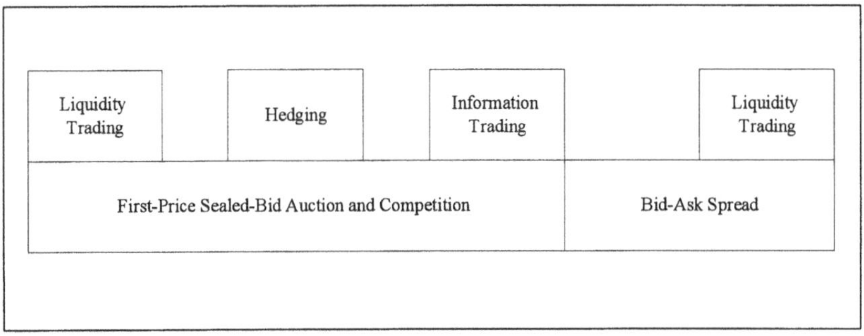

THE JOINT EFFICIENCY OF INSTITUTIONS 9-11: Compared to the pricing system, the settlement system again requires more attention since sections 1-3 above only demonstrated that

- multi-currency settlement is optimal for minimizing credit risk,
- multilateral netting is optimal for minimizing liquidity risk, and
- netting is optimal for minimizing systemic risk.

The problem of whether or not multilateral netting should be single-currency or multi-currency needed to be left to empirical research. So did the problem of whether or not netting should be multilateral in the first place (table VI.7). Consequently, it is again the integration of the results of each individual section 1-3 above that requires final attention for deriving some kind of efficiency hypothesis.

Taking the market participants' preference for the CLS Bank as the starting point, the choice of multilateral, multi-currency, and gross settlement may suggest altogether two different things in the light of proposition 9 above.

- Either the exposure to credit risk is more significant in terms of transaction costs than the one to liquidity risk and systemic risk together *and* the costs of preventing unwinding exceed the efficiency gains of multilateral netting,
- or the CLS Bank is not the efficient settlement system.

This is the case because multi-currency settlement, which is multilateral by definition, minimizes credit risk. At the same time, multilateral netting minimizes liquidity risk. However, it may not minimize systemic risk which implies that the costs of (preventing) unwinding may exceed the efficiency gains of multilateral netting.

Again, a clear-cut answer depends on empirical research. But the fact that most central banks have opted for real-time gross settlement for the design of their national payments systems[106] suggests the first view. Credit risk is the more serious risk than liquidity risk and systemic risk together *and* the costs of (preventing) unwinding are more significant than the efficiency gains of moving from multilateral and gross settlement to multilateral and net settlement. The Bank for International Settlements (1998), finally, takes the same view on this matter.

'Any sound multi-currency settlement mechanism - whether a guaranteed receipt or a guaranteed refund system, or a system that settled simultaneously or sequentially - could go directly to the heart of the problem and completely eliminate FX settlement exposures when settling individual trades. By removing the potential for settlement losses and the associated liquidity pressures, such arrangements would remove a major source of systemic risk that can arise in the settlement of FX trades. The risk-reducing benefits of any multi-currency settlement mechanism could be magnified when combined with bilateral or multilateral obligation netting of the underlying FX trades. Legally valid obligation netting (whether arranged bilaterally between pairs of individual banks or multilaterally with the aid of an industry utility) would reduce the number and size of the settlement flows and, hence, could reduce the intraday liquidity needs for settling these trades through a multi-currency settlement mechanism. Depending on the circumstances, however, problems in either the netting arrangement or the settlement mechanism could potentially impair the other. Accordingly, any guarantee underlying a payment/receipt relationship and the safety of any accompanying netting scheme must both be sufficiently strong to ensure that the combined arrangement does not create greater problems than it solves' (Bank for International Settlements 1998, p. 24).

Proposition 12, therefore, summarizes the analysis of the settlement system of the foreign exchange market as follows.

[106] See the Bank for International Settlements (1993) for details.

PROPOSITION 12: Anticipating empirical testing, the CLS Bank is efficient for the settlement of foreign exchange transactions. The statics of the future settlement system of the foreign exchange market, furthermore, resembles an arched bridge of the Roman type. Multi-currency settlement is multilateral by nature. Most effectively, it is also gross settlement for not destabilizing the settlement of foreign exchange transactions which could require corrections in the future (figures VII.3 and VII.4). Finally, therefore, the current settlement system is not efficient.

FIGURE VII.3: Statics and Efficiency of the Future Settlement System of the Foreign Exchange Market

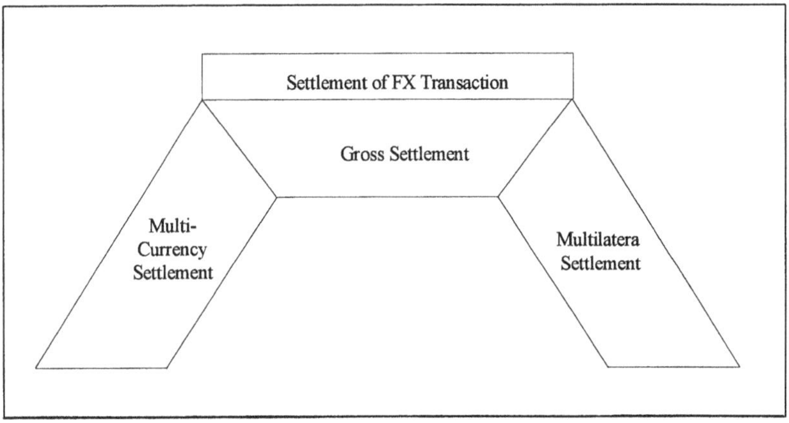

Leaving the summary of each of the analytical chapters behind, it is, finally, the chapters IV-VI themselves that need to be brought together for deriving an efficiency hypothesis concerning the entire foreign exchange market structure. The final step of the present thesis is, therefore, to analyze eventual interrelations of the search and information system, the pricing system, and/or the settlement system. In so doing, the following paragraphs finish exactly at the same point where the discussion originally started above, namely, the organization called 'foreign exchange market'.

Reviewing the set of imperfections that was discussed in chapters IV-VI above suggests three possible relations of the search and information system with the pricing system and the settlement system.

- The search and information system *and* the settlement system respond to credit risk exposure.
- The search and information system *and* the pricing system respond to position risk exposure.
- The search and information system *and* the pricing system respond to dispersed information (figure VII.5).

FIGURE VII.4: Statics and Efficiency of Multi-Currency Netting

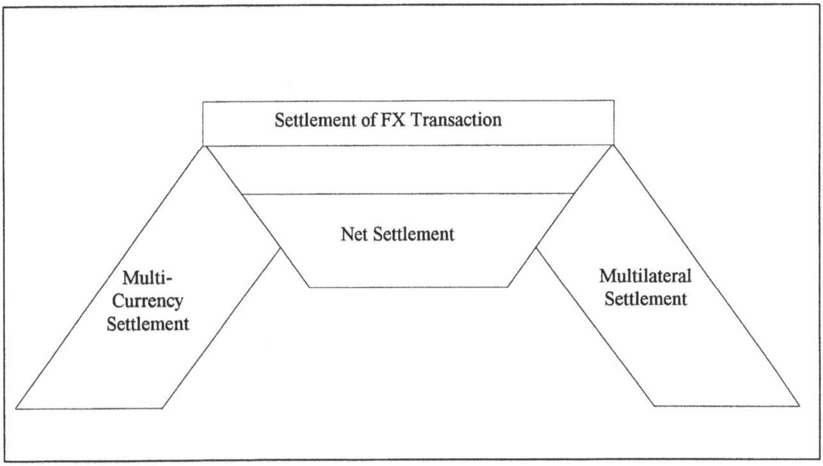

Starting with credit risk, the CLS Bank was said to eliminate it altogether. Hence, the CLS Bank may have significant external effects on the organization of the search and information system as soon as it will be operational. Agency costs of the adverse selection-type will then be equal to zero which, above all, may imply that FX dealing will no longer need to be partner-specific. In other words, the banks may no longer need to care about their reputation as much as they currently have to do, knowing that credit risk is zero at all times.

But other scenarios may also be possible such that a clear-cut answer requires continuous observation of the foreign exchange market in the close future, particularly, shortly before and after the CLS Bank will start its operations. The evolutionary approach to organizations, furthermore, may be the more appropriate theoretical background for this purpose.

FIGURE VII.5: Interrelations of the Search and Information System, the Pricing System, and the Settlement System

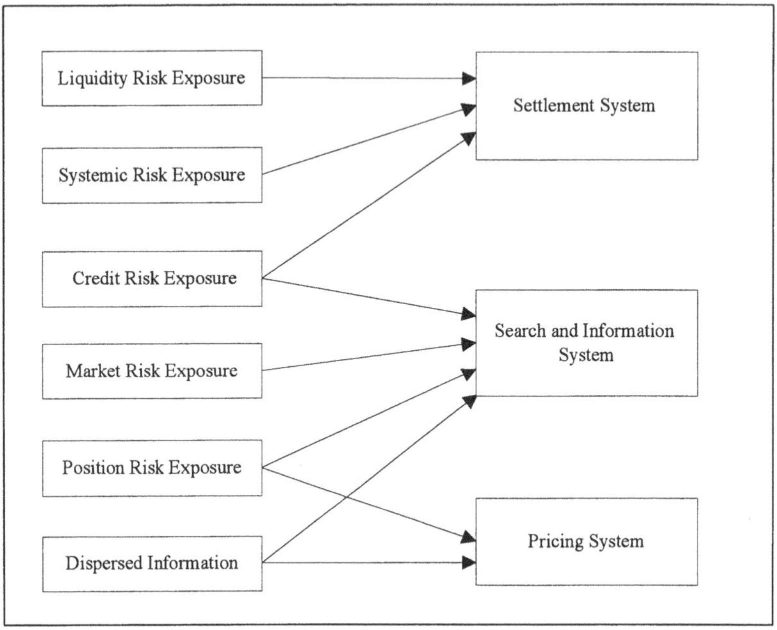

Turning from credit risk to position risk and dispersed information together, the set of institutional arrangements that the pricing system relies on is clearly independent of the one that the organization of search and information acquisition must draw from. Hence, there are no negative external effects from designing one system on designing the other. On the contrary, given that the two sets of institutional arrangements are independent, combining the efficient search and information system with the efficient pricing system should reduce transactions costs to the absolute minimum and the institutional economic analysis of the foreign exchange market can thus be concluded with the following, final proposition.

PROPOSITION 13: Focusing on the current market practice, the search and information system of the foreign exchange market is efficient, the pricing system is efficient, but the settlement system is not. Consequently, the foreign exchange market structure is not optimally designed. Focusing on the envisaged changes in the settlement system, however, the foreign exchange market moves closer to efficiency in the future, provided that the search and information system adjusts appropriately, if necessary.

Concluding Chapter VII, therefore, future research can focus on the variety of empirical problems that were mentioned throughout the analysis (anticipating the problems that normative theory brings about with respect to testing its hypotheses). One important institution, namely, the broker was also left aside. But it could find its explanation in providing anonymous trading opportunities, allowing for limit orders instead of market orders, and allowing for greater dealing amounts than the standard dealing amounts on the interbank market, a/o. Furthermore, the same comparative method as it was applied above could be applied to other international financial and commodity markets such that, eventually, a taxonomy of market structures emerges in the end. This taxonomy could subsequently serve as a guide for policy makers and regulators who are concerned with the design of markets. Ultimately, applying the evolutionary approach to institutions to the foreign exchange market could supplement the above theory. If it was correctly specified, the results should coincide.

References

Akerlof, G. (1970), The Market for Lemons: Qualitative Uncertainty and the Market Mechanism, in: Quarterly Journal of Economics, 84, 488-500.

Akerlof, G. (1985), Discriminatory Status-Based Wages Among Tradition-Oriented, Stochastically Trading Coconut Producers, in: Journal of Political Economy, 92, 265-76.

Alchian, A. and H. Demsetz (1972), Production, Information Costs, and Economic Organization, in: American Economic Review, 62, 775-95.

Amihud, Y. and H. Mendelson (1987), Trading Mechanisms and Stock Returns: An Empirical Investigation, in: Journal of Finance, 42, 533-53.

Amihud, Y. and H. Mendelson (1991), Volatility, Efficiency and Trading: Evidence from the Japanese Stock Market, in: Journal of Finance, 46, 1765-89.

Anthony, S. (1989), Foreign Exchange in Practice, North Ryde NSW: Law Book Company.

Arrow, K. J. (1972), Models of Job Discrimination, in: Racial Discrimination in Economic Life, A.H. Pascal, ed., Lexington MA: Lexington Books.

Arrow, K. J. (1974), The Limits of Organization, New York: Norton.

Arrow, K. J. (1985), The Economics of Agency, in: Principals and Agents, J. W. Pratt, ed., Boston MA: Harvard Business School Print.

Aschinger, G. (1995), Börsenkrach und Spekulation: Eine ökonomische Analyse, München: Vahlen.

Association Cambiste Internationale (1996), Code of Conduct, Paris: Association Cambiste Internationale.

Badgehot, W. (Pseudonym for Jack Treynor) (1971), The Only Game in Town, in: Financial Analysts Journal, 22, 12-14.

Bank for International Settlements (1993), Payments Systems in the Group of Ten Countries, Basle: Bank for International Settlements.

Bank for International Settlements (1996), Settlement Risk in Foreign Exchange Transactions, Basle: Bank for International Settlements.

Bank for International Settlements (1998), Reducing Foreign Exchange Settlement Risk: A Progress Report, Basle: Bank for International Settlements.

Barro, R. J. (1972), A Theory of Monopolistic Price Adjustment, in: Review of Economic Studies, 39, 17-27.

Blanchard, O. J. and S. Fischer (1989), Lectures in Macroeconomics, Cambridge MA: Massachusetts Institute of Technology Press.

Blommestein, H. J. and B. J. Summers (1994), Banking and the Payment System, in: The Payment System: Design, Management, and Supervision, B. J. Summers, ed., Washington D.C.: International Monetary Fund.

Blume, L. E. and D. Easley (1990), Implications of Walrasian Expectations Equilibria, in: Journal of Economic Theory, 51, 207-27.

Bundesaufsichtsamt für das Kreditwesen (1982), Saldierung von Devisen-Kassageschäften, die an einem Geschäftstag, in derselben Währung und mit demselben Geschäftspartner abgeschlossen werden, in: Handel und Kursbildung am Devisenmarkt, 5th (revised) ed., P. Fischer-Erlach, Stuttgart: Kohlhammer.

Burnham, J. B. (1991), Current Structure and Recent Developments in Foreign Exchange Markets, in: Recent Developments in International Banking and Finance, 4, S. J. Khoury, ed., Amsterdam: North-Holland.

Cartledge, P. C. (1991), Spot Dealing, in: The Foreign Exchange Manual, R. Weisweiller, ed., Cambridge: Woodhead-Faulkner.

Cassady, R. Jr. (1967), Auctions and Auctioneering, Berkeley: University of California Press.

Chambers, S. and C. Carter (1990), U.S. Futures Exchanges as Nonprofit Entities, in: Journal of Futures Markets, 10, 79-88.

Chandler, A. D. Jr. (1977), The Visible Hand: The Managerial Revolution in American Business, Cambridge MA: Belknap Press.

Coase, R. H. (1937), The Nature of the Firm, in: Economica, 4, 386-405.

Coase, R. H. (1960), The Problem of Social Costs, in: Journal of Law and Economics, 3, 1-44.

Coase, R. H. (1988), The Firm, the Market, and the Law, Chicago: University of Chicago Press.

Cohen, K. J. and R. A. Schwartz (1989), An Electronic Call Market: Its Design and Desirability, in: The Challenge of Information Technology for the Securities Markets, H. C. Lucas, Jr. and R. A. Schwartz, eds., Homewood: Dow Jones-Irwin.

Cohen, K. J.; Maier, S.; Schwartz, R. A. and D. K. Whitcomb (1981), Transaction Costs, Order Placement Strategy, and Existence of the Bid-Ask Spread, in: Journal of Political Economy, 89, 287-305.

Cohen, K. J.; Maier, S. F.; Schwartz, R.. A. and D. K. Whitcomb (1986), The Microstructure of Securities Markets, Englewood Cliffs: Prentice-Hall.

Commons, J. R. (1934), Institutional Economics, Madison: University of Wisconsin Press.

Copeland, T. and D. Galai (1983), Information Effects and the Bid-Ask Spread, in: Journal of Finance, 38, 1457-69.

Dahlman, C. J. (1979), The Problem of Externality, in: Journal of Law and Economics, 22, 141-162.

Deutsche Börse (1994), Börsenordnung für die Frankfurter Wertpapierbörse vom 16. Dezember 1994, in: Amtliches Kursblatt der Frankfurter Wertpapierbörse Nr. 6 vom 9. Januar 1995, revised in: Amtliches Kursblatt der Frankfurter Wertpapierbörse Nr. 46 vom 10. März 1997.

Deutsche Börse (1996), FWB - Die Frankfurter Wertpapierbörse, 2nd (revised) ed., Frankfurt am Main: Deutsche Börse AG.

Domowitz, I. (1996), An Exchange is a Many-Splendored Thing: The Classification and Regulation of Automated Trading Systems, in: The Industrial Organization of the Securities Industry, A. W. Lo, ed., Chicago: University of Chicago Press.

Easley, D. and M. O'Hara (1987), Price, Trade Size, and Information in Securities Markets, in: Journal of Financial Economics, 19, 69-90.

Einzig, P. (1970), The History of Foreign Exchange, 2nd (revised) ed., London: McMillan.

Engelbrecht-Wiggans, R.. (1980), Auctions and Bidding Models: A Survey, in: Management Science, 26, 119-42.

Engelbrecht-Wiggans, R.; Milgrom, P. and R.. Weber (1983), Competitive Bidding and Proprietary Information, in: Journal of Mathematical Economics, 11, 161-69.

Engelbrecht-Wiggans, R. (1986), Classes of Equivalent Auction Mechanisms: The Case of Risk Neutral Bidders, Urbana-Champaign: University of Illinois, College of Commerce and Business Administration, Working Paper No. 1243.

European Monetary Institute (1995), Report to the Council of the European Monetary Institute on the TARGET System, Frankfurt am Main: European Monetary Institute.

European Monetary Institute (1996), First Progress Report on the TARGET Project, Frankfurt am Main: European Monetary Institute.

European Monetary Institute (1997), Second Progress Report on the TARGET Project, Frankfurt am Main: European Monetary Institute.

Fama, E. F. (1976), Foundations of Finance, Oxford: Basic Books.

Fischer-Erlach, P. (1995), Handel und Kursbildung am Devisenmarkt, 5th (revised) ed., Stuttgart: Kohlhammer.

Flood, M. D. (1991), Microstructure Theory and the Foreign Exchange Market, in: Federal Reserve Bank of St. Louis Review, 73, 52-70.

Flood, M. D. (1992), Market Structure and Inefficiency in the Foreign Exchange Market, in: Journal of International Money and Finance, 13, 131-58.

Flood, M. D. (1996), Comment on R. K. Lyons, Foreign Exchange Volume: Sound and Fury Signifying Nothing?, in: The Microstructure of Foreign Exchange Markets, J. A. Frankel; G. Galli and A. Giovannini, eds., Chicago: University of Chicago Press.

Frank, M. (1996), Kooperation und Koordination: Eine spieltheoretische Interpretation klassischer Marktversagensgründe, Weiden: eurotrans-Verlag.

Frankel, J. A. and K. A. Froot (1990a), Chartists, Fundamentalists, and Trading in the Foreign Exchange Market, in: American Economic Review, Papers and Proceedings, 80, 181-85.

Frankel, J. A. and K. A. Froot (1990b), Chartists, Fundamentalists and the Demand for Dollars, in: Private Behaviour and Government Policy in Interdependent Economies, A. S. Courakis, ed., Oxford: Clarendon Press.

Frankel, J. A.; Galli, G. and A. Giovannini, eds. (1996), The Microstructure of Foreign Exchange Markets, Chicago: University of Chicago Press.

Frankfurter Wertpapierbörse, ed. (1991), Feststellung von Kursen und Preisen, Frankfurt am Main: Frankfurter Wertpapierbörse AG.

Fudenberg, D. and D. K. Levine (1989), Reputation and Equilibrium Selection in Games with a Patient Player, in: Econometrica, 57, 759-78.

Fudenberg, D. and E. S. Maskin (1986), The Folk Theorem in Repeated Games with Discounting or with Incomplete Information, in: Econometrica, 54, 533-54.

Furubotn, E. G. and R. Richter (1997), Institutions and Economic Theory: An Introduction to and Assessment of the New Institutional Economics, Ann Arbor: University of Michigan Press.

Gallant, P. (1991), Customer Relationships, in: The Foreign Exchange Manual, R. Weisweiller, ed., Cambridge: Woodhead-Faulkner.

Garman, M. (1976), Market Microstructure, in: Journal of Financial Economics, 3, 257-75.

Gertler, M. and A. Rose (1996), Finance, Public Policy, and Growth, in: Financial Reform: Theory and Experience, G. Caprio, Jr. and J. A. Hanson, eds., Cambridge: Cambridge University Press.

Glosten, L. and P. Milgrom (1985), Bid, Ask, and Transaction Prices in a Specialist Market with Heterogeneously Informed Traders, in: Journal of Financial Economics, 13, 71-100.

Goodhart, C. (1988), The Foreign Exchange Market: A Random Walk with a Dragging Anchor, in: Economica, 55, 437-60.

Goodhart, C.; Takatoshi, I. and R. Payne (1996), One Day in June 1993: A Study of the Working of the Reuters 2000-2 Electronic Foreign Exchange Trading System, in: The Microstructure of Foreign Exchange Markets, J. A. Frankel; G. Galli and A. Giovannini, eds., Chicago: University of Chicago Press.

Grossman, S. J. (1976), On the Efficiency of Competitive Stock Markets Where Traders have Diverse Information, in: Journal of Finance, 31, 573-85.

Grossman, S. J. (1977a), A Characterization of the Optimality of Equilibrium in Incomplete Markets, in: Journal of Economic Theory, 5, 1-15.

Grossman, S. J. (1977b), The Existence of Futures Markets, Noisy Rational Expectations and Informational Externalities, in: Review of Economic Studies, 44, 431-49.

Grossman, S. J. (1978), Further Results on the Informational Efficiency of Competitive Stock Markets, in: Journal of Economic Theory, 18, 81-101.

Grossman, S. J. and M. H. Miller (1988), Liquidity and Market Structure, in: Journal of Finance, 43, 617-33.

Grossman, S. J. and J. E. Stiglitz (1976), Information and Competitive Price Systems, in: American Economic Review, 66, 246-53.

Grossman, S. J. and J. E. Stiglitz (1980), On the Impossibility of Informationally Efficient Markets, in: American Economic Review, 70, 393-408.

Harris, L. E. (1991), Liquidity, Trading Rules and Electronic Trading Systems, New York: New York University Salomon Center.

Harris, M. and A. Raviv (1981), Allocation Mechanisms and the Design of Auctions, in: Econometrica, 49, 1477-99.

Harris, M. and R. M. Townsend (1985), Allocation Mechanisms, Asymmetric Information, and the 'Revelation Principle', in: Issues in Contemporary Microeconomics and Welfare, G. Fiewel, ed., Albany: State University if New York Press.

Hayek, F. A. v. (1945), The Use of Knowledge in Society, in: American Economic Review, 35, 519-30.

Hayek, F. A. v. (1978), New Studies in Philosophy, Politics, Economics and the History of Economic Ideas, London: Routledge & Kegan Paul.

Hicks, J. (1932), The Theory of Wages, London: McMillan (new edition, 1963, New York: McMillan).

Ho, T. and H. Stoll (1981), Optimal Dealer Pricing Under Transactions and Return Uncertainty, in: Journal of Financial Economics, 38, 1053-74.

Holmström, B. and R. B. Myerson (1983), Efficient and Durable Decision Rules with Incomplete Information, in: Econometrica, 53, 1799-1819.

Holt, C. A. Jr. (1979), Uncertainty and the Bidding for Incentive Contracts, in: American Economic Review, 69, 697-705.

Holt, C. A. Jr. (1980), Competitive Bidding for Contracts Under Alternative Auction Procedures, in: Journal of Political Economy, 88, 433-45.

Hume, D. (1739/40), A Treatise of Human Nature, London (new edition, 1911, London: Dent).

Humphrey, D. B. (1986), Payments Finality and Risk of Settlement Failure, in: Technology and the Regulation of Financial Markets, A. Saunders and L. J. White, eds., Lexington MA: Lexington Books.

Institute of International Finance (1999a), Strengthening Relations Between Emerging Market Authorities and Private Investors and Creditors, Washington D.C.: Institute of International Finance.

Institute of International Finance (1999b), Involving the Private Sector in Resolving Financial Crisis, Washington D.C.: Institute of International Finance.

International Monetary Fund (1999), Involving the Private Sector in Forestalling and Resolving Financial Crisis, Washington D.C.: International Monetary Fund.

Kennan, J. and R. Wilson (1993), Bargaining with Private Information, in: Journal of Economic Literature, 31, 45-104.

Kirman, A. P. (1995), The Behaviour of the Foreign Exchange Market, in: Bank of England Quarterly Bulletin, 15, 286-93.

Kirman, A. P. (1996), Comment on W. Perraudin and P. Vitale, Interdealer Trade and Information Flows in a Decentralized Foreign Exchange Market, in: The Microstructure of Foreign Exchange Markets, J. A. Frankel; G. Galli and A. Giovannini, eds., Chicago: University of Chicago Press.

Kolb, R. W. (1991), Understanding Futures Markets, 3rd ed., New York: New York Institute of Finance.

Kreps, D. (1990), A Course in Microeconomic Theory, Hemel Hempstead: Harvester Wheatshear.

Kreps, D. and R. Wilson (1982), Reputation and Imperfect Information, in: Journal of Economic Theory, 27, 253-79.

Kreps, D.; Milgrom, P.; Roberts, J. and R. Wilson (1982), Rational Cooperation in the Finitely Repeated Prisoners' Dilemma, in: Journal of Economic Theory, 27, 245-52.

Kyle, A. S. (1984), Market Structure, Information, Futures Markets, and Price Formation, in: International Agricultural Trade: Advanced Readings in Price Formation, Market Structure and Price Instability, G. G. Storey; A. Schmitz and A. H. Sarris, eds., London: Westview Press.

Kyle, A. S. (1985), Continuous Auctions and Insider Trading, in: Econometrica, 53, 1315-36.

Laffont, J. and E. Maskin (1980), Optimal Reservation Price in the Vickrey Auction, in: Economic Letters, 6, 309-13.

Lauterbach, B. and U. Meyer (1997), Switching to Continuous Trading and its Impact on Return Behavior and Volume of Trade, in: Journal of Financial Services Research, 12, 39-50.

London Stock Exchange (1999), The Rules and Regulations of the London Stock Exchange, in the version of April 1999, London: London Stock Exchange.

Lundberg, S. and R. Startz (1983), Private Discrimination and Social Intervention in Competitive Labor Markets, in: American Economic Review, 73, 340-47.

Lyons, R. K. (1991), Private Beliefs and Information Externalities in the Foreign Exchange Market, Cambridge MA: National Bureau of Economic Research, Working Paper No. 3889.

Lyons, R. K. (1995), A Simultaneous Trade Model of the Foreign Exchange Hot Potato, Berkeley: University of California, Business School, Typescript.

Lyons, R. K. (1996), Foreign Exchange Volume: Sound and Fury Signifying Nothing?, in: The Microstructure of Foreign Exchange Markets, J. A. Frankel; G. Galli and A. Giovannini, eds., Chicago: University of Chicago Press.

Lyons, R. K.; Melvin, M. T. and I. Takatoshi (1997), Is there Private Information in the FX Market: The Tokyo Experiment, Cambridge MA: National Bureau of Economic Research, Working Paper No. 5936.

Machiavelli, N. (1532), Il Principe, Firenze: Di Guinta (The Prince (Il Principe. English), new edition, 1988, Cambridge: Cambridge University Press).

Madhavan, A. (1992), Trading Mechanisms in Securities Markets, in: Journal of Finance, 47, 607-42.

Marquardt, J. C. (1994), Payment System Policy Issues and Analysis, in: The Payment System: Design, Management, and Supervision, B. J. Summers, ed., Washington D.C.: International Monetary Fund.

Marshall, A. (1920), Principles of Economics, 8th ed., Basingstoke: McMillan.

Matthews, S. A. (1987), Comparing Auctions for Risk Averse Buyers: A Buyer's Point of View, in: Econometrica, 55, 633-46.

McAfee, R. P. and J. McMillan (1987), Auctions and Bidding, in: Journal of Economic Literature, 25, 699-738.

Mendelson, H. (1982), Market Behavior in a Clearing House, in: Econometrica, 50, 1505-24.

Menger, C. (1883), Untersuchungen über die Methode der Socialwissenschaften und der Politischen Oekonomie insbesondere, Leipzig: Duncker & Humblot (new edition, 1969, Tübingen: Mohr).

Milgrom, R. (1981), Rational Expectations, Information Acquisition, and Competitive Bidding, in: Econometrica, 49, 921-43.

Milgrom, R. (1985), The Economics of Competitive Bidding: A Selective Survey, in: Social Goals and Social Organization, L. Hurwicz; D. Schmeidler and H. Sonnenschein, eds., Cambridge: Cambridge University Press.

Milgrom, R. (1986), Auction Theory, in: Advances in Economic Theory, T. Bewley, ed., Cambridge: Cambridge University Press.

Milgrom, P. and S. Oster (1987), Job Discrimination, Market Forces and the Invisibility Hypothesis, in: Quarterly Journal of Economics, 102, 453-76.

Milgrom P. and J. Roberts (1982), Predation, Reputation, and Entry Deterrence, in: Journal of Economic Theory, 27, 280-312.

Milgrom P. and J. Roberts (1992), Economics, Organization and Management, Englewood Cliffs: Prentice-Hall.

Milgrom, P. and R. Weber (1982), A Theory of Auctions and Competitive Bidding, in: Econometrica, 50, 1089-1122.

Mulherin, J. H.; Netter, J. M. and J. A. Overdahl (1991), Prices are Property: The Organization of Financial Exchanges from a Transaction Cost Perspective, in: Journal of Law and Economics, 34, 591-644.

Mussa, M. (1981), Sticky Prices and Disequilibrium Adjustment in a Rational Model of the Inflationary Process, in: American Economic Review, 71, 1020-27.

Myerson, R. B. (1979), Incentive Compatibility and the Bargaining Problem, in: Econometrica, 47, 61-73.

Myerson, R. B. (1981), Optimal Auction Design, in: Mathematics of Operations Research, 6, 265-81.

Myerson, R. B. (1985), Analysis of Two Bargaining Problems with Incomplete Information, in: Game-Theoretic Models of Bargaining, A. E. Roth, ed., Cambridge: Cambridge University Press.

North, D. C. (1981), Structure and Change in Economic History, New York: Norton.

North, D. C. (1990), Institutions, Institutional Change and Economic Performance, Cambridge: Cambridge University Press.

O'Hara, M. (1995), Market Microstructure Theory, Cambridge MA: Blackwell.

O'Hara, M. and G. Oldfield (1986), The Microeconomics of Market Making, in: Journal of Financial and Quantitative Analysis, 21, 361-76.

Okun, A. M. (1981), Prices and Quantities: A Macroeconomic Analysis, Oxford: Blackwell.

Osborne, M. J. and A. Rubinstein (1990), Bargaining and Markets, San Diego: Academic Press.

Ostrom, E. (1990), Governing the Commons. The Evolution of Institutions for Collective Action, Cambridge: Cambridge University Press.

Pagano, M. and A. Roell (1990), Trading Systems in European Stock Exchanges: Current Performance and Policy Options, in: Economic Policy, 10, 65-115.

Pagano, M. and A. Roell (1992), Transparency and Liquidity: A Comparison of Auction and Dealer Markets with Informed Trading, London: London School of Economics, Financial Markets Group, Discussion Paper 150.

Perraudin, W. and P. Vitale (1996), Interdealer Trade and Information Flows in a Decentralized Foreign Exchange Market, in: The Microstructure of Foreign Exchange Markets, J. A. Frankel; G. Galli and A. Giovannini, eds., Chicago: University of Chicago Press.

Rasmusen, E. (1994), Games and Information, 2nd ed., Cambridge MA: Blackwell.

Riehl, H. and R. M. Rodriguez (1983), Foreign Exchange and Money Markets: Managing Foreign and Domestic Currency Operations, New York: McGraw-Hill.

Riley, J. G. and W. F. Samuelson (1981), Optimal Auctions, in: American Economic Review, 71, 381-92.

Rochet, J. C. and J. L. Vila (1994), Insider Trading without Normality, in: Review of Economic Studies, 61, 131-52.

Rosenthal, R. W. (1981), Games of Perfect Information, Predatory Pricing and the Chain-Store Paradox, in: Journal of Economic Theory, 25, 92-100.

Schelling, T. C. (1960), The Strategy of Conflict, Cambridge MA: Harvard University Press.

Schmoller, G. v. (1900), Grundriß der allgemeinen Volkswirtschaftslehre, Leipzig: Duncker & Humblot.

Schoenmaker, D. (1995), A Comparison of Alternative Interbank Settlement Systems, London: London School of Economics, Financial Markets Group, Discussion Paper 204.

Selten, R. (1978), The Chain-Store Paradox, in: Theory and Decision, 9, 127-59.

Shell, G. R. (1991), Opportunism and Trust in the Negotiation of Commercial Contracts: Towards a New Cause of Action, in: Vanderbilt Law Review, 44, 221-82.

Shen, P. (1997), Settlement Risk in Large-Value Payments Systems, in: Federal Reserve Bank of Kansas City Economic Review, 82, 45-62.

Souren, L. (1995), Grundlagen und Praxis des Devisenhandels, Wiesbaden: Gabler.

Spatt, C. S. (1991), Preplay Communication, Participation Restrictions, and Efficiency in Initial Public Offerings, in: The Review of Financial Studies, 4, 709-26.

Spence, A.M. (1973), Market Signalling: Information Transfer in Hiring and Related Processes, Cambridge MA: Harvard University Press.

Spence, A.M. and R. Zeckhauser (1971), Insurance, Information and Individual Action, in: American Economic Review, 61, 380-87.

Stark, R. and M. H. Rothkopf (1979), Competitive Bidding: A Comprehensive Bibliography, in: Operations Research, 27, 364-91.

Stiglitz, J.E. and A. Weiss (1981), Credit Rationing in Markets with Imperfect Information, in: American Economic Review, 71, 393-409.

Stoll, H. (1978), The Supply of Dealer Services in Securities Markets, in: Journal of Finance, 33, 1133-51.

Stoll, H. R. (1992), Principles of Trading Market Structure, in: Journal of Financial Services Research, 6, 75-107.

Stoll, H. R. and R. Whaley (1990), Stock Market Structure and Volatility, in: Review of Financial Studies, 3, 37-71.

Stützel, W. (1975), Liquidität, betriebliche, in: Handwörterbuch der Betriebswirtschaft, Band 2, E. Grochla, ed., 4th (revised) ed., Stuttgart: Poeschel.

Sugden, R. (1986), The Economics of Rights, Co-operation and Welfare, Oxford: Blackwell.

Sugden, R. (1989), Spontaneous Order, in: Journal of Economic Perspectives, 3, 85-97.

Summers, B. J., ed. (1994), The Payment System: Design, Management, and Supervision, Washington D.C.: International Monetary Fund.

Telser, L. G. (1978), Economic Theory and the Core, Chicago: University of Chicago Press.

Telser, L. G. (1980), A Theory of Self-Enforcing Agreements, in: Journal of Business, 53, 27-44.

Telser, L. G. (1981), Why There are Organized Futures Markets, in: Journal of Law and Economics, 24, 1-22.

Terberger, E. (1994), Neoinstitutionalistische Ansätze: Entstehung und Wandel, Anspruch und Wirklichkeit, Wiesbaden: Gabler.

Tirole, J. (1982), On the Possibility of Speculation Under Rational Expectations, in: Econometrica, 50, 1163-82.

Varian, H. (1989), Differences of Opinion in Financial Markets, in: Financial Risk: Theory, Evidence, and Implications, C. Stone, ed., Boston: Kluwer Academic Publishers.

Van den Bergh, P. (1994), Operational and Financial Structure of the Payment System, in: The Payment System: Design, Management, and Supervision, B. J. Summers, ed., Washington D.C.: International Monetary Fund.

Van den Bergh, P. and J. M. Veale (1994), Payment System Risk and Risk Management, in: The Payment System: Design, Management, and Supervision, B. J. Summers, ed., Washington D.C.: International Monetary Fund.

Vickrey, W. (1961), Counterspeculation, Auctions, and Competitive Sealed Tenders, in: Journal of Finance, 16, 8-37.

Wagner, W. (1989), Buttonwood II: Considering Alternative Market Structures, in: The Complete Guide to Securities Transactions, W. Wagner, ed., New York: John Wiley & Sons.

Weber, M. (1990), Wirtschaft und Gesellschaft: Grundriß der verstehenden Soziologie, 5th (revised) ed., Tübingen: Mohr

Weisweiller, R. (1991), The Foreign Exchange Manual, Cambridge: Woodhead-Faulkner.

Williamson, O. (1975), Markets and Hierarchies: Analysis and Antitrust Implications, New York: The Free Press.

Williamson, O. (1979), Transaction-Cost Economics: The Governance of Contractual Relations, in: Journal of Law and Economics, 22, 233-61.

Williamson, O. (1983), Credible Commitments: Using Hostages to Support Exchange, in: American Economic Review, 73, 519-40.

Williamson, O. (1985), The Economic Institutions of Capitalism, New York: The Free Press.

Williamson, O. (1991), Economic Institutions: Spontaneous and Intentional Governance, in: Journal of Law, Economics, and Organization, 7, 159-87.

Williamson, O. (1993), Transaction Cost Economics and Organization Theory, in: Industrial and Corporate Change, 2, 107-56.

Wilson, R. (1985a), Reputation in Games and Markets, in: Game-Theoretic Models of Bargaining, A. E. Roth, ed., Cambridge: Cambridge University Press.

Wilson, R. (1985b), Incentive Efficiency of Double Auctions, in: Econometrica, 53, 1101-15.

Wolinsky, A. (1990), Information Revelation in a Market with Pairwise Meetings, in: Econometrica, 58, 1-23.

Working, H. (1958), A Theory of Anticipatory Prices, in: American Economic Review, 48, 188-99.

World Bank (1998), East Asia: The Road to Recovery, Washington D.C.: The World Bank Group.

Wunsch, S. (1989), The Single-Price Auction, in: The Complete Guide to Securities Transactions, W. Wagner, ed., New York: John Wiley & Sons.

Peter Lang · Europäischer Verlag der Wissenschaften

Petra Lietz / Dieter Kotte

The importance of economic literacy

Frankfurt/M., Berlin, Bern, Bruxelles, New York, Oxford, Wien, 2000.
XV, 142 pp., num. tab. and graf.
ISBN 3-631-36161-0 · pb. DM 54.–*
US-ISBN 0-8204-4740-4

In the world of globalization, international markets and world-wide competition it is important for students to be well informed about the underlying economic concepts. Knowledge about economics, termed 'economic literacy', has become as important as being literate in reading, writing and arithmetic. For each country and educational system the importance of economic literacy is tied to educating its youth to be capable of understanding, thinking and acting according to basic economic principles. Based on the Australian setting this book sheds light on the growing importance of economic literacy as reflected in the States' curricula and as measured in a recent survey conducted across Queensland.

Contents: Review of economic literacy world-wide · Gender differences in Economics · Content analysis of Economics curricula · Levels of economic literacy · Economics as a school subject · Economic Literacy Survey · Queensland 1998 · The internet and data collection · Literacy benchmarking using Rasch scaling · Student's attitudes towards Economics · Successful teaching strategies in Economics · School resources and Economic literacy · Policy recommendations · Hierarchical linear models · Path analysis

Frankfurt/M · Berlin · Bern · Bruxelles · New York · Oxford · Wien
Distribution: Verlag Peter Lang AG
Jupiterstr. 15, CH-3000 Bern 15
Fax (004131) 9402131
*incl. value added tax
Prices are subject to change without notice.